BASQUE
COUNTRY

WITHDRAWN

BASQUE

A Culinary Journey
Through a Food
Lover's Paradise

MARTI BUCKLEY

PHOTOGRAPHS BY SIMON BAJADA

COUNTRY

ARTISAN · NEW YORK

Library of Congress Cataloging-in-Publication Data

Names: Buckley, Marti, author.
Title: Basque country : a culinary journey through
a food lover's paradise / Marti Buckley.
Description: New York : Artisan, a division of Workman Publishing Co., Inc., 2018.|
Includes index.
Identifiers: LCCN 2017037795 | ISBN 9781579657772 (hc : alk. paper)
Subjects: LCSH: Cooking, Basque. | LCGFT: Cookbooks.
Classification: LCC TX723.5.B36 B83 2018 |
DDC 641.5929992—dc23
LC record available at https://lccn.loc.gov/2017037795

Artisan books are available at special discounts when purchased in bulk for
premiums and sales promotions as well as for fund-raising or educational use.
Special editions or book excerpts also can be created to specification. For details,
contact the Special Sales Director at the address below, or send an e-mail to
specialmarkets@workman.com.

For speaking engagements, contact speakersbureau@workman.com.

Published by Artisan
A division of Workman Publishing Co., Inc.
225 Varick Street
New York, NY 10014-4381
artisanbooks.com

Artisan is a registered trademark of
Workman Publishing Co., Inc.

Published simultaneously in Canada by
Thomas Allen & Son, Limited

Printed in China
First printing, August 2018

10 9 8 7 6 5 4 3 2 1

For the Basques and for Buckley

CONTENTS

FOREWORD

FIREWOOD IN THE OVEN, the crackle of a fire, the profound aroma of earth, and a countryside teeming with life—these are the "flavors" of the morning at Etxebarri, my restaurant in the tiny village of Axpe, Bizkaia. These smells, sounds, and sights are typical of a Basque village. You'll find them not only in my kitchen but also in the kitchens of so many Basques who have come before me.

Marti Buckley is a seeker of essences, a determined researcher, and an enthusiastic investigator. With an outsider's point of view, she has delved into a singular culture and tradition. Using her experiences in the kitchens of Basque Country, she has completed an entertaining, straightforward book that allows us to catch a glimpse and exalt the roots of Basque cuisine. Buckley captures a way of cooking that has always had respect for raw materials and humility, forging its own place on the world's culinary stage, away from the mainstream.

A unique, captivating atmosphere, natural yet powerful—this is the magic of Basque Country. The link between our food and nature remains unbroken. The result is rustic yet elegant, simple yet refined. Basque Country is rooted in tradition, and its cuisine is no different.

I hope you enjoy this book, and that you live it through your senses, which offer us new ways of perceiving things. This collection of recipes contains our most traditional dishes, those that evoke sensory memories for any Basque, whisking us straight to our grandmother's table and the dining societies, restaurants, bars, and grill houses of Basque Country.

—Bittor Arginzoniz, chef and owner, Etxebarri

INTRODUCTION:
THE BASQUE COUNTRY

Basques are uniquely obsessed with food. This is no surprise in a land so abundant in edible natural resources. Sparkling rivers, cold seas, humid forests, and lush valleys all contribute excellent-quality ingredients, arguably some of the best in the world. And the home and professional cooks inhabiting this food-loving culture know what to do with them—from brilliantly simple sauced fish to homey stews rich with peppers and onions, the Basque cuisine excels at taking a good product and enhancing, not hiding, its flavor.

Everything of importance in this small region, nestled in the north corner of Spain and the south of France, happens around the table. This table takes different forms, all of them wonderfully iconic—a bartop scattered with *pintxos* (small bites); a slab of wood with a shiny patina from years of Sunday farmhouse lunches; or a white tablecloth in a Michelin-starred restaurant. But the uniqueness of the Basque cuisine lies in its "other restaurants": homes, dining societies, cider houses, cooking competitions, and fairs that have kept a food tradition vibrant and lively, preserving dishes over hundreds of years and creating an insular recipe collection that is remade (and, consequently, improved) over and over and over.

Renowned worldwide, Basque cuisine is first and foremost about the ingredients, the freshest of raw products: just-caught seafood; excellent meat and game; produce; oils; sheep's-milk cheese; hard cider; and wine. The Basque people have cultivated a sense of taste that can distinguish between a local fish and one caught in faraway waters, further heightened by an insistence on simplistic, natural cooking. Basque cooking requires patience, employing techniques like slow poaching and simmering, rather than an excess of ingredients, to achieve depth of flavor.

The "cult of good eating," as some call it, in Basque Country has been shaped and formed by a hungry public. The champions of Basque cuisine are many—from the erudite José Maria Busca Isusi of Zumarraga (a food scholar taught and influenced by the females in his family who is considered one of the eminences of Basque cuisine) to the founders of the *nueva cocina* movement to the bloggers and about-towners who keep the traditions alive in the twenty-first century. Each is a product of their time, witness to the changing landscape of Basque culture and Basque cuisine. A cuisine first led by the hand of nature and fortune, across the wild seas and into the coldest rocky valleys, was tamed by the *etxekoandre*, the female head of the household. There is a high level of culinary literacy among

the Basques; much like the language, the cuisine was transmitted orally in home kitchens. Even young people can fend for themselves in the kitchen and enjoy food-related banter. Taught by their mothers or grandmothers, these young people go on to be *sukaldariak*, chefs, whose curiosity continues to push the cuisine to new frontiers.

The demands of the Basque diner, however, are what really keep this tradition alive. Conceiving of a relationship or a celebration without food is truly impossible for a Basque, which makes for a lot of socially coded "eating times." Morning coffee is followed by the *hamaiketako*, a light snack, usually something salty, taken around eleven a.m. or noon and often accompanied with a drink. Lunch is the largest, most important meal of the day, eaten in the neighborhood of two p.m. on the Spanish side and twelve thirty or one p.m. on the French side. On weekends, most people have a drink in a local café or bar or on any number of terraces before a family lunch, and on weekdays, it's common to grab a drink and a snack with friends after work and before (or for) dinner. The phenomenon of going out for a premeal drink and snack was what gave birth to the region's famous pintxo culture. The Basque often finishes the day with a smaller meal, perhaps calling it a night after a few pintxos.

Not all the dining is done at home or in bars, however. The *txoko*, or dining society, is a pillar of Basque cuisine even more foundational than restaurants. Behind the doors of these private clubs, techniques are practiced and perfected by the average cook, and the excitement of friendly competition and a sense of occasion keep the Basque culinary tradition alive.

My first experience in Basque Country was as a hungry university student on an exchange program in Iruña (known as Pamplona in Spanish), the capital of Nafarroa. During the semester-long experience, I barely cracked the surface, but I could sense that there was something special about this place, the people, and the land. It left me with a gnawing hunger in my belly for all things Basque. Back in the States, I attempted to satiate it by drinking Rioja, watching Spanish movies, and listening to Basque-mix CDs from friends, but deep down, I always knew I would go back.

This initial taste of Basque Country planted in me more than just a desire to return. The good eating is contagious, and after my stay, I was fully infected. Though I began my career working and writing in the magazine world, I lived a furtive life as a wannabe chef. I would spend my free time cooking, my money on kitchen gear, and my reading bandwidth on food magazines and chefs' memoirs. It didn't hurt that I worked down the hall from the Time, Inc., test kitchens in Birmingham, Alabama.

It was in a professional kitchen in Birmingham that I put my amateur love of cooking to the real test. A friend helped me to get a *stage*, an unpaid culinary internship, at Bottega Restaurant, under one of the South's most prominent chefs, Frank Stitt. My first night, spent picking parsley and wiping plates clean at the pass, turned into nearly two years cooking under Chef Stitt and his chef de cuisine, John Rolen. I learned how to really cook, perfecting technique under pressure. And it left me hungrier than ever for Spain.

When I found a way to return to Basque Country, it was to Donostia (better known by its Spanish designation, San Sebastián), a city sometimes cited as having the most bars as well as some of the best restaurants in the world. At first, every pintxo on every bar had me swooning. I couldn't get enough foie, beef cheek, potato salad. But then I began to widen my explorations and ventured out with Basque friends to special, closed-door corners of the countryside. A *babarrunada* (bean feast) in Tolosa. A cider house in Ataun. *Txuritabeltz* (a stew made from leftover lamb parts—even the intestines) in the heavenly Baztan valley. An anchovy artisan in Getaria. The food was good, of course. But the people were better—they were humble, honorable, and kind, so quick to open their homes and hearts to me. New, delicious corners of Basque culture were opening themselves to me every day.

Now, after living in the Basque Country for over eight years, I've never stopped falling in love at nearly every bite. Over the course of these years, I've recorded all the recipes, customs, and traditions I've run across. I attempted to translate these strange experiences for myself, and now I'm doing so for you. Funny enough, they've fallen all into place, around a table and deep in my heart (or is it my stomach?). Food in Basque Country is about taste, yes, but it's also about culture and patriotism. It's with that feeling of pride that I want to share the Basque world—beyond the pintxo bar—with non-Basques everywhere.

ABOUT THIS BOOK

My intention with this book is to present the real, traditional recipes of the Basque Country. You won't find avant-garde versions of dishes or concessions to global tastes, like adding a bit of black pepper or squeezing lemon where it doesn't "belong." You'll find a handful of pintxos, yes, but this book's focus is on more than these famous bites. The recipes in this book are *the* recipes of the Basque Country. Limiting the number to what could reasonably fit into the volume of a cookbook was difficult, but the recipes presented are what I consider to be the culture's most iconic dishes.

This book is made for the home cook. It includes step-by-step recipes, many of them never before outlined in such detail, organized in six chapters. These recipes are accompanied by the stories behind them, stories that have often been obscured by a mysterious language and a hard-to-reach people. Along the way, you'll find asides featuring information about the culture, customs, and characters to give context to what is happening around the tables in this corner of the world.

The Pintxos chapter is a concise, curated selection of the thousands of different pintxos that grace the bars of this region, and includes classics both new and old, as well as a balance of meat and seafood.

The Soups chapter includes recipes for warming pots of Basque-style broth, a soup born on the fishing boat, and humble, rustic, bread-based soups.

In the next two chapters, Fish and Shellfish and Vegetables and Meat, you'll find the dishes that truly form the backbone of the cuisine, from fancy preparations inspired by French technique to humble stews made with fish and garden vegetables. These dishes may be familiar, like flash-fried Gernika peppers, but they are also unique, as is the case with the striking black (yet delicious) squid in its ink.

The Sweets chapter delves deeper into the French influence in Basque cooking, this time in the pastry tradition, and also includes ancient and traditional dishes. And finally, the Drinks chapter provides the accompaniment to the food.

You should feel free to play with the formats to create your own version of the Basque dining experience—many bars and restaurants take favorite traditional dishes, such as salt cod, and serve them as small-format pintxos.

Measurements are given in cups, tablespoons, ounces, etc., that are familiar to the American cook, but also in grams and milliliters, the measurement of choice in the Basque region. Some ingredients called for may be difficult to source, or completely foreign to you—I've included a Resources section on page 316 to help you with the more hard-to-find ingredients. Happily, Basque preserves and canned foods are world class, whether you open them on Basque or American soil. And always use the absolute best raw ingredients that you have at your disposal.

Now that this book is in your hands, the control is yours. I count myself among the ranks of the Basques; but when I cook in my own home, sometimes I do improvise with a squeeze of lemon or a crack of black pepper. And if I learned anything while studying Basque cuisine, it's that there are only as many variations of a recipe as there are stoves in Basque Country. This is simple, farm-to-table cooking, so honor it and honor the time you take to enjoy your meal, in true Basque style.

BASQUE FOOD VALUES

Simple is not a synonym for *easy*. When people refer to Basque cuisine as simple, they're referencing the refined and perfected nature of the food, its pared-down aesthetic (and ingredient list). The hallmark of Basque cooking is a simplicity befitting a noble landscape. It's a refusal to hide the gifts of nature behind spices, heavy sauces, or overwrought cooking techniques. The incredible oral tradition and collective memory of the Basques has helped them hold their most ancient traditions relatively near—their spirit keeps them linked to their past.

THE PRODUCT: Basques spend time and money buying the best possible food products, especially when it comes to fish and meat. Most traditional preparations coax the innate flavor out of an ingredient rather than mask it with sauce or spice. Having the best purveyor is a point of pride, and arguments about the best stall in the market or the butcher with the tastiest *txistorra* (a quick-cured pork sausage) are common. Although the supermarket exists in modern Basque Country, many Basque people still set aside time to make trips to single-purpose stores for fish, meat, cheese, or fresh produce.

SEASONALITY: This value may seem trendy, but seasonality has been ever constant in Basque Country. Even with modern innovations, the Basque people never unlearned their taste for seasonal foods, in season. In fact, the Basques will profess that they are quite happy limiting consumption of their favorite fish or mushroom to the month or two when it is most flavorful, and then moving on to the next seasonal delicacy. They cycle from one mini season to the next, from *menestra* (vegetable stew) to anchovies to *talo* (corn flatbread), from txistorra to steaks and cider, which means a constant change of scenery when gathering around a table for shared meals.

RUSTIC OVER REFINED: Basque cooking eschews fancy touches, preferring the good char from a grill or the melding of flavors in a comforting stew. Of course the Michelin side of the cuisine has a highly refined book of tricks, but in general the Basque style leans toward primitive elements and simple garnishes.

SINGLE PLATES: You'll be hard pressed to find a meat with side dishes on a single plate in Basque Country. The principal ingredient, whether fish or beans, is given the spotlight, garnished only with a generous ladle of sauce (important!) or a pickled pepper. Much has been made over the "four colors" of Basque sauces: red, green, white, and black, which get their color from peppers, parsley, olive oil, and squid ink, respectively. In Basque cuisine, there are many examples of dishes that are nothing more than a protein swimming in a simple, lovely sauce. Vegetables are relegated to preceding courses, asparagus or artichokes destined to be openers for the main event.

POLIKI, POLIKI: This oft-repeated phrase means "little by little," and the kitchen is an ideal place to employ it. Many dishes are formed with a base of *sofrito*, a mix of sautéed vegetables, especially onions. The difference between a good dish and an incredible one is often twenty extra minutes of cooking your onions, coaxing them to a sweet, golden brown.

OIL AS AN INGREDIENT (SALT, TOO): Basque cuisine requires that you take a new view of "pantry staples." Olive oil is an ingredient. Its taste matters. Olive oil experiences great turnover in Basque kitchens, and to replicate the results achieved in those kitchens it helps to use fresh olive oil, a Spanish variety or one with a similar flavor profile. You shouldn't be afraid to use it in abundance; we all know by now that olive oil isn't what makes you fat. Salt is also an ingredient, one with different uses—it can be used to heighten flavor, or its varying textures can be employed to add an unexpected crunch to a pintxo. For suggestions on these ingredients and more, as well as favorite artisans, turn to the Resources section on page 316.

THE IMPORTANCE OF TEXTURE: Where some cultures judge a dish primarily by look and then flavor, the Basques go a step further. They are on another wavelength, one where texture is an important quality of a dish. They're much more sensitive to changes and inconsistencies in texture than they are, say, to an unbalanced acidity or an out-of-place sweetness. The gelatin in the flesh around the bones of the fish brings them a delight comparable to that of a Frenchman biting into the peppery crunch of arugula squeezed with tart lemon.

The products that mark Basque cuisine fill the pages of this book. They are land products—leeks, mushrooms, apples. They are products from the sea—anchovy, tuna, salt cod. They include cheeses—Idiazabal, Ossau-Iraty, and Roncal. They are from the farm—sausages of meat and of blood, stews of everything from beef to pork to wild game. Basque Country provides the drink for the toast, too, in the form of a wholly unique cider and world-class wines.

THE LAND

To understand Basque food, you have to understand Basque people. To understand Basque people, it helps to begin with the land, as the Basques, more than most postindustrial civilizations, maintain a strong link with the earth. Basque Country has an enchanting topography: mountains, forests, streams, meadows, oceans. Craggy cliffs and velvety green hills, over which falls an almost constant misty drizzle known as *sirimiri* in the Basque's unique language, Euskara. The sea laps against sand and crashes on rock, but most of Basque Country is mountains. Out of these mountains came a people who maintained a relative isolation from the world until modern times. They're a people with a difficult, strange language, a personality different from that of their Spanish and French neighbors, and a culture rich in mythology and tradition.

Basque Country is a well-cared-for corner of the world. It encompasses 8,000 square miles of varied terrain, with 140 miles of coastline, divided into seven provinces: Araba, Bizkaia, Gipuzkoa, Lapurdi, Nafarroa, Nafarroa Beherea, and Zuberoa. There are various geo- and sociopolitical ways to divide these provinces:

NORTHERN BASQUE COUNTRY/IPARRALDE: Lapurdi, Nafarroa Beherea, and Zuberoa in France.

SOUTHERN BASQUE COUNTRY/HEGOALDE: Araba, Bizkaia, Gipuzkoa, and Nafarroa in Spain.

EUSKADI is the Basque name for the Comunidad Autónomo Vasco, a Spanish political designation that consists of three of the four Spanish provinces with Basque heritage: Gipuzkoa, Bizkaia, and Araba.

EUSKAL HERRIA is the collective name for all seven provinces, and it carries a strong ideological nuance.

Despite living in the most industrial, wealthy region of the Iberian peninsula, the "Spanish" Basques maintain their village lifestyle, with neither the lazy spread of the French Basque countryside nor the urban stretch of the rest of Spain. The "French" Basque side, Iparralde, is still a wholly rural area, save the coast and its surfing-centered tourism. Preserving the natural parcels of land has enabled a highly populated area to hold on to its link to farming, and a mark of Basque cuisine is most definitely the fact that the link between man and nature has never been fully broken.

Basque Country's culinary divide is not by province or geopolitical nation-state, though; it is by coast and mountain. The diet of a shepherd and the diet of a fisherman, two iconic Basque professions, have very little in common. Even

nowadays, when most Basques work in globalized, digitalized industries along with the rest of the world, the marked difference remains. In Araba and lower Nafarroa, meals are meats, stews, and other foods easily captured or foraged, slowly cooked in a filling, rustic way. This is quite different from those of coastal Gipuzkoa and Bizkaia, where lighter dishes of exquisitely prepared seafood prevail. Iparralde allows a large amount of French influence in its cooking, making for luxurious, if less notably "Basque," touches: Butter replaces olive oil; pastis replaces *txakoli* (Basque white wine; see page 139). The land has, over the centuries, informed the diet of every Basque.

THE PEOPLE

Historically the Basque were, for the most part, a nautical, agricultural, and pastoral people. Their traditional occupations maintain an age-old connection to the land. They have a knack for working fields that require one-on-one, tactile fights with nature. The tradition of shepherding is deeply rooted in the culture, and shepherds receive a profound respect, their works and lifestyle having influenced the traditions of the entire Basque Country.

It's also a culture that has never been afraid of the high seas. Juan Sebastián Elcano, from Getaria, was the only captain to return from Magellan's ill-fated trip around the world—and he returned, on the ship *Victoria*, with valuable spices. Miguel López de Legazpi, from Zumarraga, went to the Philippines in search of more. The port of Baiona (in French, Bayonne) has been a center of commercial activity since the Middle Ages. This thirst for exploration later evolved into ocean foraging, earning Basques a reputation as outstanding fishermen.

The center of life for Basques has since time immemorial been the *baserri* (farm). *Baserriak*, farmhouses, were intimately linked to the name and identity of particular families over many generations. The village is another important concept in what was, until relatively recently, quite a rural population. *Auzolan* is the Euskara word for "community work," and refers to the gathering of neighbors to help with tilling the earth, gathering harvests, slaughtering animals, and other difficult jobs that typically concluded in a feast, with a few edible gifts thrown in for good measure.

The society was matriarchal, in contrast to most other traditional European societies. Strict gender roles handed the strenuous labor to the men, while women were the heads of households, carried on the family lineage, and were also able to own property. The Basque woman remains a strong character today, an imposing figure in the household, which perhaps contributed to the formation of the txoko, or *sociedad*, historically male-only dining societies where the *kuadrilla*, a Basque social group formed for life, would gather to eat, talk, and relax away from the home.

Basque traditions and mythologies were cataloged by the master ethnographer Joxemiel Barandiaran, from Ataun, and belief in these myths and in the deities that lived in the Basque lands before the arrival of Kixmi, or Christ, still forms a background to the Basque story.

The Basques are musical, dancing people, aficionados of wind instruments, accordions, and unique instruments like the *txalaparta*, a series of wooden boards that emit different tones when struck. Played in pairs like a musical game, its origins lie with the *kirikoketa*, which mimics the sounds heard during cider production, where pressing apples becomes a playful back-and-forth among workers who employ percussion to keep themselves entertained. It is often played now at Basque *jaiak*, festivals filled with traditional food, sport, dress, and music. These jaiak are an excuse, really, to remember the culture's rich traditions and gather around the table, which, even in this day and age, is still the Basques' favorite thing to do.

The distinctive modern Basque profession has also shifted—toward the kitchen. San Sebastián has held the record for having more Michelin-starred restaurants per capita than anywhere else in the world. Tourism has been a mainstay now for hundreds of years, and its modern version is highly motivated by gastronomic demands and culinary curiosity. It makes sense that the chef is the new Basque star—of all the modern professions, being a cook is surely as close as it gets to getting your hands dirty. And, of course, Basque chefs excel.

The Basques tend to enjoy entertaining mythicism surrounding their culture. Culinarily speaking, there is a belief that they have always been a region of materially blessed, amazing cooks. While the raw material has been an ever-present blessing in their corner of the world, the seas always abundant and the land always fertile, the truth is that the incredible cooking that bears the Basque label is a relatively recent invention. This hasn't stopped the Basques, however, from developing a rich, codified gastronomy that is uniquely theirs.

A BRIEF BASQUE HISTORY: CULINARY AND BEYOND

The Basques are a people who have known how to survive. Such an ancient culture must have, naturally, learned how to live off the land. The skills of unearthing mushrooms or collecting greens and the knowledge of seasons and soil allowed them to adapt the land to their survival. The ancient Basque diet was rich in chestnuts, apples, legumes, and game. Grains were also an important part of nourishment, although wheat was rare and millet predominated. Lard was the most commonly used fat.

As the Catholic Church (and its days of fasting) overtook the religious leanings of the country, from the eleventh century CE onward, fish became a more important part of the diet. In the sixteenth century, the Basque whale-fishing tradition brought a new fish to the table, one that has remained an indispensable part of Basque cuisine: cod. Salted on board the fishing vessels, cod was ideal sustenance for all the provinces, and the Basques' taste for salt cod has kept the fish at the forefront of the cuisine ever since. In an 1888 edition of the newspaper *El Eco de Navarra*, twenty recipes for bacalao appear, indicating the real roots that this salt-cured fish had in all of the Basque lands.

Basques were also one of the groups eager to make their way to the New World. The effect of the discovery of America on the Basque (and European) diet was tremendous. In terms of spices, pepper, nutmeg, clove, and cinnamon arrived. The vegetable world was revolutionized with seeds brought back from the Americas, which were slowly incorporated into the local gardens. Items from the New World are so integrated into the cuisine of the Basque Country that many locals would swear to you that corn, beans, potatoes, and peppers are native species. The face of agriculture changed greatly, the potato replacing the chestnut as the hungry man's savior, and apple trees and millet plants being supplanted by corn.

A veritable exodus of young Basques seeking their fortune in the New World had begun to evolve in the late 1600s and grew to a fever pitch by the mid-1800s. Basques made their way to the Americas, building settlements from modern-day Bolivia to the American West. Some of them, nicknamed Indianoak or Amerikanoak, would make their fortune and return to their homeland, rich

enough to build an ostentatious house and settle down. Enough of them stayed behind, however, to leave a mark in places as varied as Idaho, Nevada, Argentina, Mexico, Bolivia, and San Francisco.

With the advent of the Industrial Revolution in the 1800s, Basque society took another big step toward modernity. Industrial centers in Bizkaia and Gipuzkoa prospered. The rural populations of Iparralde, Nafarroa, and Araba, in contrast, began to vacate their villages, leaving many of them empty and abandoned. Industrialists began to accrue great wealth, and modern Basque Country was forged. This new wealth gave food obsession the opportunity to flourish, and traditional products were embraced, elevated, and shared around endless tables.

Until the twentieth century, the coals of the fire were the only source of heat for cooking in homes. Pots would bubble over them, and *burruntziak*, or skewers, were used to roast game birds and farm animals. Live-fire cooking and grilling never lost their importance, and they came back with a bang with the revolution of Basque cuisine in the 1970s. Sebastián Azcaray and Felipa Eguileor's recipes from their famous restaurant *El Amparo* had already been compiled into what is considered the first Basque cuisine cookbook. But the real bible of Basque cooking, *La Cocina de Nicolasa* (1933), was a recipe book by Nicolasa Pradera, whose now defunct establishment in the old part of San Sebastián is considered one of the key restaurants in the history of Basque cooking.

The French invasion of chefs, part of the Belle Epoque tourism boom, left its imprint on the society. A group of chefs from Gipuzkoa, born in the 1940s, was greatly inspired by Paul Bocuse and the nouvelle cuisine movement in France. A young Juan Mari Arzak had a brief sojourn in Bocuse's restaurant and carried the inspiration back home with him to Gipuzkoa, along with the devotion to market cuisine, seasonal food, and local gastronomy. Injecting these values with their own creativity became the guiding light for this group of chefs. They met with eleven of their friends and crafted a manifesto, with various points and goals, among which was the statement:

> We have putting the Basque cuisine among the best in the world as our main goal, a difficult one, since we know that the Chinese and French cuisines are recognized as the world's best. And, without arrogance, we think that the Basque cuisine can reach the same goals, thanks to its quality and its tradition.

This movement, so patriotic in nature, proved easy to digest for Basques everywhere. It gave the Basque chefs a flag to stand behind and a cause under which to unite: New Basque Cuisine. They recovered old recipes, revised traditional recipes for authenticity, and also innovated, paving the way for an entire generation of new chefs, every single one of whom has passed through at least one of these originals' kitchens. This inspired a movement across Spain, which culminated in Ferran Adrià's El Bulli. Locally, it inspired the creation of the Basque culinary scene we know today: the cult of personalities around Basque chefs, the Michelin stars, and the ever-aspiring pintxo bars.

THE LANGUAGE

Euskara, the Basque language, is the cornerstone of Basque culture. In a globalized world, with increased immigration to the Basque Country and Spain, speaking the language (being an *euskaldun*) is one of the true indicators of belonging. Euskara's origins have proved difficult to trace—it is unrelated to the Indo-European languages, with a structure totally distinct from the Romance languages that surround it. There is even a charming legend that claims Noah's grandson Tubal brought Euskara from the tower of Babel.

Basque nationalists claim unbroken descent in this place from the Cro-Magnon period, and definitive studies link the Basques back three thousand years. In the Santimamiñe caves in Bizkaia, there is evidence of ancient humans, and monolithic standing stones *harrespilak* and dolmen, prehistoric monuments that date back thousands of years, dot the hills of the Basque Country. Whether this culture dates back three thousand years or more, the telling part is that so many Basques believe a possible link to the Stone Age to be an integral part of their culture.

In reaction to the nineteenth-century mass immigration of Spanish speakers to the Basque Country's mines and factories, Basque nationalism was born. Its figurehead, Sabino de Arana y Goiri, created a movement claiming "authentic" Basqueness, with a new flag (the *ikurriña*) and a nationalist political party (the Euzko Alderdi Jeltzalea, or EAJ). The Basque Country suffered severe cultural oppression. The nationalist and separatist group Euskadi Ta Askatasuna (ETA, "Basque Homeland and Liberty") was founded in 1959 to resist this oppression. Its terrorist campaign claimed more than eight hundred lives in the name of independence, but had lost popular support by the end of the 1990s. A permanent cease-fire was declared in 2010, followed by disarmament in 2017.

The modern geopolitical divisions of the land are still highly controversial, with terrorist groups (most notoriously ETA) demanding independence from Spain. However, the unity of seven provinces that these groups seem intent upon was only briefly a reality during the eleventh century. The real unity comes in the form of Euskara, a language rich and ancient yet late to be "civilized." In the twentieth century, the language suffered greatly on the Spanish side under Franco, who persecuted Basque speakers and promoted the use of written and spoken Spanish only. An entire generation, now middle-aged, either does not speak Basque, speaks it having learned later in life, or speaks it thanks to some furtive lessons by their parents or grandparents.

Euskara's dialects have always been highly localized; residents from one side of a province may have trouble understanding those from the opposite end. However, in 1968 the language was standardized under the label Euskara Batua, and in 1982 it was made the official language of the Spanish Basque provinces, alongside Spanish. Nowadays, *ikastolak* (Basque-language schools) are the norm, with teaching almost entirely done in Euskara, raising a new generation of speakers.

A Note on Euskara, the Basque Language

The Basque language is notoriously intimidating. The sheer quantity of *X*'s next to *T*'s and unfriendly letters like *Z*'s and *K*'s might make you feel a stutter coming on before you've even begun to speak. In reality, the pronunciation is not as complicated as it looks.

Phonetically, the vowels in Euskara Batua correspond to only one sound (unlike in English). When you see *tx* together, that sound is always *ch* (as in *pintxos* [*peen-chos*]). Z, another common consonant, is a soft, snakelike *ess*. The *tt* is quite difficult to pronounce; it has a strange sound similar to a wet, muffled version of the *tx*—when in doubt, pronounce it as *ch*.

On the Spanish side of the Basque Country, Euskara is the official language along with Spanish, so one will find place names written in both Spanish and Basque. Sometimes they are similar (as in the Spanish Zarauz and the Basque Zarautz) and sometimes they are totally unrelated (as in the Spanish Vitoria and the Basque Gasteiz). For the sake of this book, all culinary terms and recipe titles are in Euskara, as well as most of the place names, save a few of the spots readers are most likely to know by their Spanish name, like San Sebastián. ✥

WHAT MAKES A PINTXO? Is it size? Is it form? Is it ingredient? Many efforts have been made to define this uniquely Basque food. A Basque carries around an innate sense of what is a pintxo and what is not. (Of course, as in any aspect of Basque cuisine, there are at least as many opinions as there are provinces.) For our purposes, a few basic facts make up a universally accepted definition:

- A pintxo is a bite of food.

- A pintxo is small; it shouldn't be any bigger than about the size of a fist.

- A pintxo is an individual portion.

- A pintxo is served in a bar. They are rarely, if ever, found in restaurants or homes.

- A pintxo can have a toothpick through it, hence the name *pintxo*, from the verb *pinchar*, "to pierce." But a pintxo can also be between or on bread or served on a plate to be eaten with a fork (or spoon).

- A pintxo is not a tapa. Why? Tapas are sometimes handed out free with drinks, something unheard of in pintxo bars. Tapas are traditionally a single-food item, in a small-plate portion, while pintxos tend to be a small sandwich or finished dish, ranging from humble to avant-garde.

Pintxos have been enjoyed in the same elegantly paced way since their inception, in part because they were born of the need to buffer alcohol intake. Their evolution has mainly been one of format. First came the *banderilla*, a small skewer typically holding vinegar-cured ingredients, from olives to onions to anchovies to peppers. They coexisted next to plates or casseroles of cooked ingredients, which could range from mushrooms to liver to salt cod. It wasn't long before these ingredients hopped onto slices of bread, secured with a toothpick. Then came the *cocina en miniatura* (literally "cuisine in miniature"), dishes worthy of restaurants, with expensive ingredients or laborious techniques, presented in pintxo size. The evolution of the pintxo continues into the modern day.

As is to be expected of a tradition with such cultural importance, there are rules for partaking of pintxos. For locals, a pintxo is often a prelude to a full meal. The custom of making a night of pintxo hopping is confined to weekends and is sometimes as exotic for a local as it is for a foreigner.

To eat a pintxo in Basque Country, you must go to a bar. It is likely to be crowded, but you can't be shy. Any square centimeter of open space is game for a wineglass, an elbow, or a person. Platters of room-temperature offerings scatter the bartop, and a menu of hot pintxos hangs behind the bar. If you want a room-temperature pintxo, ask the bartender for a plate (which should never be larger than six inches in diameter), or simply grab a napkin, and then help yourself to a pintxo. If you'd like a hot pintxo, tell the bartender, who will pass the order on to the kitchen.

When you place your pintxo order, you give your drink order, too. A pintxo is always eaten with a glass of wine, beer, or cider. Alcohol serving sizes are substantially smaller than in the United States. You won't find full wineglasses; the pour is just enough to accompany the small plate of food and move on to the next wine.

Once the pintxo is served, any napkins or toothpicks used in the process can be thrown on the floor for the bar staff to clean up later on.

When you're finished eating, ask the bartender for the bill. In Basque Country, it is considered rude, even shocking, for the waiter to charge you before the food has been consumed. When the bartender gives you the bill, settle up and head out to the next bar, which is usually just a block or two away. The rule of thumb is one bar, one pintxo, and one drink, then move on.

The recipes in this chapter are, without a doubt, classics. Some, like the *patata tortilla*, date back generations; others, like the ham, cheese, and sun-dried tomato pintxo on page 49, are recent classics. Some are not Basque in origin, but are present on nearly every bar in Basque Country. All are delicious. While pintxos might not be eaten at home in Basque Country, you can serve these recipes as appetizers before dinner. Or invite some friends over, make a few different recipes, and create your own pintxo bar on your kitchen countertop. This is social food—party food—made for eating with friends along with something good to drink.

Gilda

ANCHOVY, PEPPER, AND OLIVE SKEWER

POPULAR BASQUE LEGEND has it that the *gilda* was the first pintxo, invented and named in a bar in the center of San Sebastián. The gilda is a *banderilla*, a toothpick-skewered combination that includes pickled vegetables or seafood preserves. While these banderillas were among the first foods to find a home on bartops in San Sebastián, it's doubtful that the exact combination first created was the gilda's now signature anchovy, guindilla chile, and olive.

There are photos dating back to at least 1942 of what is now known as the gilda in emblematic bars of San Sebastián, like Bar Martínez, where they were called *torero* or banderilla (sometimes *banderilla de guindilla*), after the barbed sticks used in bullfighting. The name "gilda" came later, after the Rita Hayworth character from the 1946 film *Gilda* zoomed to popularity in Spain. The name was given because both the food and the Hayworth character are green (risqué in Spanish), salty, and a little spicy.

The perfect bite before a meal, this gilda's intense salty flavors are balanced by the sharp vinegar from the pickled peppers. The important thing is to choose a good salt-cured anchovy from Spain. The quality can vary, but the most excellent anchovies are the hand-cleaned Cantabrian kind, smaller than anchovies from other waters, and without a bone in sight. They melt like butter in your mouth and have a pleasant oceany taste. ✿

SERVES 4

8 pickled guindilla peppers
(see page 175)

8 green manzanilla olives,
pitted

4 anchovy fillets in olive oil,
preferably Cantabrian

Good-quality extra-virgin olive oil,
for garnish

Cut the stems off the peppers. Cut each pepper in half crosswise.

With a long toothpick, prick one olive through its center, followed by two pieces of pepper. Add an anchovy, threading it onto the toothpick in an "S" shape. Add two more pieces of pepper. Finish with another olive. Repeat with the remaining ingredients to make three more gildas.

Serve at room temperature on a platter, drizzled generously with olive oil.

Patata Tortilla

SPANISH OMELET

THE SPANISH OMELET, or *tortilla española*, is Spain's unofficial national dish. It is often the first cooking lesson handed down from mother to child. If a Spaniard knows how to cook only one thing, it is tortilla. If there is only one offering in a lonely corner bar, it's a round plate of tortilla. The tortilla is much, much greater than the sum of its humble parts—potato, egg, and onion. Texture can vary, but generally a perfect tortilla has a firm outer layer that, when sliced, oozes ever so slightly out of shape (as opposed to releasing a bunch of uncooked egg or, worse, being a firm, cakelike lump).

While popular in all of Spain, the *patata tortilla* may, in fact, be traceable to Nafarroa. In the anonymously authored *Memorial de Ratonera: El Comer, El Vestir, y La Vida de los Navarros de 1817*, the shepherds of the region are described as eating "two or three eggs in an omelette for five or six, because our women know how to make it big and fat with just a few eggs, mixing potatoes, bread, and other things."

It is appropriate to eat tortilla all day—for breakfast, lunch, snack, or dinner. Perhaps the most perfect time to eat tortilla is *hamaiketako*—the hallowed eleven a.m. snack break meant to tide you over until what is, by most of the world's standards, quite a late lunch (around two p.m. on the Spanish side of Basque Country). Sweet Italian green pepper is a common addition. It can be thinly sliced and added to the pan with the potatoes. ✤

SERVES 8

3 large potatoes, preferably Monalisa, Kennebec, or Yukon Gold, peeled	2 teaspoons kosher salt, plus more as needed
3 tablespoons (45 mL) extra-virgin olive oil, plus more if needed	1 cup (240 mL) sunflower or vegetable oil
2 onions, thinly sliced	10 large eggs

Halve the potatoes lengthwise and then cut each half lengthwise into quarters. Chop into pieces about ½ inch (1.5 cm) thick; you should have about 4 cups (see Notes). Put the potatoes in a bowl, add water to cover, and set aside.

In a small sauté pan, heat 2 tablespoons of the olive oil over high heat. Add the onions and sprinkle with ½ teaspoon of the salt. Lower the heat to medium and cook, stirring occasionally, for about 40 minutes, until the onions are totally soft and have taken on a deep golden color. Remove from the heat and set aside.

continued »

Meanwhile, in a separate medium skillet, heat the sunflower oil over medium heat to about 250°F (120°C). Drain the potatoes and pat them dry. To test the oil, drop in a piece of potato; if it begins to bubble and sizzle, the oil is ready. Fry the potatoes for about 15 minutes, or until a knife inserted into a larger piece comes out easily. Use a slotted spoon to remove the potatoes from the oil. Sprinkle them with ½ teaspoon of the salt.

In a large bowl, beat the eggs with the remaining 1 teaspoon salt. Add the onions and potatoes and stir to combine.

Heat a perfectly clean 10-inch (25 cm) nonstick skillet (see Notes) over high heat. (The bigger the stove burner, the more evenly the tortilla will cook, so use your largest burner.) Coat the skillet with the remaining 1 tablespoon olive oil. Add the egg-potato mixture and immediately lower the heat to medium. Stir quickly a few times, scraping along the bottom with a silicone spatula, then leave the skillet untouched, allowing the egg to cook. Move the spatula around the sides of the pan, slipping it under the omelet and loosening any stubborn stuck parts very gingerly, in an attempt to ensure the omelet is not adhering to any part of the skillet's surface. Cook for about 4 minutes, until the edges are fully cooked but the center is still a bit liquid.

Place a round plate with a diameter larger than the pan's upside down on the top of the pan. With one hand on the plate and one hand holding the pan, quickly flip the pan and plate together in one motion so that the tortilla is on the plate.

If the pan has any pieces stuck to it, quickly clean it and coat it with a bit more oil. Return the pan to the heat and slide the omelet back into the pan. Tuck the edges under with your spatula and cook for 3 minutes more.

Slide the omelet onto a clean, dry plate and let rest for 5 minutes before slicing into 8 wedges and serving.

Notes The shape of the cut potato is a highly personal preference. Some people like an irregular shape; to get it, insert a knife about ½ inch (1.5 cm) into a peeled potato and then rotate and lift the knife, breaking off an irregularly shaped piece. Rotate the potato slightly and repeat. Others prefer thin, round slices.

The choice of pan is key. It should be a 10-inch (25 cm) nonstick skillet, with its nonstick properties fully intact. In most Basque homes, there is one pan used always and sometimes exclusively for making tortilla.

Piper Beteak

STUFFED PEPPERS

EVERY PINTXO BAR OFFERS a piquillo pepper dish. With their slightly smoky flavor, unique triangular shape, and delicate texture, piquillos are perfectly at home on slices of bread, accompanied by a bit of pork loin or an anchovy. When served whole, they are often stuffed with mayonnaise and other ingredients from ham and leeks to tuna. When served warm, they are stuffed with béchamel-bound ground beef or salt cod, another common filling (see Notes). Braised meat, such as leftover stew meat, short ribs, or *txahal masailak* (beef cheeks; see page 217), is a more gourmet substitute.

While this recipe will work with any small red pepper, the authentic *pimiento del piquillo* is from Lodosa in Nafarroa (Navarre). Their smoky flavor comes from the fire used to roast off the skin. Smaller and more delicate than a red bell pepper, they make for a perfect bite-size stuffed pepper. ✿

MAKES 12

2 tablespoons extra-virgin olive oil

1 spring onion, diced

½ sweet Italian green pepper, such as Cubanelle, diced

1 garlic clove, minced

Kosher salt

10 ounces (285 g) ground beef or veal

2 tablespoons all-purpose flour, plus more for breading

1 cup (240 mL) whole milk, at room temperature

16 jarred or canned piquillo peppers (see Notes), drained

¼ cup (60 mL) tomato sauce (see page 192)

1 tablespoon heavy cream or whole milk

Olive oil or vegetable oil, for frying

2 large eggs

In a medium sauté pan, heat the olive oil over medium-high heat. Add the spring onion, green pepper, garlic, and a pinch of salt. Cook, stirring occasionally, for 5 to 7 minutes, or until the onion is translucent and tender.

Add the ground beef and another generous pinch of salt and cook, breaking up the meat with a wooden spoon as it cooks and stirring occasionally, for 7 to 8 minutes, until the meat is fully cooked. Add the flour and stir for about 1 minute. Add the milk little by little, stirring continuously. Once all the milk has been added, cook for about 2 minutes more to thicken. Remove from the heat and let cool completely. Set aside 2 tablespoons of the meat mixture.

continued »

In a blender, combine 4 piquillo peppers, the tomato sauce, the reserved 2 tablespoons meat mixture, and the cream. Add a pinch of salt and blend well. (Alternatively, combine the ingredients in a bowl and blend using an immersion blender.) Set aside.

Transfer the remaining meat mixture to a pastry bag and snip off the tip, leaving a hole large enough for the meat to pass through. (Alternatively, transfer the mixture to a resealable plastic bag and snip off one corner, or use a small spoon to fill the peppers.) Holding a pepper in one hand, insert the pastry bag tip into the open end and squeeze until the pepper is full. Place the filled pepper on a plate or platter and repeat with the remaining 11 peppers and filling.

Preheat the oven to 350°F (175°C).

Pour oil into a medium sauté pan to the depth of about an inch. Heat the oil over medium heat to about 350°F (175°C), or until a bit of flour sizzles on contact.

Fill a shallow bowl with flour and whisk in a generous pinch of salt. In a separate medium bowl, beat the eggs. Gently dredge each stuffed pepper in the flour, then roll it between your hands to remove excess flour. Dip the pepper in the eggs, allowing any excess to drip off. Carefully add the pepper to the hot oil, and repeat, dredging enough peppers to fill the pan (do not overcrowd the pan). Cook on one side until it begins to color. Turn and cook on the second side until golden. Use a slotted spoon to remove the peppers from the oil and drain on paper towels. Repeat until all peppers are fried.

Transfer the fried peppers to a casserole dish, gently ladle the pepper-tomato sauce over the top, and heat in the oven until warm. Serve.

Notes A small jar (about 200 grams) usually contains about 10 peppers. There are also larger jars available, with differing sizes and quality of pepper. It's always better to have a few extra in case any break as you're filling them.

Salt cod can be substituted for the ground beef. Typically the battering and frying step is omitted when using fish.

THE HISTORY OF THE PINTXO

1920 TO 1940

Drinking outside of the home was an established social custom well before the Spanish Civil War. People would head to the cider houses and bodegas in the old part of San Sebastián to buy their alcohol (for their home or business) and would make the most of the trip by downing a few drinks.

1940 TO 1960

Post–Spanish Civil War, *txikiteo*, the practice of traveling from bar to bar with a *kuadrilla* (a group of close friends), becomes routine. *Kuadrillak* meet at the same bar to begin the same route every night, ultimately consuming up to thirty small glasses (about a bottle) of wine a head in the process. Luckily, the wine is very cheap, around 7 pesetas (about 4 cents in today's currency).

There is also widespread scarcity. A few bars, many of them under the same ownership today, innovate by putting out a bit of food on the bartop. Bar Martinez, on Calle 31 de Agosto in San Sebastián, is one of them.

Much of the food and some of the alcohol available in the bars are contraband, smuggled from France. The police never take action, and luxuries like *txaka* (canned crab), unseen before it appeared on the bar of Borda Berri, dot the bars of the city.

The movie *Gilda* arrives in Spain, and is later the inspiration for the name of what is often purported to be the first pintxo (see page 23). A *banderilla*-style bite costs around 3 pesetas (a current value of 2 euro cents). Summer visitors from the interior of Spain are the ones who begin to refer to these toothpick-held pickles as *pinchos*.

1960 TO 1980

Life begins to get a little easier. Supply chains open up, and bars begin to develop their food offerings. Each bar has a specialty. The name "pincho" begins to catch on and circulate, but with a Basque spelling: *pintxo*.

Though the name "pintxo" has not yet reached Bilbao, familiar-looking bites begin to appear in the city's bars, among them the *bilbainito*, hard-boiled egg with mayonnaise and shrimp; *el grillo*, a piece of potato with lettuce and onion; and chunks of olive oil–preserved albacore to be grabbed with a toothpick. On Sundays, there are bars that serve fried calamari, or even *kroketak* (croquettes). The food is served off in a corner, however, not atop the bar.

In San Sebastián, the pintxo is in its full splendor, and the local municipal law enforcement doesn't know how to handle it. In the 1960s, hefty fines for setting out plates of uncovered pintxos are established—25,000 pesetas (about 150 euros today). Glass cases appear in the bars to cover the pintxos.

Bars begin to become known for their specialties: anchovies, eggs, tripe, salt cod, and more. As the pintxo business becomes more lucrative, frozen food companies begin to hock premade croquettes to bars willing to accept them.

1980 TO 2000

Creativity replaces necessity as the inspiration for pintxos as the country becomes more prosperous. Innovations such as puff pastry and egg yolks on top of mushrooms begin to spread.

Cocina en miniatura takes hold in the late 1980s. A few of San Sebastián's bars, Aloña Berri in the Gros neighborhood in particular, begin to offer miniature works of art, cooked to order. This concept attracts crowds.

Meanwhile, in Bilbao, the pintxo with bread appears, along with mushrooms and peppers. One of the first bars to bring the pintxo to Bilbao was Oriotarra. The book *Pintxos Donostiarras* by Pedro Martin Villa is released in 1992. The longest-running pintxo competition, El Concurso de Pintxos (Pintxo Txapelketa Bilbao Bizkaia), holds its first event in Bilbao in 1999.

A bar on Portu Kalea in San Sebastián begins putting out pintxos made with unorthodox combinations of ingredients, derided as "senseless mixtures" by traditionalists, but the format is quickly copied when it proves successful.

2000 TO PRESENT

Txikiteo becomes less common, a change attributed to a trend toward "cleaner" living, as well as older generations passing away and wine prices rising. It is normal to see groups of couples and friends drinking and eating pintxos for dinner, rather than groups of men drinking glass after glass of wine.

Bar owners retire and pass on their bars sometimes to outsiders. These newcomers have a more global outlook; the chefs are trained in Michelin-starred kitchens. The global explosion in popularity of pintxos and rising number of visitors to Basque Country keeps the bars full, especially in summer.

Kroketak

CROQUETTES

THE *KROKETA* is the darling of the dinner table in Basque Country and throughout Spain. Fried until golden and made to be eaten by hand, the kroketa's crunchy bread crumb exterior gives way to a thick, creamy interior that calls to mind mashed potatoes or melted cheese. They are crowd-pleasers, a standby on the wooden counters of any bar, and are even served as an entrée for children.

Classic *kroketak* are made with *jamón Ibérico de bellota*, cured ham from acorn-finished pigs, but common variations include porcini or salt cod (see page 89), and it's not difficult to find chicken and blood sausage versions as well.

One secret to croquette excellence is the extra step of infusing the dairy with the star ingredient. When made with ham-infused milk and cream, the resulting béchamel takes on a new, subtly flavored life. *Jamón Ibérico* is more flavorful than its cousin, *jamón Serrano*, but you can use either. ❧

MAKES ABOUT 30 CROQUETTES

3¼ cups (780 mL) whole milk

1 cup (240 mL) heavy cream

1 ham bone (optional), or 3 slices (50 g) Ibérico or Serrano ham

5 tablespoons (70 g) unsalted butter

½ onion, diced fine

3 cups (375 g) all-purpose flour

Kosher salt

5 ounces (140 g) Ibérico or Serrano ham, finely chopped (⅓ cup)

3 large eggs

2 cups (220 g) dry bread crumbs (see Note)

Olive oil, for frying

In a medium saucepan, combine the milk, cream, and ham bone and bring to a simmer over medium heat. Remove from the heat and set aside to infuse for at least 15 minutes before straining out the solids.

In a large sauté pan, melt the butter over medium heat. Add the onion and cook until translucent and very tender, about 15 minutes. Increase the heat to high. Add 1 cup (125 g) of the flour and stir with a whisk for about 1 minute. While whisking vigorously, add the milk-cream mixture, little by little at first, then working up to ½-cup increments, until all has been incorporated. Add a generous pinch of salt. Taste the béchamel and add a bit more salt, if desired.

Mix the chopped ham into the béchamel. Chilling the mixture in a roasting pan for at least 1 hour, or in a pastry bag overnight, will make it easier to form a perfectly shaped croquette.

continued »

Beat the eggs in a bowl. Spread the bread crumbs over a rimmed baking sheet or large plate. Spread the remaining 2 cups (250 g) flour on a separate plate.

If your croquette base is in a roasting pan, scoop about 2 tablespoons of the mixture and form it into a small ball. Dredge the ball in the flour, shaking off the excess, then dip it in the egg, allowing the excess to drip off, and finally roll it in the bread crumbs to coat. Set the coated ball on a clean, dry plate or baking sheet until ready to fry.

If your croquette base is in a pastry bag, snip the tip from the bag to leave a hole about 1 inch (2.5 cm) in diameter. Pipe roughly 3-inch (7.5 cm) logs of croquette base onto the plate with the flour, cutting them with a butter knife or other straight object. Sprinkle with more flour to coat, then, working one at a time, dip the pieces in the egg, allowing the excess to drip off, and finally roll them in the bread crumbs to coat. Set the coated pieces on a clean, dry plate or baking sheet until ready to fry.

If you aren't frying them immediately, the breaded croquettes can be refrigerated for up to 3 days. They can also be frozen for up to 3 months, and can go straight from freezer to fryer when desired. (To freeze, put the croquettes on a baking sheet, freeze until solid, then transfer to a freezer bag.)

In a heavy saucepan, heat 1 to 2 inches (3 to 5 cm) of olive oil over high heat until it reaches about 350°F (180°C). To test the oil, throw in a few bread crumbs; when they sizzle on contact, the oil is ready. Working in batches to avoid crowding the pot, fry the croquettes until golden brown, turning them occasionally to cook evenly. Remove with a slotted spoon and drain on paper towels. Sprinkle immediately with salt.

Transfer to a platter and serve warm.

Note The finer the bread crumb, the more classic the croquette. Using panko bread crumbs will result in more modern croquettes.

You can also double up on bread crumbs instead of using flour, coating the croquettes in bread crumbs, then egg, then again in bread crumbs. This results in extra-crunchy croquettes. Experiment to find your favorite texture.

Entsaladilla Errusiarra

POTATO SALAD

WHILE NOT BASQUE IN ORIGIN, *entsaladilla errusiarra* is the workhorse of virtually all pintxo bars. It's heaped high on slices of baguette and occasionally served in puff pastry or tart shells. Garnishes vary widely and are often a reflection of the aesthetic of the bar: two strips of red pepper, crossed; a green olive, cut in half; a dollop of mayonnaise, which in more old-fashioned bars is piped through a decorative pastry tip; or even a single peeled shrimp.

As its name suggests, the original dish is purportedly from 1800s Russia. Every European country has its version, always made with pantry ingredients. In Basque Country, this means potatoes, oil, eggs, carrots, and tuna.

This version features a technique inspired by savvy home cooks—adding the ingredients to the same pot of boiling water with careful timing so they all finish simultaneously—it saves you several pots and time. Don't skip the homemade mayonnaise, which takes five minutes flat using an immersion blender, and be sure to chill the salad before serving so the flavors can meld. ✿

SERVES 12

Kosher salt

3 large potatoes (450 g), preferably Yukon Gold or red potatoes, peeled

3 carrots, peeled

4 large eggs

1 cup (150 g) stuffed green olives

½ cup (50 g) frozen green peas, defrosted (or canned)

½ cup (80 g) drained canned tuna

2 cups (500 g) mayonnaise, preferably homemade (recipe follows)

Baguette slices, for serving

Olives, grated hard-boiled egg, and/ or red bell pepper strips, for serving (optional)

Bring a large pot of salted water to a boil over high heat. Add the potatoes. After 7 minutes, add the carrots. After 4 minutes more, add the eggs. Boil for exactly 9 minutes more—20 minutes total. Use a slotted spoon or a spider to remove the eggs and run them under cold water to stop the cooking. Set aside. Pierce a potato with a fork; if it comes out easily, they are ready. Drain the potatoes and carrots and let cool. When the eggs are cool enough to handle, peel them.

Cut the cooked potatoes into ½-inch (1.5 cm) cubes. Cut the carrots and 3 of the eggs to the same size. Place in a large bowl. Set aside 5 olives and coarsely chop the remainder. Add the chopped olives, peas, and tuna to the bowl. Add

continued »

1 cup of the mayonnaise and stir gently. Add the remaining mayonnaise a few tablespoons at a time until the mixture is creamy and smooth.

Cover and refrigerate for at least 1 hour before serving. If you used homemade mayo, the potato salad will keep for up to 1 day; with store-bought mayo, it will keep for up to 3 days.

To serve as a pintxo, scoop generous spoonfuls onto slices of baguette. If desired, top each with an olive (whole or halved lengthwise), a strip of pepper, or grated hard-boiled egg (grated on the small holes of a box grater). For family gatherings and group dinners, serve the salad in a single large bowl, garnished with the olives and grated hard-boiled egg or the pepper strips.

Homemade Mayonnaise

MAKES 2 CUPS

1 large egg

Apple cider vinegar

Kosher salt

2 cups (480 mL) light olive oil or vegetable oil

Combine the egg, a splash of vinegar, a pinch of salt, and a splash of the olive oil in a tall cylindrical container. Insert an immersion blender and blend to emulsify the mixture. With the blender running, add the remaining oil in a steady stream, moving the blender stick slowly up and down. (Alternatively, use a conventional blender and with the blender running, slowly stream the oil through the hole in the lid.) Taste for seasoning, adding more salt or vinegar if necessary. If it is too thick, stir in a bit of water.

Transfer to an airtight container and store in the refrigerator for up to 3 days.

Txorizoa Sagardotan

CIDER-BRAISED CHORIZO

A DISH INSPIRED by the most common of pantry staples, *txorizoa sagardotan* can save a cook in a pinch. In this recipe, Basque cider, less sweet and more sour than its Anglo-Saxon and French counterparts, simmers cured chorizo to tender perfection. This dish likely originated at rural cider houses in Basque Country and neighboring Asturias in Spain. Friends and acquaintances would gather in low-lying stone farmhouses to taste the year's vintage and select cider for purchase. The tradition of offering a bit of food to buffer the alcohol gave form to the modern-day cider house–turned–restaurant, a visit to which did—and often still does—start with a plate of steaming bites of chorizo and a basket of crusty bread.

For this dish, look for a Spanish chorizo. Mexican chorizo, widely available in the United States, is a ground meat sausage, heavily spiced and not cured or cooked. Spanish chorizo, however, features primarily paprika and is dried and cured until ready to eat. You can tell the amount of curing a chorizo has been through by simply giving it a squeeze. The harder it is, the longer it was cured. If it has a bit of give, it is ideal for this dish. ✢

SERVES 4

1 link (250 g) Spanish/Basque chorizo (see Resources, page 316)

2 cups (475 mL) Basque cider (see Resources, page 317)

1 crusty baguette, sliced into 1-inch (2.5 cm) pieces

Cut the twine from the end of the chorizo and slice the link crosswise into 2-inch-thick (5 cm) pieces. Put the chorizo in a medium saucepan, add the cider, and bring to a boil over high heat. Boil for 5 minutes. Lower the heat to maintain a lively simmer and cook until the liquid has reduced and the chorizo is nearly tender, 20 to 25 minutes, depending on the chorizo's freshness. Test for doneness by pricking with a knife; it should slide in without much resistance. Use a slotted spoon to transfer the chorizo to a plate or platter.

Serve with baguette slices and some toothpicks.

ANCHOVIES IN VINEGAR

ANCHOVIES ARE PRIZED BY THE BASQUES. In season, they are eaten fresh, but preserved or canned anchovies are enjoyed year-round. The salted brown anchovy is famously eaten on a toothpick, with pickled vegetables, while the vinegar-cured white anchovy is adored as a topping for crusty bread. The most famous white anchovies, colloquially known as *bokeroiak* (from the southern Spanish term *boquerón*), are found in San Sebastián's Old Town.

Bar Txepetxa, accented with yellow wood and framed photos of guests, makes no concessions to modernity. It is one of a nearly extinct race that has survived because of its singular commitment to specialization. Locals often refer to it as the "temple of the anchovy," and the fish are house-cured in a secret vinegar marinade, the recipe for which is locked away in the local bank. Deliciously acidic, they have an oh-so-slight salty sea taste. They are served atop bread that is always freshly cut and toasted to order, then topped with one of fourteen different mixtures, from diced vegetables to spider crab cream.

This is not the secret recipe, but when made with top-quality fresh fish, it tastes just as incredible. ✤

SERVES 4

½ cup (120 mL) apple cider vinegar

1 teaspoon (5 g) kosher salt, plus more as needed

⅓ cup (80 mL) extra-virgin olive oil

1 tablespoon finely chopped fresh parsley

1 garlic clove, minced

6 fresh anchovies (see Note)

In a shallow bowl, mix together the vinegar, salt, and ¼ cup (60 mL) water. Reserve in the refrigerator.

In a small bowl, whisk together the olive oil, parsley, and garlic. Set aside.

Fill a bowl with equal parts water and ice. Clean each anchovy by twisting the head about 90 degrees, then delicately pulling to remove it from the body. The spine and tail should follow, leaving you with two fillets. (If the head breaks off without them, simply discard it, then delicately pinch the tip of the spine and lift to remove it from the two fillets.) Run the anchovy fillets under cold water to rinse off any traces of blood. Inspect the fillets for bones and remove any you find, then put the fillets in the bowl of ice water.

continued »

Allow the anchovies to sit for a few minutes, then drain off the water and ice and refill the bowl with more ice water. Repeat this process twice more, soaking the anchovies for about 5 minutes between water changes. This will help remove all traces of blood from the fish. Drain once more.

Add the anchovies to the chilled vinegar marinade and refrigerate for about 4 hours. Check the anchovies, as their size can determine the length of time needed to marinate: The ideal marinated anchovy is almost (but not quite) totally white all the way to the center. When they have reached this point, drain off the marinade. If you're not going to use the anchovies immediately, transfer them to an airtight container, cover with a layer of good extra-virgin olive oil, and store in the refrigerator for up to 1 week.

To serve, place the anchovies on a serving dish and pour the garlic-parsley oil over the top. The anchovies can also be served individually, as pintxos, on freshly toasted baguette slices with the topping of your choice, such as a pepper-onion mixture (see page 220).

Note You can find or order fresh anchovies at your local fishmonger. The anchovies should smell fresh and oceany, not fishy. Anchovies are delicate, so they might not look perfect. Freshness is better determined by looking at the eyes; they should be clear and shiny, not cloudy.

ANTXOAK

ANCHOVIES

In the port village of Getaria, there is a simple storefront sandwiched in the port warehouse, looking out upon the boats that float in the water. It consists of three rooms: a shop, a bare room with a couple of tabletops and chairs, and a walk-in refrigerator with a few blue barrels. The table is occupied by a few middle-aged ladies, who roll and unroll towels hiding the small brown bodies of salted anchovies. They scrape a blade along the spine of each anchovy, slowly and meticulously cleaning the small fish, which have spent months in the barrels, covered in salt and leaching blood and water to form a brine that reeks of ocean and life. The simplicity is striking when you see the final product close up: small brown fillets, free of hair-thin bones. Equally beautiful are those destined for a shorter, vinegar-based cure in a comely curved glass jar.

This is the worship of the *antxoa*, an age-old tradition with roots in the Italians who came in search of seafood to preserve and found anchovies and tuna. The tiny fish live in schools, filter-feeding off zooplankton and larvae. The life span of the European anchovy (*Engraulis encrasicolus*) is about five years, and they grow to a maximum of 8 inches. The fish reproduce between May and June when the water is around 60°F (15°C), close to the coast in waters 15 to 30 meters deep. They are at the mercy of the current, so a great number die before reaching maturity. When this number is higher than average, the effect is felt in the anchovy catch two years later.

Great schools of anchovy are also found in September, although they are not as prized as the fatty summer anchovies. When they are in season, it is impossible not to know it: The fishmongers' windows are dotted with paper signs advertising ANCHOA DEL CANTABRICO, and they appear on every menu, from pintxo bars to the Michelin-starred restaurants.

GARLIC POTATOES

¡UN PLATILLO! ("A DISH!") rings out through the bar, bouncing off wooden walls. A small crowd of patrons is scattered throughout the bar, all eating the same dish: potatoes fragrant with garlic and parsley (tender after being twice-cooked—boiled then fried). The secret to these potatoes is the patina of oil that coats the pans (and the entire kitchen), but it's an easy dish to re-create at home.

Not of Basque origin, the Spanish *al ajillo* preparation consists of garlic sautéed in olive oil, often with a bit of parsley thrown in. The potatoes are tender, and although the smallest pieces have a hint of crispiness to them, they are mostly soft, melding with the garlic, parsley, and olive oil.

Serve them as they do in the bar, next to a basket of white baguette slices with a few forks, and spicy red paprika on the side. ✿

SERVES 4

Kosher salt

3 large potatoes, preferably Monalisa, Kennebec, or Yukon Gold, peeled and chopped into 1- to 1½-inch (2.5 to 5 cm) chunks

1½ cups (360 mL) olive, sunflower, or vegetable oil, for frying

¼ cup (60 mL) extra-virgin olive oil

4 garlic cloves, minced

½ bunch parsley, finely chopped

Baguette slices, for serving

Spicy paprika, for sprinkling

Bring a large pot of heavily salted water to a boil (about 2 tablespoons of salt will be sufficient). Add the potatoes and boil for exactly 10 minutes. Drain the potatoes in a colander.

In a deep, heavy-bottomed saucepan, heat the frying oil to about 250°F (120°C). To test the oil, add a small piece of potato; if it sizzles upon contact, the oil is ready. Working in batches if necessary to avoid crowding the pan, add the potatoes to the hot oil and fry for about 6 minutes. Use a slotted spoon to transfer the potatoes to a paper towel–lined plate to drain excess oil. They should be soft, not crispy, with some pieces just barely beginning to color.

In a large skillet, heat the extra-virgin olive oil over medium heat. Add the garlic. When the garlic starts to dance, add the potatoes. Taste for seasoning. Cook, stirring occasionally, for 3 to 4 minutes. Add the parsley, stir, and cook for 1 minute more. Empty the contents of the pan onto a plate.

Serve immediately with bread, toothpicks, and spicy paprika, to be sprinkled on to taste.

Ganba Brotxeta

SHRIMP KEBAB WITH PEPPER VINAIGRETTE

THE BAR THAT MADE the *ganba brotxeta* famous, Goiz Argi, is on San Sebastián's crowded Fermín Calbetón Street, where two of every three storefronts is a restaurant or bar. The flow of people begins around eleven a.m. and continues into the wee hours.

Bar Goiz Argi's specialty is this bacon-and-shrimp kebab, simply charred and topped with pepper and onion vinaigrette. To make these kebabs at home, you'll need a griddle or large, flat skillet. They also taste fantastic grilled. ❧

SERVES 4

1 sweet Italian green pepper, such as Cubanelle

½ red bell pepper

½ spring onion

1 garlic clove, minced

⅓ cup (80 mL) apple cider vinegar

Kosher salt

⅔ cup plus 1 tablespoon (175 mL) extra-virgin olive oil

12 medium shrimp, peeled and deveined

4 bacon slices, halved crosswise

½ baguette, sliced on an angle

In a food processor, combine the peppers and onion and pulse until finely chopped. (Alternatively, mince finely by hand.) Transfer the peppers and onion to a bowl, add half the minced garlic, the vinegar, and a pinch of salt, and soak for at least 10 minutes. Slowly whisk in ⅔ cup (160 mL) of the olive oil. Set aside.

Poke a wooden skewer through a shrimp from bottom to top, then thread on a piece of folded bacon, followed by another shrimp, another piece of bacon, and a final shrimp. Repeat to make three more skewers. Season with salt.

On a griddle or in a large skillet, heat the remaining 1 tablespoon olive oil over high heat. When the oil is very hot, add the remaining garlic and the kebabs to the pan. Sear for about 1 minute, or until the shrimp takes on a golden color. Flip the kebabs over and cook for about 30 seconds more. Transfer the kebabs to a plate.

Add the slices of bread to the hot pan in a single layer, toasting lightly.

Transfer the bread to a platter, place the kebabs on top, ladle a bit of the vinaigrette over, and serve.

Urdaiazpiko, Ahuntz Gazta eta Tomate Lehor Pintxoa

SPANISH HAM, GOAT CHEESE, AND SUN-DRIED TOMATO PINTXO

OFTEN, WHEN A NEW PINTXO MEETS WITH SUCCESS, it begins to pop up in other bars across town. Then it travels to a neighboring capital, trickles down to village bars, and so on, until it becomes a ubiquitous classic. That is the case with this pintxo, an easy-to-love combination of sweet sun-dried tomato, caramelized goat cheese, and soft, nutty ham, which is much greater than the sum of its parts. The original version of this pintxo was made with a seeded baguette from one of San Sebastián's best bakeries, Galparsoro. A regular baguette will also do. Splurge, if you can, on the best *jamón*. ✿

MAKES 9 PINTXOS

¼ cup (60 mL) white wine vinegar

Kosher salt

½ cup (1 ounce/28 g) dehydrated sun-dried tomatoes (see Note)

2 tablespoons extra-virgin olive oil

1 (9- to 11-ounce/250 to 315 g) log goat cheese, preferably with rind, chilled

1 tablespoon sugar

9 slices Ibérico ham

½ baguette, preferably covered in poppy, flax, or other seeds, cut into nine ½-inch-thick (1.5 cm) slices

In a small saucepan, combine the vinegar, ½ cup (120 mL) water, and a pinch of salt. Bring to a boil over medium-high heat. Place the sun-dried tomatoes in a bowl, pour the hot vinegar mixture over, and cover with plastic wrap. Soak for at least 15 minutes and up to 2 hours, until very soft. Drain, transfer to a plate, and drizzle with the olive oil. Set aside.

Preheat the broiler. Line a baking sheet with foil.

Slice the goat cheese crosswise into 9 pieces, each about ¾ inch (2 cm) thick. Arrange on the prepared baking sheet. Sprinkle the tops with the sugar. Place the baking sheet under the broiler and allow the sugar to brown, watching closely so the cheese doesn't burn. Once lightly browned and sizzling, remove from the

continued »

oven. (Alternatively, you can use a kitchen torch to brown the cheese: Hold the flame over each slice until the sugar is bubbling and beginning to brown.)

To compose the pintxos, arrange the baguette slices on a platter and place a sun-dried tomato on each slice. Using a spatula, place one slice of the goat cheese on top of each tomato, sugared-side up. Thread a piece of the ham on a skewer, forming an "S" shape. Spear the cheese, tomato, and bread with the skewer, adjusting the ham if necessary. Repeat with the remaining ham and skewers and serve.

Note You can also use oil-packed sun-dried tomatoes, in which case you can skip the soaking step.

Foie Micuit-a

FOIE GRAS TERRINE

IN THE PINTXO BARS OF BASQUE COUNTRY, you'll always find foie gras. Seared, in pâté form, stuffed in a mushroom cap, or slathered on a hunk of bread, this luxury product is omnipresent. The abundance of foie, and its special place in pintxo culture, is thanks to Basque Country's proximity to France. It has had an undeniable influence on Basque cuisine, and the appetite created for foie has led to Spain being in the world's top five producers of the fatty liver.

This recipe, taken from the kitchen of one of San Sebastián's most popular pintxo bars, Atari, is foolproof. When making their foie *mi-cuit* (French for "half-cooked"), they use a quick method that results in a silky-smooth foie pâté. The presentation on raisin-nut bread evokes the Basque holiday table, where a can of foie gras and toasted raisin bread are a sign of the season. To gild the liver, garnish with apple or pear compote, balsamic glaze (see Notes), or even banana puree. ✿

SERVES 8 TO 10

1 (1-pound) piece duck liver, fresh or frozen and thawed (see Notes)

1 teaspoon table salt, plus more if needed

1 loaf raisin-walnut bread

Olive oil

Flaky sea salt and freshly cracked black pepper

Choose a container that will create the final form of the foie—a small loaf pan, rectangular mold, or small bowl will do. Line it with plastic wrap.

Cut the duck liver into large pieces. Remove any prominent veins. Put the pieces of liver in a saucepan and cook over medium-high heat, stirring, until all the pieces of liver have melted. You want to keep the foie at a just-warm temperature; if you see that the melting foie is getting too hot (steaming or bubbling), remove it from the heat and stir before putting it back on the heat. This process takes about 3 minutes. Stir in the table salt, taste, and adjust the seasoning.

Pour the foie into a fine-mesh sieve set over a bowl and push it through with a whisk, stirring and scraping until the liquid has passed through and any veins remain behind. Discard the solids in the sieve.

Transfer the strained foie to the prepared mold. Cover tightly and refrigerate until completely cool, at least a few hours.

When ready to serve, preheat the broiler.

continued »

Slice the raisin bread into thin slices, about ½ inch (1.5 cm) thick, lay them on a baking sheet, and drizzle with olive oil. Toast under the broiler until crunchy. Transfer to a serving platter.

Slice the foie into thin pieces (less than ¼ inch/6 mm thick) and place a slice on each piece of bread. Sprinkle with flaky sea salt and cracked black pepper. Serve while still warm. Any leftover foie can be wrapped well and frozen for up to three months and defrosted to serve when desired.

Notes This recipe can be adjusted to use smaller or larger quantities of liver; just be sure to season to taste.

To make a classic balsamic glaze, in a small saucepan, combine 4 parts balsamic vinegar with 1 part sugar and heat over medium-high heat, stirring frequently to dissolve the sugar, until the liquid reduces and a thick syrup forms. Drizzle the glaze on the plate before arranging the toasts on top.

GIPUZKOA

*It would be difficult for the planet Earth to offer up a place with
a greater density of grand restaurants and temples of good eating,
including the dining societies, like there is in the 1,997 km² of its territory,
in the heart of which come the best products from the farm, gardens,
vineyards, sea, and coops. Gipuzkoans have known how to approach
the stove with veneration.—*JOSÉ LUIS ITURRIETA

A SMALL YET BEAUTIFUL PROVINCE, GIPUZKOA HAS A DRAMATIC VERDANT
and rocky coast that gives way to rolling hills dotted with livestock, clusters of
village homes, and lonely white *baserriak* (farmhouses). The inhabitants are united
by a fierce sense of pride in their culture and their food. The pride seems to be
justified, whether one counts in Michelin-starred restaurants (seventeen) or in
unique heritage food products (cheese, cider, sausages, and on and on).

The irony of all this is that the local
approach to cooking, at least when it comes
to seafood, is the following: Do as little as
possible. The grill men of Orio, Getaria, and
the other villages of the coast see themselves
as conduits for the fish they place over the fire,
some preparations of which they are said to
have invented, like the whole grilled turbot
(see page 126). The same goes for the steak, the

green peppers from Ibarra, the preserved tuna
and anchovy: All food preparation is done with
an eye to not messing up the good thing this
region has going on. No strong flavors detract
from the tender white fish or minuscule local
malko ilarrak, the lauded teardrop peas, aside
from perhaps a bit of parsley.

Before the Gipuzkoan stars of fine dining—
Luis Irizar, Juan Mari Arzak, Hilario Arbelaitz,

Karlos Arguiñano, Martín Berasategui, Pedro Subijana, Andoni Luis Aduriz, and others—brought about a culinary renaissance, there were those who sowed the seeds: Nicolasa Pradera, Félix Ibarguren (known as Shishito), and José Castillo. But before the culinary seed was planted by these hands, there was a long-standing tradition of eating and appreciation that still marks tables today. The style of eating in Gipuzkoa has a markedly social component, most perfectly expressed in the *elkartea* (sociedad), or the dining society (see page 91).

Also known as *txoko*, the dining society is an example of the concept of the "other restaurant," which comes in a wide variety of forms: cider houses, *txakolindegiak* (wineries that open for eating and drinking in the same way cider houses do), pilgrimages followed by open-air picnics, town squares holding cooking competitions. Any gathering is nearly always accompanied by food and drink. Inhabitants love to celebrate their product, whether it is *txakoli* (the region's white wine; see page 139), cider, *txistorra* (quick-cured pork sausage; see page 200), anchovy, beans, or blood sausage. Every local specialty comes with a dedicated day and, often, a *kofradia*, or society. The

local cheese, Idiazabal, is produced around a quiet inland village that shares its name, and it is celebrated both in the village and in Ordizia, the famous market town, on the Day of the Shepherd. The celebration culminates in a competition, with distinctive red plastic cheese markers and a line of celebrity judges who smell and taste chunks of cheese before bestowing the highest honor possible to the winning shepherd or cheese maker.

The cuisine of Gipuzkoa carries a significant French influence compared with the other Basque provinces. In the Belle Epoque, its capital, San Sebastián, was a summer playground for royalty, who brought their French or French-trained chefs to cook for them. Hotels were also staffed with foreign chefs and were the site of the white-tablecloth dining of the times. These immigrants left behind their know-how or, in the case of wartime, stayed behind to further influence everything from saucing to pastry.

The most important holiday in the province is San Sebastián Day, January 20. The *danborrada* (drum festival) kicks off with the *izada*, the hoisting of the flag in the Plaza de la Constitución at midnight on the night of January 19. Members of the dining societies, dressed as cooks and soldiers, march in groups through the streets of the city, playing traditional songs written by the town's favorite composer, Raimundo Sarriegui. The drums sound for twenty-four straight hours in what is one of the world's most unique festivals.

San Sebastián is also the birthplace of the pintxo—a small bite of food that has the ability to charm diners the world over. Pintxos line the bars and, along with the city's fine dining prowess, have contributed to a growing culinary fame that has converted the province into a center for culinary tourism.

AFTER THE SUN GOES DOWN, Basque Country comes into its own. Its mountain passes are draped in fog, and peaceful waves lap the shore; there's a permanent chill in the air, dramatic shadows, and a general sense of mystery.

This permanent chill has hollowed out a special place for bone-warming pots of soup. Until modern times, soup was often served for breakfast, at lunch, and solo as a dinner. The emblematic soups of Basque cuisine have occupied an important part of daily nutrition for centuries: *Marmitako* (a thick tuna and potato stew) originated on a ship deck, when fishermen needed a one-pot meal made from readily available ingredients. *Zurrukutun* (a bread soup made with salt cod) is a humble "stone soup" eaten by inlanders. Even city dwellers hang on tight to the connection of healing, homey broths, looking forward in winter to the signs in bars announcing the presence of the Basque *salda*, a warming broth.

"Spoon dishes," as they are referred to, are lovely examples of economy, balance, and taste all in one dish. One pot was the most efficient use of energy when cooking was done over a fire, and a one-pot meal by definition needed a variety of nutrients: carbohydrates, vegetables, and protein. That efficiency and nutritional completeness have kept these soups in rotation in Basque kitchens.

Visitors will be hard pressed to find these traditional soups on restaurant menus, though, as soups are mostly a home affair, apart from winter salda and *arrai zopa* (fish soup). Most of these soups are even better the day after they are made, making them perfect for comforting weeknight dinners and next-day lunches.

Salda

BEEF AND CHICKEN BROTH

SALDA BADAGO. It means "There is broth," and you'll see it in capital letters, printed on a sheet of loose-leaf paper and fixed to the wall or shelf in bars across Basque Country when temperatures begin to drop. When salda is ordered, the bartender ducks into the kitchen, ladles a bit of warm liquid out of an ever-simmering pot into a short ceramic mug, and serves it perched on a paper napkin.

Basque salda is a lovely, amber-toned broth born of an unrefined jumble of meats and vegetables. In cities, the broth has become something of a novelty, but in rural areas it has never lost its relevance. Not surprising, given that nothing tastes better on a cold day than this restorative liquid, filling and warming to the bone. ✤

SERVES 6

7 ounces (200 g) beef trimmings or shank

1 pound beef bones (a mixture of whatever is available)

1 bone-in, skin-on chicken thigh (see Notes)

2 leeks, halved and rinsed well

2 carrots

1 onion, quartered

3 parsley sprigs

1 teaspoon kosher salt

7 ounces (200 g) dried chickpeas, soaked in water to cover overnight (optional; see Notes)

In a stockpot, combine the beef trimmings, beef bones, chicken, and 12 cups (2.8 L) water. Set over high heat and bring just to a boil. Lower the heat to medium and simmer, skimming any foam off the top as it rises.

Add the leeks, carrots, onion, parsley, salt, and chickpeas (if using; see Notes) and return the liquid to a simmer, skimming off any foam that forms. Reduce the heat to maintain a gentle simmer and cook for about 2 hours.

Strain the broth through a fine-mesh sieve and return it to the pot, discarding the solids. Serve warm.

Notes Feel free to substitute the pieces of chicken you have available: a leftover chicken carcass or whatever you have on hand.

Using chickpeas in the broth will lend it a bit of viscosity and deepen the flavor. If using, place the drained soaked chickpeas in a piece of cheesecloth and tie the top with kitchen twine. Add the bundle to the pot when you add the vegetables. Before straining the broth, remove the chickpea bundle; you can use them where you would canned chickpeas.

TRAINERUAK
ROWBOATS

Hundreds of years ago, the capture of a whale off the Cantabrian coast meant wealth for an entire village. Stakes were high, and it all depended on the strength and endurance of the men who rowed out in *txalupak*, smaller boats manned by just a few men, and *traineruak*, fourteen-man rowboats. The first to harpoon the whale would later enjoy a higher portion of the wealth when the value of the catch was divvied up. Every part of the whale, from the skin to the blubber, was put to use, often in culinary applications. When it came to fishing for other species, speed was also important; the first boat back to the port would get a higher price for its catch. Eventually, these informal contests evolved into rowing clubs.

Celebrations related to the *traineru* are many and varied: In the town of Orio, every five years the catch of the last Cantabrian whale (in 1901) is celebrated and the departure of five boats reenacted by the whole town, dressed in the traditional port clothes of the region. *Estropadak* (regattas) are held every summer in San Sebastián and are the culmination of the rowing season. Bright yellow boats from Orio, purple from Pasaia, blue from San Sebastián, and the colors from a handful of other coastal villages (Hondarribia, Getaria, Zumaia, and Ondarroa) row around Mount Urgull and the Concha Bay as onlookers in the port and on the beach drink cider and *txakoli* from the bottle and cheer on their favorite team. The wildly popular boat races were first organized in 1879 as an official version of the bets made between rowers about who could go from one town to the next the fastest—labor turned competitive leisure.

Arrai Salda

FISH BROTH

WITH AN ABUNDANCE OF SEAFOOD DISHES, from fish soup (see page 72) to rice with clams (see page 140), many Basque recipes rely heavily on a good fish broth. A basic building block, it is unceremoniously present in every Basque kitchen, something an *etxekoandre* (the lady of the house) doesn't think twice about preparing in a pinch. Fish broth doesn't need to simmer for more than 20 minutes, making it the best stock for last-minute cooking.

In Basque Country, fishmongers keep hake heads and tails in the back as a favor to customers. With any purchase, you can ask for bones and, with a bit of luck and if it's early in the day, the fishmonger will pull out a hake head and tail, then clean the carcass and rid it of anything that might cloud the broth or turn it bitter. After a good rinse, the head and tail are wrapped up and handed over, free of charge. If you can't find hake bones, you can use snapper, bass, tilefish, halibut, or cod instead. ✤

MAKES ABOUT 2 QUARTS (1.9 L)

Bones, head, and tail from 1 fish, preferably hake

1 carrot, chopped

1 leek, chopped and rinsed well

½ spring onion, chopped

3 parsley sprigs

Kosher salt

Rinse all the fish pieces until they're clean of any residue. Combine the fish pieces, carrot, leek, spring onion, and parsley in a stockpot. Add enough water to cover completely and a generous pinch of salt. Bring the water to a boil, then reduce the heat to maintain a gentle simmer and cook for 20 minutes, skimming off any foam that forms on the top as it rises.

Remove the broth from the heat and allow it to steep a bit; about 10 minutes is sufficient. Strain through a fine-mesh sieve, discarding the solids (if you're making the broth expressly for a fish soup, you can pick through the bones and remove any scraps of meat to add to the soup).

Use immediately or let cool completely and transfer to airtight containers. It will keep in the refrigerator for up to 5 days or in the freezer for at least 6 months.

Porrusalda

LEEK AND POTATO SOUP

IN THE VILLAGES OF BASQUE COUNTRY, nearly every home has a small garden. Even the blocks of more modern apartments often come with a parcel of land, a corner that some landowner rents out so that apartment dwellers can grow their own vegetables. This comforting and healthy vegetable soup is made with a mix of basic garden vegetables. Literally translated, *porrusalda* means "leek broth," and this classic soup is not much more than that: leeks, with a hint of garlic, potatoes for body, and sometimes, as in this recipe, carrots; some cooks also sprinkle a bit of salt cod in the finished soup. Play with the size and cut of the vegetables: the bigger the chunks, the more rustic the soup. ✤

SERVES 6

¼ cup (60 mL) extra-virgin olive oil

6 leeks, white and light green parts only, chopped and rinsed well

1 garlic clove, minced

¼ teaspoon kosher salt, plus more as needed

3 potatoes, peeled and cut into ½- to 1-inch (1.5 to 2 cm) pieces

2 carrots, cut into ½- to 1-inch (1.5 to 2 cm) pieces (optional)

In a large saucepan, heat the olive oil over medium-high heat. Add the leeks, garlic, and salt and cook, stirring occasionally, until the leeks are tender and translucent, about 10 minutes.

Add the potatoes, carrots (if using), another pinch of salt, and water to just cover the vegetables. Bring the water to a boil, then reduce the heat to maintain a simmer and cook for about 10 minutes.

Smash a few potatoes with the back of a fork to help thicken the broth and cook until the potatoes are completely tender, about 5 minutes more. Taste the soup and add more salt if necessary. Serve warm.

FARMHOUSE

Basque life has always centered around the *etxea*, the house, and especially the *baserri*, farmhouse. It was the heart of all political, social, and economic activity of rural life. Families took their surname from the name of the house, which is why so many Basque last names are location markers or nature related (like Goikoetxea, "the top house," or Mendialdea, "on the mountainside"). In fact, before last names became common legal practice, moving houses because of marriage or for another reason meant changing one's surname. The baserri was passed down, generation to generation, with a feeling of permanence beyond its inhabitants—the oldest baserri visible in Basque Country dates all the way back to the sixteenth century. Only one child received the house as inheritance, since the priority was maintaining it whole. The heads of the household were the *etxekojaun* (man of the house) and *etxekoandre* (lady of the house).

The wide-set, rectangular structures, made of stone and wood, traditionally face east. Each province has different design tendencies: The picturesque white country house with red trim is a classic image from the Lapurdi countryside; in the south, they lean toward gray stone structures. Many of the houses have an *eguzki lore*, a type of sun-shaped flowered thistle, hung over the door to trick dangerous night spirits into thinking it is daytime.

Despite its enormous appearance, the baserri of old was not an expansive home for a well-off family. The family members were crammed in a corner of the house while the majority of the space was dedicated to animals, food and grain storage, and perhaps a *lagar*, an apple press for making cider. The *ezkaratza* was the center of the house, for work and storage. Family would gather and spend time around the fireplace. The furniture was simple—*kutxak* (trunks) decorated with carvings depicting nature or religious scenes or, from the sixteenth century on, the *lauburu*, a pattern that looks like four commas placed together at their tails. The animals lived on the grounds—sheep (*ardiak*), used for milk and cheesemaking; sometimes cows, like the native *behigorri* variety or *betizu* (wild cows); the *txerri* (pig) that would stock the pantry after the winter slaughter; and *oiloak* (chickens) for eggs. Working the land was the major labor on the baserri, shared among the men and the women.

Baratxuri Zopa

GARLIC SOUP

AT SIX O'CLOCK IN THE MORNING in Spanish Basque Country, there are two kinds of people awake: partygoers, stumbling home after a night of dancing and drinking, and laborers, traditionally fishermen and shepherds, obliged to greet the morning before the sunrise. And for all these people, there is *baratxuri zopa*.

The soup is at once hearty and warming, and its curative nature, with ten cloves of garlic, is said to be great for hangovers. Hence the double life led by this peasant-style dish. An integral characteristic of the soup, and perhaps the best part, is that its taste improves with time. The *etxekoandre* (lady of the house) makes the soup at the same time she makes dinner and leaves it out on the counter for partygoing offspring, hardworking spouses, or the next day's midmorning snack, called the *hamaiketako*.

Said to have originated in Castile, this soup has been adopted and adapted by each region of Spain. What makes a baratxuri zopa more Basque than Castilian is the *zopako ogia*, a bread crafted specifically to soak in soup and thicken traditional sauces. The name of this Basque bread literally translates to "bread of the soup" and it is ugly, overly toasted, and has almost no crumb; you can use a well-toasted baguette as a good substitute. The paprika in the broth provides both color and flavor (so try to use a fresh jar, not that dusty old tin in the spice cabinet). The splash of sherry vinegar is an unconventional touch that takes this soup from necessity to star of the dinner table. ✤

SERVES 4 TO 6

4 ounces (113 g) zopako or baguette bread

½ cup (120 mL) olive oil

10 garlic cloves, minced

1 rounded tablespoon Spanish paprika

8 cups (2 L) meat broth or salda (see page 63)

2 teaspoons kosher salt, plus more if needed

2 tablespoons (30 mL) sherry vinegar (optional)

3 large eggs

If using a regular baguette, preheat the oven to 450°F (225°C). Toast the baguette for 20 to 25 minutes, until it's so brown, it's verging on burnt. Remove from the oven and let cool before slicing or breaking into pieces.

Break or slice your zopako or baguette into largish pieces, 1- to 2-inch (2.5 to 5 cm) cubes or 1-inch (2.5 cm) slices.

Reserve 1 tablespoon of the olive oil and warm the remainder in a large pot over medium-high heat.

Add the bread pieces and reduce the heat to medium. Cook the bread, turning it to allow it to soak up the oil and toast, for about 2 minutes. Remove and set aside.

Add the reserved 1 tablespoon olive oil and the garlic to the pot. Cook, stirring, until the garlic begins to turn golden, 30 seconds to 1 minute. Stir in the paprika.

When the garlic is uniformly golden, add the broth and salt and bring the mixture to a boil.

Return the bread to the pot. Reduce the heat to maintain a simmer, add the vinegar (if using), and cook, stirring occasionally to help break up the bread, for 20 to 30 minutes. Taste and add more salt if necessary.

For best results, allow the soup to sit overnight, refrigerated or at room temperature. When ready to serve, bring the soup to a simmer over medium-high heat. Beat the eggs in a small bowl. While stirring, pour the beaten eggs into the hot soup; they will thicken the broth and even form small pieces of cooked egg. If any large pieces of bread remain, cut them with kitchen scissors or dismantle them with a spoon.

Serve hot. Garlic soup is best eaten a day or two after it was made.

FISH SOUP

THE BASQUE COAST STRETCHES from Spain to France with 150 miles of ports and cliffs and mountains and coves. Depending on where along the coastline you are, this fish soup can vary widely, veering from red to brown, from brothy to almost stewlike.

This recipe is from the Spanish Basque coast, noticeably so thanks to the inclusion of the darkly toasted *zopako* bread. The French Basque coast has its own, slightly more refined version—*ttoro*. The firm, white fish commonly used along the Spanish Basque coast is *perlón*, or gurnard, but you can use red mullet, whiting, or even tilapia. The addition of luxurious *zigala* (Norway lobster; a misleading name, as the crustacean is actually closer to a langoustine) takes this soup to a level worthy of a celebration.

Fish broth (see page 65) is an essential component, but a real Basque would never sweat a missing ingredient. If you don't have fish broth on hand, you can simply toss leftover fish scraps and whatever vegetables you have in the fridge into a pot with water, simmer, and use this as the base for the soup. Make this soup a day before serving to allow the flavors to meld. ❧ PICTURED ON PAGE 58

SERVES 6 TO 8

10 clams

¼ loaf (50 g) zopako or baguette bread

5½ cups (1⅓ L) fish broth (see page 65)

3 tablespoons extra-virgin olive oil

10 shrimp, peeled, heads removed and reserved

¼ cup brandy

3 garlic cloves, minced

1 onion, diced

1 leek, diced and rinsed well

1 sweet Italian green pepper, such as Cubanelle, diced

¼ teaspoon kosher salt

Leaves from 3 parsley sprigs

½ cup (120 mL) tomato sauce (see page 192)

½ dried red chile, preferably guindilla

½ cup (120 mL) white wine

½ pound (225 g) monkfish, cut into roughly 2-inch (5 cm) pieces

1 pound (450 g) firm white-fleshed fish, cut into roughly 2-inch (5 cm) pieces

6 Norway lobsters (see Note), heads removed

Place the clams in a bowl of water and soak until ready to use, to release any dirt or sand.

If using a regular baguette, preheat the oven to 450°F (225°C). Toast the baguette for 20 to 25 minutes, until it's so brown, it's verging on burnt. Remove from the oven and let cool before slicing or breaking into pieces.

Break or slice your zopako or baguette into largish pieces, 1- to 2-inch (2.5 to 5 cm) cubes or 1-inch (2.5 cm) slices.

Warm the broth in a stockpot over medium heat.

In a medium skillet, heat 1 tablespoon of the olive oil over medium-high heat. Add the shrimp heads and cook, stirring occasionally, for about 5 minutes.

Pour in the brandy and carefully, with a long match or a long lighter held near the liquid, set the mixture on fire. Allow it to burn until it goes out, about 15 seconds.

Add the pan's contents to the pot with the broth and simmer for about 10 minutes. Strain the broth through a fine-mesh sieve, reserving the shrimp heads.

In a clean large pot, heat the remaining 2 tablespoons olive oil over medium-high heat. Add the garlic, onion, leek, pepper, and salt. Add the parsley and reduce the heat to medium. Cook until the mixture begins to turn a light golden color, about 20 minutes.

Add the bread and cook, stirring occasionally, for about 2 minutes. Add the tomato sauce and the chile and stir until everything is well mixed. Increase the heat to medium-high, add the wine, and cook for about 1 minute to burn off the alcohol.

Squeeze any liquid from the reserved shrimp heads into the pot, discarding the heads when no more liquid comes out. Cook the mixture for about 5 minutes more.

Add the strained broth and increase the heat to high. Add the monkfish and the white fish to the broth and bring to a boil. Remove the monkfish after 5 minutes and set aside. After 20 minutes total of cooking time, remove the remaining whole pieces of fish and set aside with the monkfish. Any bits of skin and unsightly pieces can stay in the stockpot. Puree the mixture directly in the pot with an immersion blender or pass it through a food mill into a bowl. Push the puree through a fine-mesh sieve, return it to the pot, and place it over medium-high heat. Taste the puree and add salt if necessary.

Drain the clams, scrubbing them to remove any visible dirt, and discard any clams with broken shells. Add the clams, cooked fish, Norway lobsters, and shrimp to the soup and simmer until the clams open, about 3 minutes. Discard any that do not open. Stir and serve immediately.

Note If you cannot find Norway lobsters, use more shrimp.

Zurrukutuna

SALT COD AND BREAD SOUP

THIS IS MOST DEFINITELY A HOMEY, HUMBLE SOUP. Similar in makeup to *baratxuri zopa* (see page 70), *zurrukutun* was a long-forgotten staple of Basque homes before it was rescued from obscurity by culinary patriots in the second half of the twentieth century. Now, curiously enough, it has resurfaced in Michelin-starred restaurants, modernist plays on a rustic dish once difficult to spot outside the home kitchen.

Zurrukutun is defined by the presence of salt cod and a poached egg. At the turn of the nineteenth century, the soup was often made with milk instead of water, and scraps of fish instead of big pieces of salt cod. Eggs were a weekend addition, or for special occasions when company came. Farmers and shepherds who spent mornings working in the cold, misty fields would return to the house for a plate of zurrukutun midmorning, and then put in a few more hours of work before lunch. This versatile, savory soup is made to warm you from the inside out. It makes great leftovers as well; just reheat and add a bit more water to thin it as desired. Desalting the salt cod will take 12 to 48 hours, so plan ahead. ✣

SERVES 4

9 ounces (250 g) flaked or whole fillet salt cod, desalted (see page 77)

4 dried choricero peppers, or 2 tablespoons choricero pepper puree (see Note)

5 tablespoons (75 mL) extra-virgin olive oil

4 garlic cloves, sliced

½ dried red chile, preferably guindilla

½ loaf (3½ ounces/100 g) zopako or baguette bread

4 large eggs

Kosher salt

If you're working with a whole salt cod fillet, once it's desalted, shred it with your hands and set aside.

If you're using dried choricero peppers, heat 4 cups (1 L) water in a saucepan. Put the peppers in a bowl and pour enough hot water over the peppers to cover. Soak until they are soft, up to 1 hour, depending on the pepper. Drain and pat dry with a paper towel. Open each pepper with a knife, discarding the stems and seeds. Scrape the pulp from the skin of the peppers with the knife and discard the skin. Set the choricero pulp aside.

continued »

If using a regular baguette, preheat the oven to 450°F (225°C). Toast the baguette for 20 to 25 minutes, until it's so brown, it's verging on burnt. Remove from the oven and let cool before slicing or breaking into pieces.

Break or slice the zopako or baguette into largish pieces, 1- to 2-inch (2.5 to 5 cm) cubes or 1-inch (2.5 cm) slices.

In a large pot, heat 3 tablespoons of the olive oil over medium heat. Add the garlic and cook until it begins to brown. Remove the garlic with a slotted spoon and set aside.

Turn the heat to low and add the salt cod and the dried chile to the garlic-infused olive oil. Stir gently, allowing the salt cod to warm slowly, releasing its liquid and gelatin. Remove from the pan and set aside.

Add the remaining 2 tablespoons olive oil to the same pot. Add the bread pieces and the choricero pulp (or puree, if using), and cook, stirring, for 1 to 2 minutes, allowing the bread and the chile to toast and begin to color a bit. Return the salt cod and garlic to the pot. Add enough water to just cover the ingredients. Cover the pot and simmer, stirring occasionally to help break up the bread, for about 20 minutes.

Crack each egg carefully into the soup. Sprinkle a bit of salt over each yolk and allow the eggs to simmer intact in the soup for 3 to 4 minutes, or until the whites are fully cooked.

Ladle the soup between four bowls, adding one egg to each bowl once full.

Note Choricero peppers are a cook's secret weapon, adding a deep, smoky, sweet note to sauces, stews, and everything in between. They are peppers that have been dried, concentrating their flavor into what is, once reconstituted, an intensely flavored layer of flesh waiting to be scraped from the dry skin. If you're unable to find dried choricero peppers, you can substitute 2 tablespoons jarred choricero puree, which is easy to find or order online (see Resources, page 316). It is often sold labeled "*pulpa de pimiento choricero*" or "*carne de pimiento choricero*."

BAKAILAOA GEZATZEN

PREPARING SALT COD

Salt-crusted and dry, *bakailao* (salt cod) can be a bit frightening to look at. The key to using it is desalting, which may sound intimidating but is extremely simple, requiring nothing more than cool water and time. When you plan to serve a recipe that calls for salt cod, be sure to incorporate the 12 to 48 hours it takes to draw out the excess salt into your prep timeline.

Twenty-four to 48 hours before you are going to use the salt cod, run it under cold water to take off excess salt on its surface. If necessary, cut the cod so the pieces are evenly sized (always work with similar-size pieces, or they will end up unevenly salty). Place it in a large bowl and add cold water to cover. Set aside to soak in a cool place—generally, desalting will take longer in the refrigerator than at cool room temperature. Depending on the size of the cod and its saltiness, desalting may take 12 to 48 hours. Change the water every 8 to 12 hours. After 12 hours, taste a piece of the cod for saltiness. When it tastes well-seasoned, neither overly salty nor bland, drain the water, pat the cod dry with paper towels, and use it as directed in your recipe. If you must store it after desalting, treat it like fresh fish and store it for no more than a couple of days.

ALBACORE WHITE TUNA

The prized fresh fish of Basque waters is the tuna. Not just any tuna, however. This is not the beautiful ruby red tuna that Asian and Western cultures treat with such reverence. For the Basques, there is only one: *hegaluze*—albacore white tuna.

Confusion abounds, in part because the fish is known as *bonito del norte* in Spanish, and another fish also goes by the name of *bonito*. However, that bonito is *Sarda sarda*, a striped fish similar to mackerel, while bonito del norte or hegaluze (*Thunnus alalunga*) is the white-fleshed, aromatic, and savory albacore. It has dark blue, almost black skin, which fades to white along its underside. Its meat is juicy and flavorful, and gathers quite a bit of fat, especially along the belly. The red-fleshed Atlantic bluefin tuna (*Thunnus thynnus*) can increasingly be found in markets and on menus, but it is generally viewed as secondary in quality. Apart from the color of their meat, red tuna and hegaluze can be distinguished by the size of their wing fin—on the hegaluze, it is longer and more slender. A hegaluze rarely weighs over 50 pounds; a red tuna can reach 550.

In July, hegaluze begin to flow into the ports: Bermeo and Ondarroa in Bizkaia and Getaria and Hondarribia in Gipuzkoa. Catching them is a long, demanding job. Large fishing boats head out for weeks at a time, sometimes traveling up to a thousand miles away in the early part of the season, when tuna are still migrating. The tuna are traditionally line caught, one at a time. Hauled in rubber and plastic crates packed with ice, they get distributed from low-lying warehouses, where they are divided by size and freshness, determined by the color of the fish's gills. It is a loud, official business, with fishermen and foremen and auctioneers dealing with such brusque quickness that the beauty of each individual fish blurs into a mess of fresh, shiny skin.

Curiously, fresh, unadorned hegaluze is a rarity. It is much more common preserved in olive oil as part of a pintxo or a salad, stewed in tomato sauce, or as part of a *marmitako* (see page 79), that warm summer soup that originated with the local fishermen.

TUNA AND POTATO STEW

THE HUNT FOR TUNA, albacore in particular, is a summer venture in Basque culture. Fishermen sail off into the temperate nights or chilly mornings of the Cantabrian Sea and begin their trolling, rowing smaller boats slowly through the water, dragging baited lines behind them, fishing the tuna one by one.

Hegaluze (albacore tuna; *bonito del norte*, in Spanish; see page 78) is a prized catch, but it is also the sustenance for the fishermen at sea. In Basque, *marmitako* literally means "from the pot." Historically, fishermen would sauté onions in a *marmita*, a metal pot, and add some dried pepper, garlic, and potatoes, which were introduced to Basque Country from the Americas about two hundred years ago (before that time, bread, chestnuts, or turnips were the favored carbohydrate in the preparation of the soup).

In this recipe, the fish broth is fortified with the bones of the tuna, although you can make the soup without this step. Adding the tuna at the last minute ensures that it never dries out. You could also sear the tuna before adding it to the broth, if you want the meat to have a golden crust. ✥

SERVES 4 TO 6

2 dried choricero peppers, or 1 tablespoon choricero pepper puree (see Note, page 76)

1¼ pounds (565 g) albacore or bonito tuna (with bones, if possible)

5¼ cups (1.25 L) fish broth (see page 65)

3 tablespoons extra-virgin olive oil

1 onion, chopped

2 sweet Italian green peppers, such as Cubanelle, chopped

1 garlic clove, minced

5 potatoes (about 2 pounds/900 g), preferably Monalisa, Kennebec, or Yukon Gold, peeled

½ cup (120 mL) tomato sauce (see page 192)

Kosher salt

If you're using dried choricero peppers, heat 4 cups (1 L) water in a saucepan. Put the peppers in a bowl and pour enough hot water over the peppers to cover. Soak until they are soft, up to 1 hour, depending on the pepper. Drain and pat dry with a paper towel. Open each pepper with a knife, discarding the stems and seeds. Scrape the pulp from the skin of the peppers with the knife and discard the skin. Set the choricero pulp aside.

continued »

Remove the bones from the tuna and set the meat aside. Rinse the bones under cold water and put them in a large pot. Add the fish broth. Bring just to a boil, remove from the heat, and steep for 10 minutes. Strain the broth through a fine-mesh sieve and set aside; discard the solids.

In a large pot, heat the olive oil over medium-high heat. Add the onion, green peppers, and garlic. Reduce the heat to medium and cook, stirring, for 20 to 25 minutes, until the vegetables begin to caramelize.

Meanwhile, cut the potatoes into 1-inch (2.5 cm) chunks. To get the most authentic shape, insert a knife about ½ inch (1.5 cm) into a peeled potato and then rotate and lift the knife, breaking the potato into an irregularly shaped piece. Rotate the potato slightly and repeat; repeat with the remaining potatoes. This is the traditionally preferred method because it avoids the need for a cutting board or level surface and because uneven edges are thought to help release the starch.

Add the potatoes to the pot and cook, stirring, for a minute or two. Add the choricero pulp (or choricero puree, if using) and the tomato sauce and cook, stirring, for 1 minute more.

Add the broth. If the broth doesn't cover the ingredients completely, add a bit of water. Bring to a simmer and cook for about 20 minutes, until the potatoes are tender enough to easily insert a knife or fork. Mash a few of the potatoes with the back of a spoon to help thicken the soup and cook for 5 minutes more. Taste the soup and add a bit more salt if necessary.

Meanwhile, cut the tuna into large, bite-size chunks. Add it to the pot, stir, and allow to sit for a few minutes for the tuna to cook in the residual heat. Serve warm.

BIZKAIA

BIZKAIA

THE WESTERNMOST OF THE SEVEN BASQUE PROVINCES, BIZKAIA IS about tradition. Bizkaia is fish cooked just hours off the boat. It is dramatic cliffsides of gray, craggy stone, rising from the greenest valleys one could ever imagine, with an omnipresent fog that somehow increases the region's majestic beauty. The food history of Bizkaia centers heavily on salt cod, due to the immense amount passing through the port of Bilbao.

Bizkaia has always been a relatively well-off province, rich in ingredients and later in industry, on both land and sea. In the 1800s, the level of wealth generated by the Industrial Revolution allowed well-off families to bring in cooks, many of them French, who in turn brought their subtle, elegant touch to the local cuisine. Up until this point, the cuisine of the province was most assuredly homey, one of hearths stocked with earthenware pots and products from the farm. At the turn of the century, restaurants were touting their prix fixe menus; a general trend of buying the best line-caught fish was established; and legendary restaurants, like El Amparo, had opened their doors.

The capital of Bizkaia is Bilbao, the city in a hole, tucked between mountains, with the river Nervíon running through the middle, snaking its way around the Casco Viejo and past La Ribera market. La Ribera is one of the largest markets in Europe, and continues to be a working window into the foodways of Basque Country after a renovation in the 2000s, with stalls upon stalls of the fish, leeks, potatoes, mushrooms, apples, kiwi, fresh peppers, and strings of dried dark red choricero peppers that form the hallmark of Bizkaia cuisine.

In 1997, the Guggenheim Museum, designed by American architect Frank Gehry, opened its doors on a then sketchy river promenade. What has followed has been a transformation—a grungy city whose focus was on factories and fishing has, little by little, grown more glamorous. From restaurants to hotels, big-name design is a must in Bilbao, the museum having cleared the way for experimental architecture in a city, the biggest in Basque Country, that only keeps growing.

The products and way of eating in Bizkaia resemble those of Gipuzkoa, thanks to a similar terrain, affinity for the sea, and economy. Where Gipuzkoa has a twinge of French influence, Bizkaia fills in culinary gaps with tastes of neighboring Burgos, such as an affinity for blood sausage (*morcilla de Burgos*, made with rice) that comes from Castilla y León. Bizkaia particularly stands out for the elvers (young eels) fished in its river; sardines, carried by basket on the heads of women and grilled in the open air; sweet red onions from Zalla; and scaly, black-skinned hake line-caught one by one off the coast of Bermeo.

Bizkaia's wine tradition was in place by the nineteenth century, but after a plague ravaged the vines, it took nearly one hundred years to get back on track. Bizkaia also has a strong history of *txakoli* (Basque white wine; see page 139) making and its own protected Designation of Origin (Jatorri Izendapena/ Denominación de Origen), Bizkaia Txakolina, albeit with a lower production than that of Gipuzkoa. And ordering "water" from Bilbao (*agua de Bilbao*) will get you champagne. The famous anecdote goes that Bilbaine visitors to Casa Nicolasa in San Sebastián ordered agua de Bilbao, perplexing the waiters, until they explained they meant champagne, which they said Bilbao residents drank like water. The story is a typical *bilbainada*, a genre of jokes widely told in which a *bilbotarra* (someone from Bilbao) typically attributes the invention of everything to his beloved city. One nonexaggerated contribution of Bizkaia, and of Bilbao in particular, to the world is *kalimotxo* (see page 309), that beloved mixed drink of cola and red wine. A dubious mixture, but famous enough to be dubbed a modern classic.

With its lovely fishing villages, striking peaks (like Mount Oiz), the hermitage of San Juan de Gaztelugatxe, and the town of Gernika (Guernica, made famous by the bombing later depicted by Pablo Picasso), Bizkaia has larger-than-life drama and larger-than-life eating, too.

BAKAILAO KROKETAK
Salt Cod Croquettes | 89

ANGULAK
Elvers (Young Eel) | 92

KRABARROKA PASTELA
Scorpion Fish Pâté | 95

BAKAILAO TORTILLA
Salt Cod Omelet | 97

AJOARRIERO BAKAILAOA
Salt Cod Stew | 101

SARDINAK PARRILAN
Grilled Sardines | 117

HEGALUZE ONTZIRATUA
Oil-Cured Tuna | 118

HEGALUZE ETA TOMATE ENTSALADA
Tuna and Tomato Salad | 121

HEGALUZEA TOMATEAREKIN
Tuna with Tomato Sauce | 122

LEGATZA TXIRLEKIN SALTSA BERDEAN
Hake with Clams in Salsa Verde | 135

ARROZA TXIRLEKIN
Rice with Clams | 140

ZAPO FRIJITUA
Fried Monkfish | 143

AMUARRAINA NAFAR ERARA
Navarre-Style Trout | 145

ARRAINAK ETA ITSASKIAK

FISH AND SHELLFISH

BAKAILAOA BIZKAIKO ERARA
Salt Cod in Biscayne Sauce | 103

TXANGURROA DONOSTIAR ERARA
San Sebastían–Style Spider Crab | 109

ANTXOA FRIJITUAK
Fried Anchovies | 112

KOKOTXAK PIL-PIL ERAN
Kokotxas in Pil-Pil Sauce | 115

HEGALUZE MENDREZKA
Grilled Tuna Belly | 124

ERREBOILOA PARRILAN
Grilled Turbot | 126

TXIPIROIAK PELAIO ERARA
Squid with Caramelized Onions | 128

TXIPIROIAK BERE TINTAN
Squid in Ink Sauce | 133

BASQUE COASTAL DWELLERS live and breathe seafood. They have always had an intimate relationship with the sea, gaining fame worldwide as the best naval navigators and fishermen. A Basque was the first to circumnavigate the globe. Basque whalers were renowned far and wide, and have even been said to be the ones who discovered the Americas on their hunt for whale (and, incidentally, cod—see page 106). And recreational fishing is a universally beloved activity.

A visit to the market or a stroll down to the port is all it takes for locals to get their hands on fish that is exponentially fresher than what most people have ever tasted in their lives. The beauty of the Cantabrian Sea, dark blue, wild, and noble, pounding the dramatic cliffs and rocky shores, is second only to the quality of the fish that thrive in it. Its cold, very salty water constitutes a superior environment and yields superior fish. Markets from La Bretxa in San Sebastián to La Ribera in Bilbao buzz with activity from Tuesday through Saturday. The markets are wall to wall with fishmongers, who buy their fish at auction in nearby ports that morning and tote them to the stalls to be placed over ice in beautiful, glistening arrangements of whole fish, mollusks, and crustaceans.

A brief glance through any market reveals piles and piles of an amazing variety of fish plucked straight from the sea: anchovy, monkfish, tuna, hake, mackerel, mullet, sea bream, turbot, scorpion fish, cod, sardine, sole, eel, shark, corvina, trout, swordfish, grouper, salmon, and more. Then there are the trays and tanks of crustaceans and mollusks: spider crab, lobster, langoustine, baby eel, shrimp, brown crab, Norway lobster, goose barnacles, sea urchins, clams, scallops, octopus, squid, cuttlefish, razor clams, and mussels—the list goes on.

One fish, however, occupies an outsized place of importance in the Basque diet: cod. More than any other fish, cod has driven the Basque economy. Originally salted on the boat to preserve the fish on long journeys, cod became a mainstay in the local diet and remains so. Although fresh cod made its way to the market with the advent of refrigeration, there is a strong preference for the mellowed flavor and chewier texture of the salted stuff.

Before mechanical transportation, fresh seafood didn't make it far inland. And in small towns as close as thirty minutes to the sea, one still hears the refrain, perhaps repeated so many times it has stuck, that "we don't get much fresh fish all the way out here." These mountain dwellers instead rely on recipes like Navarre-style trout and varied dishes, from stew to omelet, made from the very hardy salted cod.

Salsa verde and rich red Biscayne sauce can happily dress all different types of fish. An average weeknight meal in Basque homes is often a baked, fried, or grilled fish, like anchovies or turbot, dressed with a simple sauce.

When dining out, fish and shellfish take on many forms. Oil-cured tuna and anchovy feature in cold pintxos. Nearly every fish gets the grill treatment, from sardines to tuna belly. There are some unique dishes for you to try at home, like *marmitako* (see page 79), a hot tuna soup made only in summertime, and squid in ink sauce (see page 133), one of the world's only black dishes.

The key to making the recipes from this chapter is finding the freshest fish available. The seafood fanatics of Basque Country talk of the region's much celebrated marine *terroir*, and in that spirit you should use fish from your local waters, substituting something similar when those I've called for aren't available. You can't hide bad flavor with a sauce; therefore, sourcing is vital, as are high-quality—and, whenever possible, organic or local—olive oil and other ingredients.

SALT COD CROQUETTES

KROKETAK are the Iberian peninsula's equivalent of the Proustian madeleine. Each Basque has their favorite (usually their mother's). The secret is in the béchamel, made thicker than normal, so that it firms up to a solid mixture when cool. These croquettes, with their crunchy exterior and creamy filling, are a good way to convince skeptics of the deliciousness of salt cod.

This recipe calls for a fillet of salt cod cooked especially for the croquettes, but the truth is, croquettes are prized for their economy. Most cooks, from housewives to chefs, put scraps from other salt cod dishes to good use in croquettes. Take a page from their book and make several batches of croquettes at once, and freeze extras after breading for ready-to-fry appetizers.

Desalting the cod will take 12 to 48 hours, so plan ahead. ✤

MAKES ABOUT 30 CROQUETTES

1⅓ pounds (600 g) salt cod fillet, desalted (see page 77)

1 cup (240 mL) extra-virgin olive oil

5 garlic cloves

2 tablespoons unsalted butter

1 spring onion, cut into small dice

1 sweet Italian green pepper, such as Cubanelle, cut into small dice

3 cups (375 g) all-purpose flour

4¼ cups (1 L) whole milk

Kosher salt

3 large eggs, beaten

2 cups (240 g) dry bread crumbs (see Note)

Olive oil, for frying

If using a whole salt cod fillet, shred the desalted cod into pieces with your hands. Place the pieces of salt cod between two clean, dry kitchen towels or stacks of paper towels and press well, drying the cod as much as possible. If necessary, repeat with more dry towels.

In a small sauté pan, heat the extra-virgin olive oil and garlic over medium-low heat, allowing the garlic to slowly color. Once the garlic is beginning to take on a golden shade, remove it and add the cod pieces, skin-side up. The oil should be hot, but not too hot; it should bubble occasionally. Cook the cod for 7 to 8 minutes. Remove the cod from the oil and flake it into small pieces, removing any bones and the skin. Set aside. Pass the oil through a fine-mesh sieve and set aside.

In a large sauté pan, melt the butter with 2 tablespoons of the cod-cooking oil over medium heat. Add the onion and pepper and cook, stirring, until translucent and tender, about 15 minutes. Increase the heat to high. Add 1 cup (125 g) of the flour and stir with a whisk for about 1 minute. While whisking vigorously, add the milk, little by little at first, then working up to ½-cup (120 mL) increments, until all has been incorporated and the mixture is bubbling. Season with salt to taste.

Add the cod pieces (make sure there are no large pieces, as they will interfere with shaping) and stir them into the béchamel. Taste and adjust the seasoning.

Pour the mixture into a roasting pan and refrigerate for at least 1 hour, or transfer it to a pastry bag and refrigerate overnight, which makes for a perfectly shaped croquette.

Beat the eggs in a bowl. Spread the bread crumbs over a rimmed baking sheet or large plate. Spread the remaining 2 cups (250 g) flour on a separate plate.

If your croquette base is in a roasting pan, scoop about 2 tablespoons of the mixture and form it into a small ball. Dredge the ball in the flour, shaking off the excess, then dip it in the egg, allowing the excess to drip off, and finally roll it in the bread crumbs to coat. Set the coated ball on a clean, dry plate or baking sheet until ready to fry.

If your croquette base is in a pastry bag, snip the tip from the bag to leave a hole about 1 inch (2.5 cm) in diameter. Pipe roughly 3-inch (7.5 cm) logs of croquette base onto the plate with the flour, cutting them with a butter knife. Sprinkle with more flour to coat, then, working one at a time, dip the pieces in the egg, allowing the excess to drip off, and finally roll them in the bread crumbs to coat. Set the coated pieces on a clean, dry plate or baking sheet until ready to fry.

If you aren't frying them immediately, the croquettes can be refrigerated for up to 3 days. They can also be frozen for up to 3 months, and can go straight from freezer to fryer when desired. (To freeze, put the croquettes on a baking sheet, freeze until solid, then transfer to a freezer bag.)

In a heavy saucepan, heat 2 inches (5 cm) of olive oil over high heat until it reaches about 350°F (180°C). To test the oil, throw in a bit of bread crumbs; when it sizzles on contact, the oil is ready. Working in batches to avoid crowding the pot, fry the croquettes until golden brown, turning them occasionally to cook evenly. Remove with a slotted spoon and drain on paper towels. Sprinkle immediately with salt.

Transfer to a platter and serve warm.

Note You can also double up on bread crumbs instead of using flour, coating the croquettes in bread crumbs, then egg, then again in bread crumbs. This results in extra-crunchy croquettes. Experiment to find your favorite texture.

DINING SOCIETY

Basque cuisine's foundations are its "other restaurants"—one of which is the dining society. Traditionally called *elkartea* in Gipuzkoa and in Bizkaia *txoko*, which literally means "corner," these societies are rented spaces in a busy part of town, usually on the ground-floor level, outfitted with professional stainless-steel kitchens and an adjoining room with rows and rows of tables. At these tables and around the stoves, members gather to cook, talk, and socialize. These societies were traditionally the men's domain; women were invited in only on certain days, and never into the kitchen. That has changed in the last couple of decades, and more and more dining societies have no restrictions on gender.

The first elkartea, La Fraternal, was founded in 1843 in San Sebastián. Its statutes stated that it was founded to serve as a place to "eat and sing." The oldest continuously running society is the Unión Artesana in San Sebastián, founded in 1870 when La Fraternal suffered a destructive fire. Later, in 1900, Kañoietan opened its doors as the first society founded solely as an eating space, giving birth to the next phase in its evolution. There are now more than 1,300 registered societies.

Members invite friends or schedule a dinner with other members, and the day of the dinner they go shopping for the fresh ingredients. Lugging them through the streets to the txoko's headquarters, they get to cooking after opening a few beers and bottles of wine. The food prepared is nearly always traditional, carried out by the designated cook of the night in a giant earthenware vessel or stainless-steel pot and served on a wooden table.

Respect and the honor system are the only rules of the society; members are expected to tally up the wine, oil, stove time, and anything else consumed at the end of the night. Empty wine bottles are saved in a line on the table to help make the job easier. The bill is subsequently paid or added to the member's account. It is a truly Basque way of dining: cooking in company, paying on the honor system, and enjoying a good *sobremesa*, the time spent around the table chatting and imbibing after a meal, with *patxaran* and gin-tonic and a side of communal singing—this is where traditional cuisine is alive and well.

Angulak

ELVERS (YOUNG EEL)

ANGULAK (ELVERS, OR BABY EELS), often referred to as glass eels, are a mythologized product in Basque cuisine. Once, as the story goes, they were food for the poor. Dredged up from the rivers, after hatching but before heading out to sea, the baby eels were taken home while the more valuable catch was sold at market.

However, scarcity of angulak hit in the 1980s, and prices began to skyrocket. Now these tiny fish are the focus of culinary worship, the peak of which is reached on January 19, the eve of San Sebastián Day (see page 57). Having an earthenware dish of eels, the cost of which typically hovers around 275 euros a pound, on the table is a status symbol.

Elvers are fished in the northern United States. An economic substitution is the widely popular "fake" version, made from surimi. It's significantly cheaper, and often served in Spain as *gulas*. Elvers don't need much more than a quick sauté in olive oil infused with garlic and spice. The magic lies in their texture, a sensual slipperiness with a pleasing, subtle crunch. ✤

SERVES 3 OR 4

½ dried guindilla chile (see Notes)

1 tablespoon mild olive oil

1 garlic clove, thinly sliced

7 ounces (200 g) elvers, fresh, frozen, or preserved (see Notes)

Slice the chile into thin rings. In a medium skillet, heat the olive oil over high heat. Add the garlic and 2 rings of the chile (or more, if desired, depending on the heat of the chile and personal preference). Cook, stirring, for about 30 seconds, then remove the chile rings with a slotted spoon and set aside.

When the garlic slices begin to turn golden, about 30 seconds more, remove the skillet from the heat. Add the elvers and mix gently, ideally tossing by hand or very delicately with a wooden spoon. Allow them to cook in the residual heat of the skillet for about 1 minute.

Transfer to a serving dish and serve warm, garnishing with reserved chile rings.

Notes You can substitute another dried mild red chile, such as guajillo, for the guindilla. A milder chile is preferable over chile de árbol or other spicier dried chiles.

Most elvers are sold precooked. If using frozen eels, thaw them first. If using preserved eels, drain them and pat dry before proceeding with the recipe.

Krabarroka Pastela

SCORPION FISH PÂTÉ

FISH *PASTELA* ("CAKE") certainly departs from the Basque tradition of taking a fish from the ocean and immediately cooking it with no adornment, but it was a traditional way to take advantage of scraps. Its fame skyrocketed when one of Basque Country's culinary godfathers, Juan Mari Arzak, decided to update it in a distinctly French way in the 1970s. With a splash of cream and a more refined pâté-like texture, it became a ubiquitous hit.

While this pastela has reached a sort of iconic, retro fame, it has never stopped gracing the counters of local bars or being served at home. It can be quite elegant, too; you can serve it arranged in slices, to be scooped onto bread or crackers, or on individual serving spoons, topped with a dollop of homemade mayonnaise (see page 36). Baked in small ramekins, it is ready to be served individually at a dinner party or as part of an arrangement of pintxos. A small scorpion fish yields about 7 ounces (200 g) cooked, picked meat, but feel free to substitute the same amount of meat from another rockfish or white-fleshed fish. ✤

SERVES 6

Unsalted butter, for greasing

Kosher salt

1 red scorpion fish or other rockfish or white-fleshed fish (1¼ pounds/565 g)

1 carrot, coarsely chopped

1 leek, coarsely chopped and rinsed well

1 spring onion, halved

3 or 4 parsley sprigs

4 large eggs

½ cup (120 mL) heavy cream

½ cup (120 mL) tomato sauce (see page 192)

Freshly ground black pepper

Preheat the oven to 400°F (200°C). Grease six 4-ounce (115 mL) ramekins with butter. (A greased 8½ × 4½-inch—22 by 12 cm—loaf pan can also be used.)

Bring a pot of salted water to a boil. Add the scorpion fish, carrot, leek, onion, and parsley, reduce the heat to a simmer, and cook for about 20 minutes. Drain, discarding the liquid and vegetables, and set aside the fish until cool enough to handle. Pick all the usable meat off the fish, being careful to avoid any small bones. You should end up with about 7 ounces (200 g) of meat. Very finely chop the meat.

continued »

In a large bowl, beat the eggs. Add the cream and tomato sauce and whisk well. Add the finely chopped fish, season with salt, and grind a generous amount of pepper into the mixture. Whisk to combine.

Divide the mixture evenly among the ramekins or pour it into the loaf pan. Set a roasting pan in the oven, then put the ramekins or loaf pan in the roasting pan. Pour in hot water to come about halfway up the sides of the ramekins. Bake for 25 minutes. To test for doneness, you can insert a toothpick; once it comes out clean, the pastela is ready. Carefully remove the ramekins or loaf pan from the water bath and set aside to cool.

Unmold onto individual serving plates or a serving platter. Top with mayonnaise if desired. Serve with crusty bread or crackers for spreading.

Bakailao Tortilla

SALT COD OMELET

AN ESSENTIAL PART OF ANY CIDER HOUSE MENU, the *bakailao tortilla* was surely born of rural pantry staples: onions, eggs, and salt cod.

The most famous by far, and the star of the menu at Roxario restaurant in the cider town of Astigarraga, is the tortilla made by Txaro Zapiain, a cook devoted to serving the most traditional dishes, from "old" sardines to "crystal" peppers. She can be seen between meal services sitting on the porch, shelling beans, or taking care of some other daily task. Txaro's mother, María Goñi, wife of the cidermaker, first taught her how to make this tortilla when the family's cider house had an adjoining restaurant.

This recipe makes the creamiest, most delicious tortilla. It just barely sets so that when you dig into it, it gives way to juicy perfection studded with beautifully caramelized onions and perfectly desalted cod. Serve it family-style, with pieces of crusty bread to scoop it up.

Desalting the cod will take 12 to 48 hours, so plan ahead. ❖

SERVES 4

8 ounces (225 g) shredded or whole fillet salt cod, desalted (see page 77)

4 tablespoons (60 mL) extra-virgin olive oil, plus more if needed

2 onions, thinly sliced

½ teaspoon kosher salt, plus a pinch

1 dried guindilla chile

2 tablespoons chopped fresh parsley

8 large eggs

Crusty bread, for serving

If you're working with a whole salt cod fillet, once it's desalted, shred it with your hands and set aside.

In a medium skillet, heat 2 tablespoons of the olive oil over medium-high heat. Add the onions and the pinch of salt and cook, stirring occasionally, for about 10 minutes. Add the chile, reduce the heat to medium, and cook, stirring occasionally, until the onions have a nice, deep golden color, 15 to 20 minutes more.

Add the remaining 2 tablespoons olive oil to the pan. Add the shredded salt cod and reduce the heat to low. Cook for a few minutes more, allowing the salt cod to let out any water and cook a bit in the oil. Remove the chile and discard. Sprinkle the parsley into the mixture.

Meanwhile, beat the eggs in a bowl with the remaining ½ teaspoon salt.

continued »

Raise the heat to high and, when the pan is hot, add the eggs. Stir continuously with a wooden spoon or silicone spatula for about 20 seconds. Let set without stirring for a few seconds, then run a spatula under the tortilla and around the sides to make sure it is not sticking. Place a round plate with a diameter larger than the pan's upside down on the top of the pan. With one hand on the plate and one hand holding the pan, quickly flip them together in one motion so the tortilla is on the plate.

If the pan has any pieces stuck to it, quickly clean it and coat it with a bit more oil. Return to the heat and slide the tortilla back into the pan. Tuck the edges under with your spatula and cook for 10 to 20 seconds more. Do not overcook; the tortilla should remain creamy and not be cooked all the way through.

Slide the tortilla onto a platter and serve immediately, with crusty bread alongside.

Ajoarriero Bakailaoa

SALT COD STEW

NAFARROA is not known for seafood recipes, but this is one of its most popular, invented on the overland trading routes by *arrieros* (Spanish for "muleteer"). These transporters of goods employed mules as their beasts of burden on long journeys, and their food supply was limited to what could be stored at any temperature and cooked in a pinch: preserved fish, peppers, garlic (the *ajo* in *ajoarriero*), and tomato.

On the trail, these travelers would quickly desalt the cod by charring it to sweat out the salt and then purging it in running water. Sometimes, while rinsing the charred cod in the river, an arriero would nab a few freshwater crabs and add them to the stew as well. You can take a page from their book and add crab or lobster to transform this rustic dish into a special occasion–worthy main. You could also add potatoes, cut into small pieces, to make the dish more of a complete meal. A poached egg served on top is also a common addition and, like the potato, is in line with the humble rural origins of the dish.

Desalting the cod will take 12 to 48 hours, so plan ahead. ✿

SERVES 3 OR 4

12 ounces (340 g) shredded or whole fillet salt cod, desalted (see page 77)

4 dried choricero peppers, or 2 tablespoons choricero pepper puree (see Note, page 76)

5 tablespoons (75 mL) extra-virgin olive oil

3 sweet Italian green peppers, such as Cubanelle, diced

1 red bell pepper or 4 piquillo peppers, diced

1 onion, diced

3 garlic cloves, minced

¾ cup (180 mL) tomato sauce (see page 192)

If you're working with a whole salt cod fillet, once it's desalted, shred it with your hands and set aside (you should have about 2 cups).

If you're using dried choricero peppers, heat 4 cups (1 L) water in a saucepan. Put the peppers in a bowl and pour enough hot water over the peppers to cover. Soak until they are soft, up to 1 hour, depending on the pepper. Drain and pat dry with a paper towel. Open each pepper with a knife, discarding the stems and seeds. Scrape the pulp from the skin of the peppers with the knife and discard the skin. Set the choricero pulp aside.

continued »

In a medium skillet, heat 3 tablespoons of the olive oil over medium-high heat. Add the green and red peppers and the onion. Reduce the heat to medium and cook, stirring, until tender and beginning to caramelize, 20 to 30 minutes.

In a separate skillet, heat the remaining 2 tablespoons olive oil over medium-high heat. Add the garlic. When it begins to color, add the salt cod and cook, allowing it to take on some of the garlic-oil flavor and to cook out any water, for about 5 minutes. Add the tomato sauce and the choricero pulp (or puree, if using). Cook, stirring, until the mixture comes together nicely, then add the peppers and onion to the mixture. Cook for about 5 minutes more.

Serve hot. This dish is even better the day after it is made. Reheat and add a bit of water if it is drying out.

SALT COD IN BISCAYNE SAUCE

THIS ICONIC DISH, from the province of Bizkaia, is made from common pantry ingredients—salted fish, dried peppers, onions, garlic, and olive oil—yet in it the Basques managed to make something new and fully theirs. Dried choricero peppers and their distinct, deep pepper flavor are the star of this dish. The Biscayne sauce is often made with a local red onion, the Zalla violet, which is prized for its mild, sweet flavor, but any onion will produce a rich, lovely sauce.

Respected writer Ángel Muro said there are more variations of this dish "than there are holy day vigils in seven whole years." The truth is, this highly personal dish is shrouded in mystery, from its origins to the little touches each cook gives to their version. Home cooks might add a bit of bread or flour to thicken the sauce. Before olive oil was commonly available, pork fat was widely used in the dish, and there are those who still incorporate ham. Curiously, the farther away one gets from Bizkaia, the more adulterations this sauce suffers.

Another habitual variation is the addition of tomato to the choricero pepper sauce. Purists squarely deny its place in the recipe and many locals who *do* add it aren't likely to admit it. In this recipe, the tomato is optional, so you're free to skip it, add it and admit it, or deny with a wry smile.

Desalting the cod will take 12 to 48 hours, so plan ahead. ✿

SERVES 4

12 dried choricero peppers, or 6 tablespoons (about 100 g) choricero pepper puree (see Note, page 76)

⅔ cup (160 mL) mild olive oil

2 garlic cloves, sliced

4 (7-ounce/200 g) salt cod fillets, desalted (see page 77 and Notes, below)

3 yellow or red onions, finely chopped

1 sprig parsley

1½ cups (360 mL) fish broth (see page 65 and Notes, below)

½ cup (120 mL) tomato sauce (see page 192; optional)

If you're using dried choricero peppers, heat 4 cups (1 L) water in a saucepan. Put the peppers in a bowl and pour enough hot water over the peppers to cover. Soak until they are soft, up to 1 hour, depending on the pepper. Drain and pat dry with

continued »

a paper towel. Open each pepper with a knife, discarding the stems and seeds. Scrape the pulp from the skin of the peppers with the knife and discard the skin. Set the choricero pulp aside.

In a medium sauté pan, heat the olive oil and the garlic slices over medium heat. When the garlic starts to "dance" and the oil bubbles, add the salt cod, skin-side down, and cook for about 4 minutes. Gelatin will start to bubble out of the cod. Flip the cod and cook for about 2 minutes more. Remove the cod and garlic and set aside on a plate.

Return the pan to the heat. Add the onions and parsley and cook, stirring occasionally, for about 25 minutes, until tender and golden. Remove the pan from the heat and drain any excess oil, keeping the onions in the pan. Return the pan to medium-high heat and add the choricero pulp (or puree, if using). Cook, stirring, for about 30 seconds.

Add the fish broth (see Notes) and the tomato sauce (if using) and stir until combined. Add any juices the salt cod has released. Cook for about 5 minutes, until the sauce begins to come together and thicken.

Strain the sauce through a fine-mesh sieve or chinois, pushing it through with the back of a ladle and pressing hard to squeeze out every bit of sauce; discard the solids. (Alternatively, pass the sauce through a food mill and discard the solids that remain.) Return the sauce to the pan and simmer until it is nice and thick, anywhere from just a few minutes to up to 10. Return the salt cod to the pan and cook to warm it, about 3 minutes.

Serve warm, family-style, or plate each fillet individually, with the sauce ladled over.

Notes You can use the water from the last round of soaking the salt cod in place of the fish broth.

If you're working without a chinois or food mill, it may be difficult to get the right amount of sauce from the onion mixture. A good solution is to take about half the onions left in the sieve (no more than ½ cup) and blend them with the liquid that has already passed through. If the sauce becomes too light, add another tablespoon choricero pepper puree before returning it to the heat.

SALT COD

It is impossible to exaggerate the importance of cod (*Gadus morhua*) in Basque history. Not only has this fish defined Basque cuisine, but its capture has defined Basque culture, made men wealthy and famous, fed them, and driven them crazy.

When a Basque talks about cod, he talks only about salt cod. The Basques were initially whalers, renowned for their skill at pursuing the sea mammal. They would make long voyages to the cold waters of the North Atlantic in their search, but the boats that rowed out to chase whales also fished for cod. Sailors used the same methods to preserve the cod as they used for the whale meat, and in doing so, they not only generated a way to sustain themselves on extended whaling trips but also created a massive industry in the process. The cod were gutted and butterflied on board, then salted heavily and stored in vats. As whale fishing died out, Basque fishermen began seeking out cod in earnest, and by the end of the 1700s, demand for whale had already been replaced by the highly desired salt cod. Without whaling, there would be no salt cod.

The influence of the Catholic Church in Europe, and over the Basques, also contributed to the importance of salt cod. On days when meat was prohibited, cod became the protein of choice, and among this food-loving culture, cooking it well was a priority.

Pasaia, near San Sebastián, is one of the most important ports in Basque Country. Nearly one hundred cod-fishing ships floated there in the 1970s, bringing in boatfuls of the prized Atlantic cod, which typically ranges from 2 to 4 feet long, with greenish-brown spotted skin. More than half the cod fished in Spain was unloaded on its docks. But by the 1990s, overfishing, diminishing prices, and new technologies led to the disappearance of the cod-fishing fleet. The introduction of oft-imported fresh cod is a modernity in Basque Country, and it is viewed as less desirable.

Bizkaia has its own claim to salt cod fame, a story that sounds more like fiction than fact but has been corroborated to a fault. In the mid-1830s, the trader Simón Gurtubay sent a telegram asking to be sent "*100 o 120 bacaladas.*" An error in the telegram, however, turned the *o* into a zero, the recipient interpreted the number as "1,000,120," and that was how many *bakailao* he received in the port of Bilbao. Fortuitously, around the same time this massive shipment landed at Gurtubay's feet, the city was besieged by troops in the First Carlist War. Gurtubay's salt cod fed the people through that time of scarcity, making him a very rich man.

In bigger cities in Basque Country, there are dedicated salt cod stores. In these shops, their windows hung with the characteristic triangular salted skins, clients can purchase an entire hide of cod, although sales tend to be for specific cuts. Loins, jowls, tails, and more sit in plastic trays or baskets, their prices varying widely according to desirability. A bestseller in these bakailao shops is pre-desalted cod, ready for cooking the day of purchase.

When purchasing salt cod, which is available in local fish markets as well as online, look for pieces with dark skin and white flesh. Avoid any with flesh that has reddish or yellow tones. A rigid piece has been stored in excessive dryness; a piece that has a dewy look is overly damp. The perfect salted cod will be somewhere in between, with a lovely white tone.

Txangurroa Donostiar Erara

SAN SEBASTIÁN-STYLE SPIDER CRAB

SPIDER CRAB À LA *DONOSTIARRA* (San Sebastián–style) is a truly unique Basque dish. And unlike most Basque dishes, its roots lie in haute cuisine rather than in humble cooking. San Sebastián became a destination for royalty when King Alfonso XII's wife, María Cristina, decided to pass her summers in the seaside town. The royal court and its hangers-on followed, and the city was built up with lovely, regal Belle Epoque buildings, like the casino that now houses city hall and the Victoria Eugenia theater. Of course, among the royal entourage were cooks schooled in Escoffier's cooking methods. Félix Ibarguren, aka Xixito, was a local cooking instructor who gave classes in the former Palacio de Bellas Artes at the beginning of the 1900s, and he was the first to make this riff on the popular *langoustines à l'américaine.*

When possible, purchase live crabs—the meat will still be full and plump inside the shell. You can substitute less expensive brown crab for the spider crab. Because of the kitchen time involved, most Basques reserve this dish for Christmas and other holidays. Cracking open each crab leg and picking through for the meat is best done in a group. The labor is worth it, however, for this stunning and delicious showstopper. ❧

SERVES 4

¼ cup (75 g) kosher salt, plus more as needed

2 (2-pound/900 g) spider crabs, or substitute your local crabs

½ cup (120 mL) extra-virgin olive oil

1 carrot, minced

2 onions, minced

1 leek, minced and rinsed well

½ cup (120 mL) tomato sauce (see page 192), or 1 tomato, peeled and minced

¼ cup (60 mL) brandy

Dried bread crumbs

Butter

Bring a stockpot of heavily salted water to a boil; you want at least ¼ cup (75 g) salt in the water.

Add the crab to the boiling water and cook it according to the times indicated in the Note. Remove and set aside. When the crab is cool enough to handle, pick out all the meat: Holding the body in one hand, use all your fingers to squeeze on

continued »

opposite ends of the head to open. Reserve the shell to fill later, and reserve any liquid inside. Cut the body in half and then in quarters and patiently pick out all the meat. Crack the claws and pick the meat as well, being careful to remove and discard any bits of shell. Set the crabmeat aside in a bowl.

In a large skillet, heat the olive oil over medium heat. Add the carrot, onions, and leek along with a pinch of salt. Cook, stirring occasionally, until the onions are golden and tender, about 45 minutes.

Meanwhile, preheat the broiler.

Add the tomato sauce to the pan with the onions and cook for about 3 minutes. Add the brandy and simmer to cook out the alcohol. Add the crabmeat and the liquid from the body to the skillet. Bring to a lively simmer and cook for a few minutes more, until the sauce has thickened a bit and has a pleasant consistency—not soupy but thickly saucy.

Stuff the reserved shells with the crab mixture, dividing it evenly between the two. Sprinkle the bread crumbs on top and dot with butter. Place the crabs on a baking sheet or broiler pan and broil until the top of the crust begins to bubble and turn golden, about 5 minutes.

Serve immediately.

Note To know how long to boil your crab, use these weight and time ratios:

21 ounces (600 g) = 8 minutes

35 ounces (1 kg) = 12 minutes

52 ounces (1.5 kg) = 15 minutes

COOKING COMPETITIONS

The *lehiaketa*, cooking competition, is a thoroughly Basque tradition. Most of the time the cooking is done by an individual, but sometimes a *kuadrilla* (a group of close friends) joins in. There are more serious food competitions, such as the Idiazabal cheese contest held in Ordizia, but most village lehiaketak are warmer, informal, and a downright party (and a good excuse to gather and to put all that boasting from the dining society to the test). Each competitor or group is assigned a number, designating their soup or omelet or *pil-pil* for the judges. The competitor cooks through the morning until the dish is prepared, then sets it out to be judged. The jury members pass by one by one to try his dish, and the next hundred or so entries down the line. Coming in first place might mean a cash or material prize, but most of the time it means bragging rights, which are fundamentally much more valuable.

There are too many food competitions to name, and contests of omelets, pil-pil, and pintxos count off into Basque gastronomic infinity. Here is a small sampling of towns that hold cooking contests for particular foods or dishes.

ANOETA: Salt cod in *salsa verde*

ATARRABIA (VILLAVA): *Rellenos*, a sausage similar to *mondeju* (see page 206)

BAKIO (BAQUIO): *Marmitako* (see page 79), an important contest

ENKARTERRI (LAS ENCARTACIONES): *Putxera*, a stew of beans

IEKORA (YÉCORA): *Rancho o caldereta* (the stew that was eaten among the vineyards at midday in the Rioja Álavesa)

KARRANTZA (CARRANZA): Karrantza sheep stew

LIZARRA (ESTELLA): *Ajoarriero bakailaoa* (see page 101)

LAUDIO (LLODIO): Pig's feet

MENAKA (MEÑACA): *Sukalki*, a beef stew

ORIO: Grilled sea bream

TOLOSA: The local bean

Antxoa Frijituak

FRIED ANCHOVIES

ANCHOVIES ARE A HARBINGER of spring in Basque Country, and spring is when their flesh is at its best, firm and flavorful. They are an economical purchase—about thirty-three cents each—yet prized nonetheless. It is often said that if anchovies were as rare as *angulak* (baby eels; see page 92), Basques would be more than happy to pay a higher price for them.

Fresh anchovies are shiny, beautiful things and require nothing more than a simple fry, but with a bit of care in the execution and attention to detail, you can turn them into the most delicious light dinner or appetizer. You can fry the anchovies in olive oil without any coating, as the purists do, but they're better if you coat them with some flour before frying, as in this recipe. The flour adds an addictive crunch and a richness to the salty fish. ❧

SERVES 4

16 anchovies (about 9 ounces/255 g), heads and guts removed	1 large dried guindilla chile, cut into rings
Kosher salt	4 garlic cloves, sliced
½ cup (60 g) all-purpose flour	Chopped fresh parsley
½ cup (120 mL) extra-virgin olive oil	

Rinse the anchovies under cold water to clean thoroughly. Pat dry. Season the anchovies with salt and set aside for about 15 minutes.

Place the flour on a plate or shallow bowl. Dredge each anchovy through the flour, shaking off any excess.

In a large skillet, heat the olive oil and the chile over high heat. When the olive oil is so hot it is almost smoking (about 400°F/200°C), add the garlic. It will brown quickly, so add the anchovies immediately, carefully placing them in the pan in a single layer. Do not crowd the pan. (It might be necessary to cook them in two or three batches.) After 30 seconds, turn the anchovies with a spatula or a slotted spoon. Fry for 30 seconds more and remove. Arrange the anchovies on a serving plate along with the garlic and chile. Fry the remaining anchovies, adding the parsley in the last moment of cooking.

To serve, pour the parsley oil over all the anchovies. It should be abundant, forming a bed of oil under the anchovies.

Kokotxak Pil-Pil Eran

KOKOTXAS IN PIL-PIL SAUCE

PIL-PIL SAUCE is one of the emblematic elements of Basque cuisine. Its ingredients are few—nothing more than olive oil, garlic, and a bit of fish—but it becomes something greater than the sum of its parts. The word *pil* has no meaning; it is an onomatopoeia for the sound the garlic-infused olive oil makes as it bubbles around the salt cod, coaxing out the fish's naturally occurring gelatin to create a thick, emulsified sauce.

The movement required to emulsify (*loditu*, in Basque) the sauce is a back-and-forth motion that enjoys the same spectacle and debate among Basques as a golf swing or a baseball pitching style. You have to patiently watch the temperature, keeping it at a nice, low heat as you move the pan in a circle, like a wheel, a motion the Basques call *gurpilada*.

Kokotxak have various poor translations into English: neck, jowl, cheek, chin, and tongue being the most common, if slightly inaccurate. The *kokotxa* is actually the flesh on the underside of a fish's mouth, a V-shaped, gelatinous piece that sits between the chin and the throat. Two types of kokotxak are typically used: hake, which are smaller and more expensive, and salt cod, which can be used fresh or desalted. If you can't find kokotxak, cod or hake loin can be used instead. ✿

SERVES 4

1 cup (240 mL) extra-virgin olive oil

3 garlic cloves, minced or sliced

18 ounces (510 g) hake or cod kokotxak

½ teaspoon kosher salt

1 small whole guindilla chile, or 1 large guindilla, sliced into rings

Chopped fresh parsley, for garnish (optional)

In a large sauté pan or pot with straight sides, heat the olive oil and the garlic over medium heat. When the garlic starts to "dance," bubbling in the oil, add the kokotxak and reduce the heat to low. Immediately add the salt and the chile.

Begin to move the kokotxak in a back-and-forth motion over the low heat, gently but continuously. Keep the motion going until the sauce begins to emulsify, anywhere from 5 to 20 minutes, depending on the quality and quantity of gelatin in the kokotxak.

continued »

Ideally, the kokotxak should be served after just under 10 minutes of slowly cooking and moving back and forth. If the sauce gets too thick, add a bit of fish stock to thin it out.

Garnish with fresh parsley, if desired, and serve warm, family-style, or divide into individual portions.

Variation

To make this dish with cod fillets, the process is similar, but requires a bit more work. Place the cod skin-side up in the pan with the olive oil and garlic and begin to warm it over low heat; it should never sizzle when added to the olive oil. When bubbles start to flow from the skin of the cod, take the pan off the heat and begin to move it back and forth. Pressing the pieces of cod with a spatula to release more gelatin can help.

Note If the pil-pil sauce doesn't emulsify to your liking, don't worry. Savvy cooks have a whole litany of tricks to help ease the process:

· Whisk only the sauce until it emulsifies to the desired texture.

· Add ¼ cup fish broth (see page 65) and whisk vigorously until the sauce is emulsified.

· Begin the process with a few extra gelatinous parts (bones, extra skin) in the pot and remove and discard them once you get the emulsification.

· Another good trick is to cook the salt cod separately and slowly incorporate the garlic-infused olive oil, as you would with a mayonnaise. This method is the one often used in restaurant kitchens.

· An immersion blender can bring together the sauce if all else fails. Be careful not to blend too much or the pil-pil will overthicken to a mayonnaise-like consistency.

Sardinak Parrilan

GRILLED SARDINES

SARDINES ARE A COMMON CATCH in the waters off the Basque coast. The season to eat them is mid-July to mid-August, when the warmer waters are teeming with life and the sardines are fatter than ever. In Santurtzi, home of the most famous sardines in all of Basque Country, the Day of the Sardine is celebrated on July 16, but the feast continues all summer long.

In Santurtzi, the figure of the *sardin saltzailea* (sardine seller) was all-important. These women awaited the signal of a raised net from an approaching boat, meaning it was coming in with a catch, and carried the fish in baskets balanced on their head to the auctioneer. But the advent of cars and trains changed their way of working and now modern European Union regulations have made them obsolete.

Fishermen in the port heft plastic bags or crates full of sardines not destined for auction to nearby *txiringitoak*, beach huts that dot the coast and serve the bare necessities: cold drinks, sandwiches, and the freshest seafood. The fire of the grill converts the humble, silvery sardine into something luxurious, a melt-in-your-mouth meat with beautiful charred flavor. ⚙

SERVES 4

12 whole fresh sardines, scaled

Sea salt

Generously salt both sides of each sardine and let rest at room temperature for 30 minutes to 1 hour.

Meanwhile, prepare a grill to high heat, but with no live flame. If using a charcoal grill, place the grill grate 4 to 6 inches (10 to 15 cm) above the coals, so that if fat drips from the sardines, the resulting flare-up doesn't reach the fish.

Grill the sardines until lightly charred and firm to the touch, turning occasionally, 5 to 7 minutes.

Hegaluze Ontziratua

OIL-CURED TUNA

THE EPHEMERAL FISHING SEASON for albacore tuna is one of the factors that has made this fish one of the most commonly preserved in Basque Country. It is the so-called "chicken of the sea" of supermarket fame, but when made with high-quality tuna and oil, the result can convert even a professed tuna hater.

Many people in Basque Country make their own oil-packed tuna at home. The fish must rest for about three months before it can be eaten; it's an important step that allows the tuna to "cure" in the olive oil. Most boil the fish before canning, but it can also be canned raw—proponents of this method swear it gives the tuna a juicier texture. I've tried both, and the differences are minuscule; the real factor here is the quality of both the tuna and the olive oil. Use this tuna in all types of salads and sandwiches, or even as an ingredient in a pasta dish. Or do what the Basques do and eat it on its own, balanced on a piece of crusty bread. ✿

MAKES ONE 16-OUNCE JAR

2 teaspoons kosher salt, plus more as needed

1 pound (450 g) albacore tuna loins

1 to 1½ cups (240 to 360 mL) extra-virgin olive oil, preferably mildly flavored

Sterilize a 16-ounce glass jar and its lid and ring.

Salt a pot of water generously (use about ½ tablespoon salt for every cup of water) and bring to a boil over high heat. Cut the tuna into a few pieces, no larger than the diameter of the canning jar, and add to the water. Maintain at a gentle simmer for 30 minutes. Drain and set aside until cool enough to handle.

Pack the tuna in the sterilized jar as tightly as possible, using smaller chunks to fill any holes. Add enough of the olive oil to cover the tuna. Add the salt. Refrigerate, uncovered, for 12 hours.

Fill a pot with water to the height of your canning jar and bring to a boil. Remove the jar from the refrigerator and top it off with olive oil, as the tuna will have absorbed some. Leave ½ inch (1.5 cm) of space at the top of the jar. Seal the jar airtight and place it upside down in the boiling water. Boil for 30 minutes, adding hot water if the level ever drops below the height of the jar. Turn off the heat and let cool in the pot.

Remove the jar, wipe it clean, and store in a cool, dark place at room temperature for at least 3 months before opening. Refrigerate after opening. The jars keep, unopened, for up to 1 year.

Hegaluze eta Tomate Entsalada

TUNA AND TOMATO SALAD

TOMATO MAKES ITS SUMMER APPEARANCE in Basque Country from late June through October. The idea of eating tomato raw, as in this salad, is a relatively recent one in Basque Country. Until after the Spanish Civil War ended in 1939, it was unheard of, viewed as something foreign, a habit of Spaniards. The custom of eating tomatoes was likely something adopted first by Basques who fought in the war.

Nowadays, a respectable variety of tomatoes is cultivated in the sunnier parts of the region: pear, Raf, and Kumato, along with local varieties like Saint-Michel, Morado de Aretxabaleta, and Pikoluze. Along with the acceptance of the tomato has come its use in salads: naked, with a bit of olive oil and flaky salt, or served as in this recipe, a gardenlike base for stellar oil-cured tuna (see page 118). The vinegary peppers provide acidic bite to the salad, although you could cut it with an extra drizzle of apple cider vinegar or white wine vinegar. Choose a fresh, good-quality extra-virgin olive oil and be ridiculously generous with it. ✥

SERVES 4

1 jar or can (about 7.7 ounces/220 g) preserved tuna in olive oil (see page 118)

3 tomatoes

Flaky sea salt

1 spring onion

15 pickled guindilla chiles (2.4 ounces/75 g)

Extra-virgin olive oil

Remove the tuna from the can or jar and drain well.

Slice the tomatoes into thick wedges. Arrange them in a single layer on a serving platter and sprinkle lightly with salt.

Gently breaking up the tuna, arrange it on top of the tomatoes, leaving a generous border.

Thinly slice the spring onion using a knife or, better, a mandoline and sprinkle it across the top.

If desired, cut the guindilla peppers into ½-inch (1.5 cm) pieces, discarding the stem. For a more rustic presentation, leave the peppers whole. Place across the center of the salad.

To finish, sprinkle with salt and drizzle generously with olive oil. Serve.

Hegaluzea Tomatearekin

TUNA WITH TOMATO SAUCE

THIS DISH IS SIMPLICITY EPITOMIZED: the freshest tuna, barely seared and warmed through in tomato sauce. One bite will take any Basque straight back to the childhood dinner table, where this dish was omnipresent. It's a quick yet satisfying meal; make it a weeknight go-to dinner for your family. This recipe, which includes a tomato sauce made from scratch, gives the ingredients their due respect, bringing the dish up to modern culinary speed. ✤

SERVES 4

1½ pounds (680 g) albacore tuna loin, about 1½ inches (4 cm) thick, cut into 4 medium pieces (ask your fishmonger to do this)

Kosher salt

1 tablespoon extra-virgin olive oil

1 recipe tomato sauce (see page 192), prepared but not passed through a sieve

Season the tuna with salt.

In a large skillet, heat the olive oil over high heat. One at a time, quickly sear each piece of tuna, only 20 to 30 seconds on each side. Remove the tuna and set aside on a platter.

Reduce the heat to low. Add the tomato sauce and cook for a couple of minutes. Return the tuna to the pan and remove from the heat. Cover until ready to serve.

This dish can also be eaten the next day, though the flavor of the tuna intensifies from one day to the next.

THE GRILL

Grilling is exactly the kind of primordial cooking that suits the Basques: Simple and tactile, it allows the excellence of the raw ingredient to shine through.

The Basque working the grill sees himself as more of a conduit than a cook. Using the best possible product, he watches carefully, safeguarding the natural assets of the meat or fish, learning to adjust the grill's height and position and the cook time to perfectly crisp the outside and leave the inside succulent and tender. Dressings and grilling liquids—such as *ajilimójili*, a sauce of blended and emulsified olive oil, lemon juice, and garlic—are dispensed generously from an anonymous plastic bottle.

Until the twentieth century, the coals of the fire were the only source of heat for cooking in Spanish homes. Pots would bubble over them, grills would be placed on top to roast sausages, and skewers/pokers (called *burruntziak*) were used to roast game birds and farm animals. Whole lambs were skewered and driven into the ground to roast, a method called *zikiro jate* that Basques who had spent time in the Americas brought back with them, purportedly from Argentina.

An important evolution of the Basque grill was the rise in popularity of grilled seabream. In the mid-1950s, the Gipuzkoan village of Orio was its mecca. What could perhaps be referred to in Spanish as the *nueva parrilla* ("new grilling") movement began at Elkano in neighboring Getaria, when the first hake neck and then the first turbot were grilled whole. Now whole lobsters, shrimp, and monkfish are fair game for the grill, and the skill of grilling has become an entrenched value in Basque cuisine. In 1990, a humble restaurant, Etxebarri, opened in Axpe, Bizkaia, and ten years later its chef-owner, Bittor Arginzoniz, began to experiment with the unique qualities of his ingredients, custom-crafting grillware for each item and using carbonized wood that he dry-ages before sealing it hermetically in an oven to begin smoldering. It now ranks in the top ten of the world's best restaurants. The indisputable ability of the grill to convert the most simple ingredient into pure luxury has resulted in a cooking style as at home in four-walled mountain huts as in the finest restaurants of Basque Country.

Hegaluze Mendrezka

GRILLED TUNA BELLY

WHILE THE REST OF THE WORLD eats grilled tuna steaks, Basques grill only the *mendrezka* (belly). Long and triangular, the belly is a curiously shaped piece. You'll want to buy it super fresh, as the fatty belly degrades quickly.

The key to a perfect grilled tuna belly is pulling it off the grill the moment the thinnest part is done. Hot olive oil, infused with garlic and spicy red guindilla chile, is then poured over the thicker parts of the cut, ensuring that each square inch is perfectly cooked. The resulting sauce is called *olio errea*, or *refrito* in Spanish. This fatty tuna belly is unctuous, creamy, and delicious. It is a dish redolent of summertime, perfect served with a glass of cold *txakoli*.

If you have a *besuguera*, the name used generally to refer to wire cages designed for grilling fish, use that to help keep the fish together and easy to turn on the grill. If you grill directly on the grates, just make sure they are very hot before you put the fish on, to help prevent sticking. ✿

SERVES 4

1 whole skin-on tuna belly, about 2 pounds (900 g)

Kosher salt

¼ cup (60 mL) extra-virgin olive oil

2 garlic cloves, sliced

1 small guindilla chile

2 tablespoons white wine vinegar or apple cider vinegar

Bring the tuna belly to room temperature. Prepare a grill to high heat but with no live flames. Place the grate 6 to 8 inches (15 to 20 cm) above the heat source.

Sprinkle the tuna belly generously with salt on both sides.

Place the tuna belly in a grilling basket, if you have one, and lay it skin-side down on the grill (otherwise, make sure the grill is very hot, then place the fish directly on the grates). Grill until you see that the skin is browning, 2 to 3 minutes. Flip gently and cook for 2 to 3 minutes more. Remove from the grill when the thinnest part of the belly is cooked. Place on a serving platter, skin-side down.

Meanwhile, in a small skillet, combine the olive oil, garlic, and chile and heat over medium-high heat. When the garlic begins to brown, remove from the heat.

Pour the hot chile-garlic oil over the fat parts of the fish to help continue the cooking. Carefully tilt the platter so the oil falls back into the skillet.

Add the vinegar to the skillet and bring the mixture to a simmer, swirling to mix. Pour the oil mixture over the fat parts of the tuna for a second time.

Serve warm on a large serving platter with a simple salad and crusty bread.

Erreboiloa Parrilan

GRILLED TURBOT

TURBOT ON THE GRILL originated in the seaside town of Getaria, still one of the busier ports of the Basque Country. It hums with the activity of small boats puttering in and out and large fishing boats manned by several men, a mess of nets and shouting. The port and the old town are lined with grills, simple little caves built into the walls of the buildings. These grills are nothing more than a metal basket at thigh height, filled with ash and coals; a wheel, for adjusting the height of the grates from the embers; and the black grates themselves.

Pedro Arregui, of Elkano, one of the masters of the Basque grill, pioneered the grilled turbot. Instead of filleting it, as was customary with flat fish, Pedro grilled it whole. Instead of adding the traditional garlicky *olio errea* sauce (see page 124), his wife, Mari Jose, whipped up a vinegar-oil mixture, which combines perfectly with the unctuous oils the turbot releases. Known as *agua de Lourdes*, it is still served today at the restaurant, now run by their son Aitor.

A wild turbot is easily identified by its price, up to four times more than that of a farmed turbot. The texture of the skin is another telltale sign: Instead of slimy smooth, it will be bumpy and uneven, a mark of natural quality. When choosing the fish, look for lovely red gills, clear and fresh eyes, and an underside that is rosy, not pallid; allot about a pound per person. You can make this recipe on the grill *or* in the oven, which means you can cook it all year long. ❧

SERVES 2

¼ cup (60 mL) extra-virgin olive oil, plus more as needed

1 tablespoon white wine vinegar

¼ teaspoon kosher salt, plus more as needed

1 (1½- to 2-pound/680 to 900 g) whole turbot (wild if available), cleaned

In a blender or in a high-sided container using an immersion blender, blend together the olive oil, vinegar, and salt. A squirt bottle comes in handy for storing and dispensing the mixture. Set aside until ready to use.

ON THE GRILL:
Prepare a grill to high heat but with no live flame (this is best done an hour or two before use, so the charcoal is smoldering and very hot). Place the grate 5 to 6 inches (13 to 15 cm) above the heat source.

Bring the turbot to room temperature 15 to 30 minutes before grilling. Salt the turbot very heavily on each side.

Place the fish in a grilling basket, if you have one, and lay it dark-skin-side down on the grill (otherwise, make sure the grill is very hot, then place the fish directly on the grates). Grill for 7 minutes, then flip, scraping off the excess salt on the dark side. The skin should be bubbling in places.

Squirt the fish with about one-third of the vinegar mixture, letting it run off the fish. Grill for about 7 minutes more. Lift off the grill, squirting both sides generously with about half the remaining vinegar mixture, and place on a rimmed serving platter.

If desired, prepare the fish for the table by cutting down the middle of the loin, along the spine, and separating the head. Douse it with the remaining vinegar mixture, then at the table, with a spoon, tilt the platter so the juice running off the fish mixes with the vinegar mixture and pools around the base of the rimmed serving platter. Beat it lightly to combine and ladle it back over the fish as you would a serving sauce right before serving.

IN THE OVEN:
Preheat the oven to 430°F (220°C). Line a baking sheet with aluminum foil and set it in the oven to preheat.

Rinse the turbot with cool water and pat dry. Season both sides generously with salt and set aside.

Remove the hot baking sheet from the oven. Drizzle it with a bit of olive oil, distributing it evenly with a kitchen brush or folded paper towel. Place the turbot, lighter-side down, in the middle of the baking sheet and return it to the oven.

Bake for 5 minutes. Pull the baking sheet far enough out of the oven to access the fish, and squirt or pour about two-thirds of the vinegar mixture over the fish. Return the fish to the oven for about 7 minutes more.

Switch the oven to broil. Pull the baking sheet far enough out of the oven to access the fish again and with a spoon or baster, collect the juices and olive oil from the pan and redistribute them over the fish. Baste the fish several times. Position the baking sheet under the broiler and broil for about 5 minutes, until the skin is bubbling and turning gold in some places.

Remove from the oven and transfer carefully to a large serving platter. If desired, prepare the fish for the table by cutting down the middle of the loin, along the spine, and separating the head. Pour all the liquid from the baking sheet into a small bowl and blend with an immersion blender to emulsify. Pour the liquid back over the fish and serve immediately.

Txipiroiak Pelaio Erara

SQUID WITH CARAMELIZED ONIONS

PELAYO WAS A BAR IN THE TOWN OF GETARIA, where so much of Basque seafood innovation happens. Supposedly, the bar's owner was up to his ears in the summer squid catch. He asked his wife to prepare the baby squid in a new way, and this dish, literally named "Pelayo-style squid," was born. The bar, located on Calle Elkano in the little town, closed after the Spanish Civil War, but the dish lives on. The ingredients are similar to squid in its ink (see page 133), but the eating experience is totally different: beautifully seared squid, served with golden, meltingly caramelized vegetables.

Txipiroiak (squid) are well loved and highly regarded in Basque cuisine. They are at their best in the height of summer, and are generally enjoyed in season only. The tiny ones are most prized for this recipe, although larger squid, those that reach six inches or so, can also be used. Look for the freshest squid you can get at your fishmonger; however, this dish can be made with frozen squid in a pinch. ❧

SERVES 4

4 tablespoons (60 mL) extra-virgin olive oil

3 spring onions, thinly sliced

2 sweet Italian green peppers, such as Cubanelle, thinly sliced

Kosher salt

3 garlic cloves

24 fresh baby squid, or 12 larger (6 inches/15 cm or larger) squid

½ cup (120 mL) txakoli or other acidic white wine

In a medium sauté pan, heat 3 tablespoons of the olive oil over medium heat. Add the onions and peppers, along with a generous pinch of salt. Mince two of the garlic cloves and add them to the pan. Reduce the heat to medium-low and cook, stirring occasionally, until the mixture is a deep golden brown, 45 minutes to 1 hour. Remove from the heat and set aside.

Meanwhile, working over the sink, clean the squid by first removing the finned tube from the tentacles. With the head section in one hand, grasp the tail section and pull gently. Reserve the silvery ink bag that comes out with the innards; it can be frozen for another use. Pull out and discard the hard beak in the

continued »

center of the tentacles. On a cutting board, cut the tentacles just below the eyes, and rinse the tentacles under cold water. Set the tentacles aside on a plate.

Reaching inside the tube, pull out the cartilage and discard. At this point, removing the film of outer skin is an optional step, and one often skipped by Basque cooks. Rinse the tubes under cold water. Remove the fins and discard. Stuff the body tubes with the tentacles.

Place the pan with the peppers and onions back over medium heat. Thinly slice the remaining garlic clove.

In a separate medium sauté pan, heat the remaining 1 tablespoon olive oil over high heat. Season the stuffed squid with salt. When the oil is very hot, add the squid to the pan. Cook without disturbing for 1 minute, then turn the squid. Add the garlic slices and cook for 1 to 2 minutes more, until well browned on both sides.

Transfer the squid to the pan with the onions and peppers. Pour in the txakoli and simmer over low heat until the mixture comes together, about 3 minutes.

To serve, on a platter, arrange the vegetables under or on top of the squid. If you have any leftovers, the flavors will improve the next day.

TXIPIROI BILA

SQUID FISHING

When the waters around Basque Country are calm, fishermen and hobbyists rise with the dawn or set out at dusk in their *txipironerak*, small and simple squid-fishing boats, to search for squid. They fish with nothing more than a string or a pole and some bait, typically a *potera*, a squid jig with an array of upward-slanting hooks. Some also carry a *tutua*, a bamboo case with a cork top, used to carry the sharp lures. The fisherman thrusts out the pole or string with the brightly colored potera attached and moves it with a quick, jerking motion, hoping for the most prized catch—squid babies, only a few inches long.

Once caught, the pure white squid are gently removed from the hook and placed in a plastic bag to carry home. After a little while, their skin develops spots in a lovely brilliant reddish-purple pattern. These babies are most numerous in the late spring and summer months, and even the fisherman who sticks close to land might bring in enough to make a sale to a local restaurant. Baby squid are worth more by weight than larger ones, and a chef pays around 2 euros per *txipiroia*. Visually, there is no mistaking them for the ones that were dragged in a net with other sea refuse, their skin battered and torn. And the taste is pure, clean sea with a taut yet tender skin—a real treasure.

Txipiroiak Bere Tintan

SQUID IN INK SAUCE

THE SHOCKING COLOR of this dish may strike you at first—it seems to be pure black ink. The color comes from the ink of the squid, but the sauce is essentially a delicious tinted vegetable puree. The Italians are the only other culture in the world with a totally black dish, and it is likely they introduced the idea to the Basques when they immigrated to the Basque coast to open fish-preserving factories.

Look for small (2- to 3-inch/5 to 7.5 cm) baby squid for this dish. Larger squid can be used when the babies are unavailable; slice them and incorporate into the sauce. Don't be afraid to let the pan get quite hot, as the combination of a hard sear followed by slow stewing makes for the most tender squid you'll ever try.

Optimally, make this dish the day before you want to serve it, as it improves in taste from one day to the next. If the sauce thickens too much overnight, just add a bit more fish broth or water.

Serve it with toasted bread or even rice for a more filling main course.

SERVES 4

24 fresh baby squid, or 12 small squid, with ink (see Note)

¾ cup (180 mL) olive oil

2 spring onions, finely diced

2 garlic cloves, minced

2 onions, diced

1 sweet Italian green pepper, such as Cubanelle, diced

1 cup (240 mL) txakoli or other acidic white wine

½ cup (120 mL) tomato sauce (see page 192)

Fish broth (see page 65)

Working over the sink, clean the squid by first removing the finned tube from the tentacles. With the head section in one hand, grasp the tail section and pull gently. Reserve the silvery ink bag that comes out with the innards for the sauce. Pull out and discard the hard beak in the center of the tentacles. On a cutting board, cut the tentacles just below the eyes, and rinse the tentacles under cold water. Set the tentacles aside on a plate.

Reaching inside the tube, pull out the cartilage and discard. At this point, removing the film of outer skin is an optional step, and one often skipped by Basque cooks. Rinse the tubes under cold water. Remove the fins and finely dice them. Finely dice the tentacles. Set aside.

continued »

In a large sauté pan, heat 3 tablespoons of the olive oil over medium heat. Add the spring onions and garlic and cook, stirring occasionally, until tender. Add the squid tentacles and fins and cook for 10 to 15 minutes, until the liquid the squid releases has reduced. Taste and adjust the seasoning. Let cool.

Fill each individual squid body with the mixture. Stick a toothpick through the open end of the body to close it.

In a clean large sauté pan, heat 1 tablespoon of the olive oil over high heat. When the oil is extremely hot, add the squid and cook, searing them deeply, for about 3 minutes. Transfer the squid and any liquid they let out to a plate and set aside.

In the same pan, heat the remaining ½ cup (120 mL) olive oil over medium-high heat. Add the onions and pepper, along with a pinch of salt. Cook until the onions are translucent, add the wine, and simmer for about 5 minutes, until the mixture has reduced slightly. Add the tomato sauce and a splash of fish broth and simmer. Add the ink bags and simmer for 15 minutes more. Carefully pass the mixture through a food mill or blend directly in the pan with an immersion blender and then pass it through a fine-mesh sieve; discard the solids. Return the sauce to the pan.

Remove the toothpicks from the squid and add them to the sauce, along with any liquid that has collected on the plate. Cover over low heat until tender, 15 to 20 minutes. Let rest for at least 10 minutes before serving.

Note If your squid come without ink bags, squid ink can be purchased from your fishmonger or online.

Legatza Txirlekin Saltsa Berdean

HAKE WITH CLAMS IN SALSA VERDE

WHILE SAUCES IN BIZKAIA AND ARABA are marked by peppers and tomatoes, the coastal province of Gipuzkoa, on the Spanish-French border, is known for light *saltsa berdean* (*salsa verde*), a sauce of olive oil, parsley, garlic, and white wine. Though it pairs well with any seafood, it is most often served with hake. In other parts of Spain, this dish goes by the name Basque hake. Written recipes for the dish date back to 1723. In *La Cocina Vasca*, the authoritative classic for Basque home cooks, there are no fewer than seven recipes for this dish; one of them, called the "economical" version, calls for only four ingredients: potato, fish, parsley, and a garlic clove.

In this recipe, the clams open to release their briny juices, which boost the flavor of the sauce and enhance the hake perfectly. If you can't find fresh hake, cod and flounder make nice substitutes. Traditionally, this (and most other saucy dishes in Basque cuisine) is served in earthenware casserole dishes, but use any vessel with a bit of a lip for retaining the luscious sauce. ✿

SERVES 4

20 clams

Bones, head, and tail from 1 fish, preferably hake

4 skin-on hake fillets, about 7 ounces (200 g) each

Kosher salt

½ cup (120 mL) extra-virgin olive oil

2 garlic cloves, minced

1 tablespoon all-purpose flour (see Note)

½ cup (120 mL) txakoli or other acidic white wine

4 teaspoons finely chopped fresh parsley

Place the clams in a bowl, add cold water to cover, and set aside.

Rinse the bones, head, or whatever scraps you have from the hake with cold water. Place in a medium pot and add water to cover. Bring to a boil over high heat, reduce the heat to low, and simmer for about 20 minutes. Strain the liquid (called fumet) through a fine-mesh sieve and discard the solids. Set the fumet aside.

Scrub and drain the clams; set aside.

Rinse the hake fillets and pat them dry. Season the skin-free side of each fillet with salt.

continued »

In an earthenware casserole or a large sauté pan, heat the olive oil and garlic over medium-high heat. When the garlic starts to "dance," add the flour and cook, stirring, for about 30 seconds. Pour in the wine and simmer for about 30 seconds to cook off the alcohol. Add 1 cup (240 mL) of the fumet and simmer for about 1 minute.

Add the hake fillets to the pan, skin-side up. Simmer for about 3 minutes. Gently turn the hake fillets over. Add the clams, placing them around the pot, and cook for about 5 minutes. Should the pan begin to look dry, add more fumet.

Sprinkle the parsley over the pan. Remove from the heat and move the pan in a circular motion until the sauce begins to come together and emulsify, 1 to 2 minutes. Taste and adjust the seasoning.

Serve in individual bowls or family-style. You can reserve the remaining fumet for another use.

Note The inclusion of flour in the salsa verde is a matter of debate. It helps to thicken the sauce, but purists say "less flour, more wrist," insistent that the correct stirring technique will result in perfectly emulsified sauce. Experiment to see which version you like best.

TXAKOLI

Cool, crisp, and refreshing. Easy to drink, with sour and salty notes. White wine, but not quite white in color, *txakoli* has long been the wine of choice for Basques, served up with informality and a sense of patriotism.

A wine whose written references date back to the sixteenth century, txakoli was produced in farmhouses by families and used, along with other homemade products, as currency. But this table wine didn't get much credibility until it was granted its first protected classification (Jatorri Deitura/Denominación de Origen/Designation of Origin), Getariako Txakolina, in 1990. Previously, txakoli had been a rough, wild wine, produced in uncared-for vineyards and sold in recycled glass bottles with no labels. After a handful of proponents, such as the Txueka brothers from the Txomin Etxaniz winery, bet on improvements and more "serious" installations, the DO was formed and served to regulate the vines of *hondarrabi zuri* and *hondarrabi beltza* (literally, hondarrabi white and black grapes). Two other DOs quickly followed: Bizkaiko Txakolina (which incorporated the grape *munematsa*) and Txakolí de Álava, though Gipuzkoa's txakoli remains the most consumed, with the highest average quality, for now. In total, there are more than eighty wineries (*bodegas* in Spanish) across the DOs.

Txakoli grapes are harvested, often manually, from the vines in September. The grapes are pressed quickly and then transferred to stainless-steel tanks. The must ferments on its lees for two to three weeks at 55 to 60°F (13 to 16°C). At this point, some wineries leave it longer on its lees, while others filter and send the wine off to storage, to be bottled to order. Traditionally, new txakoli is tasted on January 17, the day of San Antonio, Txakoli Eguna.

Serve this young wine when the Basques do—on a hot day, as an aperitif with a small bite or two. Its *bizigarri*, a Basque word that means both "fizz" and "that special something," makes it a perfect match for fresh grilled fish. Take sides on the pouring style—in Bizkaia, the txakoli is often poured as any other white wine, gently and low to the glass. In Gipuzkoa, however, the farther the bottle is held from the glass, the better, and a specially designed stopper is often used to control the pour, allowing the txakoli to bubble, fizz, and open up.

Arroza Txirlekin

RICE WITH CLAMS

THE BASQUE CUISINE isn't much for bivalves, but clams hold a special place in the culinary repertoire. Rice with clams is an emblematic Basque dish, and its simple name doesn't do it justice. The rice is very creamy, made with more liquid than a rice or risotto. The juice of the clams goes into the fish broth, and the resulting liquid, thickened by the starch from the rice, is truly a revelation. ❦

SERVES 3 OR 4

1½ pounds (680 g) clams

3 tablespoons olive oil

2 spring onions, diced

2 garlic cloves, minced

2 tablespoons chopped fresh parsley (see Note)

1 cup (240 mL) white wine

1 cup (7 ounces/200 g) short-grain rice, preferably bomba

1 teaspoon kosher salt

2 to 3 cups (480 to 620 mL) fish broth (see page 65)

Place the clams in a bowl, add cold water to cover, and set aside. After 20 minutes, scrub and drain the clams; set aside.

In a medium pot, heat 1 tablespoon of the olive oil over medium heat. Add half the onions and half the garlic. Cook, stirring occasionally, until the vegetables begin to turn translucent, just a few minutes. Add the clams and 1 tablespoon of the parsley. Stir. Add ½ cup (120 mL) of the wine and bring to a simmer. When the clams begin to open, after about 2 minutes, remove from the heat. Reserve.

In a separate large pot, heat the remaining 2 tablespoons olive oil over medium heat. Add the remaining garlic and onion. Cook, stirring, until tender, about 10 minutes. Add the rice and salt and cook, stirring, for about 1 minute.

Add the remaining ½ cup (120 mL) wine and bring the mixture back to a simmer. Measure the clam cooking liquid and add enough fish broth so that you have 2¾ cups (660 mL) of liquid total. Once the alcohol has cooked off, add the broth mixture and reduce the heat to maintain a simmer. Cook, stirring occasionally, for 17 minutes. The rice should still be brothy and a touch al dente. Remove the pot from the heat. Add the clams and the remaining 1 tablespoon parsley and cover. Let rest for 5 minutes.

Serve, dividing the clams evenly between plates, arranged atop the rice.

Note Chop the parsley with a knife, or try what I've seen Basque housewives do: stuff the leaves into a glass and cut into them with scissors, a mess-free method.

THE FISHERMAN

From Ziburu to Santurtzi, the Basque fisherman cuts the same humble figure in blue overalls with a *boina* beret, ever knowledgeable about the moon, the tides, and the health of local marine life. For the Basque, fishing was a form of sustenance, not a job but a way of living. Until the mid-twentieth century, it was a distinctly low-tech proposition, with fish caught one by one on the line, which remains a prized fishing method today. The most traditional and respected method of fishing is coastal fishing, done in boats that are typically smaller and float along the coast. *Kofradiak*, fishermen's associations, date back to the fourteenth century. Majorly influential in everything from lobbying for steady paychecks to setting the yearly fishing calendar, they carry the names of saints and still occupy sixteen of the fishing villages today. These fishing villages feature rows of houses, often built into the steep cliffs of the coastline, with little to no space between the rows. These are the traditional abodes of the fishermen, white-walled houses with wooden beams painted blue, green, and red.

A fisherman's work schedule varies: The hours can be infinite, the results all that matter. In spring, the fisherman may set out in the evening, casting about during the night for fish and heading back to port midmorning to unload his catch. Depending on his success, he'll have lunch and a nap until it is time to head out again. In the winter, he might set out at dawn and spend the whole day in search of sardines or mackerel, returning at dark. A great many culinary traditions—among them the grilling of whole fish, the salting of cod (see page 106), and the invention of *marmitako* (see page 79)—were begotten by necessity and cemented aboard ships.

Recent laws put in place by the European Union restrict coastal fishing, endangering the livelihood of traditional fishermen in Basque Country. Mysterious changes prompted by man and climate contribute to shortages of fish that have never been in short supply, from anchovy to crab, and invasions by species like triggerfish, which the Basques disdain as inedible. With an increase in immigrant fishermen and young people's increased education and decreased interest in the trade, the future of fishing is uncertain, if not bleak.

Zapo Frijitua

FRIED MONKFISH

THE BASQUE ANSWER to a simple lunch or dinner is fresh fish, baked in the oven or fried in olive oil. *Etxekoandreak* (the female heads of the house) don't think twice about frying up white-fleshed fish, from hake to cod. The process is instinctive: Crack a few eggs for battering, heat a generous glug of olive oil, and *ala!*, to the table. It may seem a waste to fry with high-quality olive oil, but the economy comes from saving it in a bottle next to the stove, to be reused several times.

Monkfish has tender, meaty flesh, often compared with lobster. Coating the fish in flour, then dipping it in egg, is the most widely used way to prepare fried fish. This method, more battering than breading, results in a pillowy, golden exterior instead of the crispy one you might be accustomed to. Serve the fish with a bit of mayonnaise for dipping. ✤

SERVES 4

1 pound (450 g) monkfish, skin and bones removed

Kosher salt

Olive oil, for frying

2 garlic cloves, whole

2 large eggs

About 1 cup (125 g) all-purpose flour, for breading

Cut the fish into large bite-size pieces and season with salt.

Pour 1 inch (2.5 cm) of olive oil into a high-sided skillet and add the garlic. Heat the oil over high heat to about 300°F (150°C); when the oil reaches temperature and the garlic has browned, remove the garlic with a slotted spoon.

Meanwhile, put the eggs in a shallow bowl and beat with a fork. Season with salt. Spread the flour over a shallow bowl or plate.

Dredge each piece of fish in the flour, shaking off any excess, then dip it in the egg wash and allow any excess to drip off. Carefully add the fish to the hot oil; work in batches as necessary to avoid crowding the pan. Fry for about 1 minute, flip each piece, and fry for another minute or two, until golden. Remove with a slotted spoon and drain on paper towels. Sprinkle with a bit of salt. Repeat to fry the remaining fish.

Serve warm, solo or with mayonnaise for dipping.

NAVARRE-STYLE TROUT

TROUT IS, WITHOUT A DOUBT, A CELEBRATED FISH in Nafarroa's cuisine. This region has no coastline, so river fish have always had a special place at the table. A relative of salmon, the trout that dots the rivers of Nafarroa is the brown trout (*Salmo trutta*), silver and speckled and quite challenging to catch. Just after the winter thaw, fishermen make daytime trips to the riverbed, wading in the cool waters and catching trout with a rod, traditionally wrapping it in ferns to keep the skin moist.

This dish of ham-stuffed fish is a classic, appearing in the oldest recipe books from the region. Some recipes include an addition of lovely red piquillo peppers (see page 170). Nowadays, the trout is often served with roasted potato slices. Moister, mild *jamón Serrano* is used in this recipe, but you could also use the more luxurious *jamón Ibérico*. ❧

SERVES 4

4 small trout (about 8 ounces/226 g each), cleaned and butterflied

Kosher salt

6 slices Serrano ham (about 100 g)

2 tablespoons milk

All-purpose flour, for coating

3 tablespoons extra-virgin olive oil or lard

Preheat the oven to 400°F (200°C).

Rinse the trout with cool water and pat dry with a paper towel. Sprinkle the interior generously with salt and place 1 slice of ham in each fish.

Using a kitchen brush, paint each fish with a bit of milk. Mix the flour and a pinch of salt on a plate and dredge each trout in the flour to evenly coat, shaking off any excess.

In a large skillet, heat the olive oil over medium-high heat. Add the remaining 2 slices ham and cook until its fat begins to render and its edges begin to approach crispiness. Remove and set aside. Add one or two trout to the pan and cook for a few minutes on each side, until the fish gains a bit of color. Transfer to a baking sheet and repeat to cook the remaining fish.

Transfer the baking sheet to the oven and bake for about 5 minutes. Turn the fish and bake for 5 minutes more.

Transfer the fish to a platter. Serve garnished with the reserved ham.

NAFARROA

NAFARROA

NAFARROA (NAVARRE IN SPANISH) IS REGAL. PARADOXICALLY, IT IS NOT part of País Vasco, the Spanish autonomous community, although it is considered the birthplace of the Basque people. The Vascones were a pre-Roman tribe that inhabited the area, and they quietly endured occupation by the Romans and the Franks before electing a chieftain as their leader and giving a name to their country around the turn of the first century. Land disputes plagued Nafarroa's desirable geography—the Spanish royalty were always attempting to snatch the juiciest corners, and part of Nafarroa (Basse-Navarre) remained in French power—but a *fuero* system (a municipal franchise) allowed the region great control over its politics and economics.

Nafarroa has a varied geography: pale gray peaks to the north, dewy valleys with rivers abundant with trout, dry Mediterranean-style land dotted with olive groves, and even a Sahara-like desert region, making it the most agriculturally diverse region in Basque Country. Culinarily speaking, it is the vegetable basket of the Basque Country.

Nafarroa has fifteen government-protected products, including ruby red piquillo peppers (see page 170), Roncal and Idiazabal cheeses,

rosé wine, white asparagus (see page 159), artichokes (see page 155), and *patxaran*, the famed Basque digestif (see page 306), among others. It also boasts an important olive oil production, and the Bidasoa river has been a recorded source of salmon for the Basque Country since medieval times.

Nafarroa's cultural diversity also results in different eating habits in the region: The northern part is distinctly more Basque, and is known for the sausage *txistorra* (see page 200).

Sheep also dominate, forming the backbone of traditional dishes from the Baztan valley. Dishes like *baztan zopa*, a dish of stewed lamb's head served with a big piece of week-old bread to soak up the juices (more delicious than it sounds), and *txuritabeltz*, literally "white and black," a stew of lamb stomach sausage and boiled blood (also delicious), dominate festivities. However, closer to the Ribera and the Spanish Rioja, the dishes are more focused on lamb, roasted *chilindrón*-style (see page 211), or served from the inside out as in *patorillo* or *menudico*, a stew of peppers and what seems like every internal organ of the sheep, as well as other Castilian-flavored specialties.

Nafarroa even has a wine country, dating back to before the Middle Ages and especially noted for its rosés. The *rosado* of the region is primarily made with garnacha grapes, which yield a light, aromatic, and fruity dark pink wine locally known as *clarete*. The Day of the Navarran Rosado is celebrated on the last Sunday of May in San Martín de Unx, and upward of one thousand bottles of rosado are opened for tasting on the streets of the village.

The capital of Nafarroa is Iruña—more commonly known by its Spanish moniker, Pamplona. It's a lovely city whose old part is marked with an ancient cathedral and the infamous bull ring. The festival of San Fermín, colloquially known as the running of the bulls, which begins on July 7, is one of the world's most famous. Each year, the city is inundated with aspiring runners from all over the world, but the festival has quite a local, private side that is somewhat more civilized: long lunches featuring rich oxtail stew and robust reds from the region, and socializing on friends' balconies along Estafeta Street. Pamplona has its own namesake charcuterie, *chorizo de pamplona*, a mix of beef and pork with loads of paprika that is a favorite snack among children. Sweets include the famous *pastillas de café con leche*, rectangular hard caramels, and mini *pains au chocolat* called *garroticos* from Pastas Beatriz, which are served warm and sell out before they have a chance to cool.

In this more agrarian society less influenced by the dining societies (see page 91), women have remained at the forefront of the food scene, though more recently, male chefs have crowded into the kitchen. More than in neighboring provinces, the cooking of Nafarroa is female-led, with the men holding up their end by hunting game and fowl, fishing for trout and salmon, and collecting wild mushrooms. The restaurants that uphold traditional cooking (like Tubal) or shine with Michelin stars (like Europa) have had a woman at the helm. These and more of the region's most emblematic restaurants, from the old Santesteban to Las Potxolas at number 6 Sarasate Street in Pamplona, were all run by matriarchs whose culinary stardom came before its time. This feminine touch almost certainly served to reinforce Nafarroa's now-famous vegetable-based traditional cuisine.

BARAZKI MENESTRA
Spring Vegetable
Stew | 155

ZAINZURIAK MAIONESAREKIN
White Asparagus
with Mayonnaise | 159

BABAK "VITORIANA" ERARA
Vitoria-Style Fava
Beans | 162

BARRASKILOAK
Snails | 164

GERNIKAKO PIPERRAK
Gernika Peppers | 169

POTXAK NAFAR ERARA
Navarre-Style
White Beans | 183

ENTSALADA
Simple Basque
Salad | 185

ONDDOAK GORRINGOAREKIN
Porcini Mushrooms
with Egg Yolk | 186

PATATAK ERRIOXAR ERARA
Riojan Potato-Chorizo
Stew | 189

PERRETXIKO NAHASKIA
Mushroom Eggs | 190

TXISTORRA
Basque Chorizo | 200

ODOLKIA
Blood Sausage | 203

MONDEJUA
Lamb Tripe and
Egg Sausage | 206

ARKUMEA
TXILINDRON ERARA
Lamb in Chilindrón
Sauce | 211

TXITXIKIS
Pork Hash
with Paprika | 214

BARAZKIAK ETA HARAGIAK

VEGETABLES AND MEAT

PIQUILLO PIPERRAK
Piquillo Peppers | 170

PIPERMINAK
Pickled Guindilla
Peppers | 175

TOLOSAKO BABARRUNAK
Tolosa Beans | 176

AZA
Cabbage | 178

PIPERRADA
Tomato-Pepper
Stew | 180

TOMATE FRIJITUA
Tomato Sauce | 192

XIPISTER
Herb-Pepper
Vinegar Sauce | 195

TALOA
Basque Corn
Flatbread | 196

TXAHAL MASAILAK
Beef Cheeks | 217

AXOA
Veal Stew with
Peppers | 220

TXULETA
Steak | 223

THERE ARE FEW MODERN CULTURES that remain as linked to the land as that of the Basques. The people of the *mendi* (mountain) live in a world of early-morning fog, entrapped between steep cliffs and sweeping valleys. The *baserri*, the Basque farmhouse, marks the rhythms of the mountain way of life, although with each passing generation you need to go deeper and deeper inland to find fully functioning *baserriak*.

Nevertheless, the changing of the seasons and its effect on the *terroir* remains deeply observed and felt. Every new wind blows in a different round of traditions and festivals, each observed with a sense of surety that can only come from repeating the same tradition over generations.

Spring ushers in the feasts of Carnaval, San Prudentzio and mountain snails, mushrooms (specifically *perretxikoak*, St. George's mushrooms), and plates of the vegetable stew *menestra*. When summer hits, there is an instinct buried within every Basque to head to the nearest sun-soaked outdoor table for a glass of *txakoli* and a salad with tomato, tuna, and vinegary peppers (see page 121). Then the days of fall come around, the harvest from the vines and the beginning of winemaking seasons, the apples heavy on the trees awaiting their conversion into cider (*sagardo*), and olives ready to be pressed into oil.

A pig slaughter (known as *txerriboda*) traditionally marked the arrival of fall and winter and would bring together an entire village in a group effort. Fresh sausages that were traditionally by-products of the family pig, such as *txistorra*, *morcilla*, and *txitxikis*, are the feature of winter celebrations.

Winter also means a trip to taste the fresh cider, which for the last half century has been accompanied by mandatory salt cod omelets (see page 97) and *txuleta* (see page 223), a Basque-size steak served wonderfully rare. Excuses to gather often base themselves around menus, like the *babarrunada*, a party with friends revolving around a stew of beans served with pickled guindilla chiles and morcilla.

Hunting wild birds, deer, and rabbit has always been a source of food primarily associated with the winter. Foraging for wild mushrooms, especially the prized *onddoak* (porcini), is still a popular pastime among

Basques of all ages, and their contraband findings can be seen entering the back doors of restaurants across Basque Country.

Basque traditions and the land are deeply, inextricably intertwined. However, modern times have seen the Basque relationship with the terrain evolve. Nowadays, modern farming techniques are used, with the old manual ways of working relegated to individuals tending their home gardens. Advances in farming technology have been used to bring back heirloom varieties, though eating local vegetables was never erased from the collective habit. The Basques maintain a living, breathing relationship with their surroundings that is authentic and universal, and it plays out across tables everywhere.

Barazki Menestra

SPRING VEGETABLE STEW

MENESTRA COULD BE CONSIDERED Nafarroa's signature dish: a vegetable medley draped in nothing more than a simple, earthy, béchamel-like vegetable sauce. Spring's culinary calling card comes in many styles, but this is the classic menestra from the area around the town of Tudela. It includes four vegetables—artichokes, white asparagus, peas, and fava beans. As the seasons turn, you can substitute green beans for peas and borage for fava beans. In Nafarroa, the reigning meat is sheep, and menestra with lamb is almost as common as the vegetable version. A native of Tudela might swear that the secret is using the same water to cook as you did to water the plants. But the true keys to this simple dish are procuring the freshest, best produce possible and adequately seasoning the blanching water as well as the thickened broth. ✿ PICTURED ON PAGES 150 AND 157

SERVES 4

Kosher salt

18 ounces (510 g) green peas in the pod, shelled (about 1½ cups shelled)

4 pounds (900 g) fava beans in the pod, shelled (about 2 cups shelled; see Notes)

6 artichokes

8 fresh white asparagus spears (see Notes)

9 ounces (255 g) Ibérico ham, sliced (about 11 slices)

2 tablespoons extra-virgin olive oil, plus more for drizzling

2 garlic cloves, sliced

2 tablespoons all-purpose flour

Bring a pot of salted water to a boil. Add the peas little by little to avoid breaking the boil. Boil for about 3 minutes and drain. Run the peas under cold water or drop into a bowl of ice water to cool. Drain and set aside.

Refill the pot with water, add salt, and bring to a boil. Add the fava beans little by little to avoid breaking the boil. If you plan to peel the favas, boil them for 3 minutes, drain, and run under cold water. Peel the beans, pinching to squeeze them out of the shell. Set aside.

Refill the pot with water, add salt, and bring to a boil. Clean the artichokes quickly by trimming the bottom stalk and removing the outermost leaves until you get to the white-yellow interior leaves. Chop off the top third of the artichoke. Add to the salted water and boil until a knife is easily inserted into and removed from each artichoke. The cooking time can vary widely according to the type

continued »

of artichoke, so start checking after 10 minutes. Drain and let cool. Cut each artichoke into quarters, removing the choke.

Refill the pot with water, add salt, and bring to a boil. Trim the bottom of each asparagus spear, cutting off an inch or two. Peel the bottom half with a vegetable peeler. Add to the boiling water. Boil until totally tender, 12 to 15 minutes. Drain, reserving the cooking liquid.

Set 4 slices of the ham aside in a warm place to bring to room temperature. Cut the remaining ham into thin strips.

In a large pot, heat the olive oil over medium-high heat. Add the garlic and cook, stirring, until it begins to color. Add the sliced ham to the pot and stir. Sprinkle the flour over the mixture and cook, stirring for 1 to 2 minutes to remove the raw flour taste. Gradually add 2 to 3 cups (480 to 720 mL) of the warm vegetable cooking liquid and stir until it is incorporated. Add the blanched vegetables to the pot, stirring gently to coat in the sauce, and bring to a boil. Cook for a couple of minutes. Taste and adjust the seasoning, adding salt if necessary.

To serve, scoop the smaller vegetables onto plates and arrange the artichokes and asparagus on top, dividing the sauce evenly. Drizzle with a bit of olive oil. Place one piece of the reserved ham, folded delicately, on top of each dish. Serve.

Notes You can leave the shelled fava beans unpeeled, but peeling the outer layer of each bean results in a greener appearance and a more refined taste.

You can replace the fresh white asparagus with canned; incorporate it carefully into the menestra in the last step. In the accept-it-all spirit of menestra, green asparagus can also be added, although it's not commonly used in Basque Country.

MARKETS

One of Basque Country's most famous markets sits under a roof supported by huge Corinthian columns, in the town of Ordizia in Gipuzkoa. Mushrooms with dirt on their stems, leeks, gigantic chard, preserves, cheeses in all shades of cream, walnuts, Reinette apples wonderfully irregular in shape, green peppers, red peppers, wicker baskets, cabbages, cauliflower, tomatoes, green cider bottles without labels—it is a richness contained by the limits of Basque cuisine, but one that delves deep into its different shades and textures. The prices set in this market serve as a benchmark across the province, and it's also where the most important contest to judge the Idiazabal cheese is held.

On the French side of the border, products take a turn for the divine. Foie is fresher and on eye-catching display; cheeses are stinkier and available in incredible variety. Les Halles in Biarritz, staffed by impossibly handsome young people, sits in the middle of a bustling square of streets where bars specialize in champagne and oysters, the making of a perfect morning market transition to lunch.

Basques shop at these markets. They enjoy bantering with the people they are buying from, making inquiries about the weather, the aspect of today's catch, and the dish they plan to make. This transaction—the gathering of the walnuts, the slicing of the cheese wheel, the removal of the dried pepper from the strand—is a tactile memory, one that feels familiar for nearly all generations. Markets are centrally located and accessible on foot, making them a more efficient food stop than a supermarket.

The continuing importance of markets in daily life is reflected in the fact that they have evolved with the times, for better or for worse. Mercado de la Bretxa in San Sebastián, formerly an enormous fish market, was converted to an American-style mall that never met with much acceptance, but Mercado de San Martín, in San Sebastián's Centro neighborhood, is a success story. It has co-opted the recent trend of a happy hour special of a pintxo for 2 euros, which patrons can enjoy to the soundtrack of live concerts.

Zainzuriak Maionesarekin

WHITE ASPARAGUS WITH MAYONNAISE

IT TAKES TWO YEARS to grow white asparagus to maturity. The roots of the young asparagus plant begin to sprout small stalks. The roots and small stalks make up what is called the *zarpa* (Spanish for "claw," as they bear a striking resemblance), and the zarpa is harvested and then replanted around February. The plant begins to mature, but under the surface the roots are putting away reserves to sprout the following year. In the second year, farmers work to pile up the soil over the asparagus plants, preventing sunlight from reaching the plants and thus the production of chlorophyll that would turn the asparagus green. The majority of white asparagus picked are destined to be preserved. They are washed, peeled, and trimmed to a uniform height, then blanched, shocked, and bottled simply with water and salt.

Fresh asparagus is available in Basque Country in April, May, and June, although it is at its best earlier in springtime (hence a popular saying that goes, "The ones from April for me, the ones from May for my love, the ones from June for nobody"). When fresh white asparagus is unavailable either near you or imported online, you can substitute canned; drain the spears well before serving as described in the recipe. ✿

SERVES 4

Kosher salt

16 white asparagus spears
(about 2 pounds/900 g)

4 tablespoons (60 mL) extra-virgin olive oil

½ cup (115 g) homemade mayonnaise
(see page 36)

Fill a pot halfway with water, salt it generously, and bring to a boil. Fill a large bowl with ice and water and set it nearby.

Meanwhile, trim about 2 inches (5 cm) off the tough, woody bottom of the asparagus spears. Working with one at a time, hold the asparagus just below the tip. With a vegetable peeler, begin to peel from the top downward, rotating the stalk as you go. Be careful not to touch the delicate tip. Repeat with the remaining asparagus. Rinse with water.

continued »

Add the asparagus to the boiling water. Boil until tender, about 20 minutes, depending on size and freshness. Test by pricking with a fork: You should be able to pierce them without force and remove the asparagus easily. Transfer to the ice water to cool them quickly, then drain.

Divide the asparagus spears among four plates and drizzle each with 1 tablespoon of the olive oil. Serve with the mayonnaise alongside, at room temperature. These asparagus are also delicious served with a vinaigrette (see page 195).

Note If you're going to cook the asparagus further, on the grill or battered and fried for tempura, for example, reduce the cooking time to about 7 minutes.

Babak "Vitoriana" Erara

VITORIA-STYLE FAVA BEANS

PEOPLE BORN IN ARABA (especially around Vitoria) are known as *babazorro*, which means "sack of beans" in Basque. It can be used affectionately or more pointedly as a term for a rustic, poorly bred country person. Fava beans once held a stigma as poor people's food and were meagerly enjoyed with a corn *talo* (flatbread; see page 196) when meat and white bread were unavailable.

Ancient recipes for this dish call for making a sort of ham broth for cooking the beans, often without removing the individual casing of each fava bean. In Araba, the beans are traditionally eaten with this outer layer, which, on smaller (or very fresh) beans, is still quite edible. You can take the rustic approach, too, and save yourself a lot of time. Instead of briefly blanching them as directed in the recipe, boil the beans for about 30 minutes before proceeding. If you do go to the trouble of peeling each fava bean, it makes this dish even more remarkable. ✿

SERVES 4

Kosher salt

8 pounds (3.6 kg) fava beans in the pod, shelled (about 4 cups shelled)

2 tablespoons extra-virgin olive oil

1 onion, finely chopped

6 ounces (170 g) Ibérico ham, sliced (about 7 slices) and cut into thin strips

1 tablespoon all-purpose flour

Bring about 2 quarts (1.9 L) lightly salted water to a boil. Add the fava beans and cook for about 3 minutes. Drain, reserving the cooking liquid in a bowl or pitcher, and rinse the beans under cold water. Peel the beans, pinching to squeeze them out of the shell. Set aside.

In a large skillet, heat the olive oil over medium heat. Add the onion and cook, stirring, until transparent, about 10 minutes. Add the ham and cook until the fat begins to render. Add the flour and cook, stirring, for 1 to 2 minutes to remove the raw flour taste. Gradually add 2 cups (480 mL) of the fava cooking liquid, stirring continuously until incorporated. Bring to a simmer, then add the fava beans. Simmer for a couple of minutes. Taste, adjust the seasoning, and serve.

Barraskiloak

SNAILS

BARAKURKUILO, BARAKUILO, BARRASKILO . . . the snail is an animal so widely and anciently consumed in Basque Country that it has almost as many names as there are villages. *Iberus alonensis* is one of the most prized specimens, found in the dry areas of the Rioja Alavesa and the Bardenas in Nafarroa, made especially savory by a diet of herbs, fig trees, olive plants, and other aromatics.

The recipe here is traditional: stewed with chorizo, peppers, and *tomate frijitua*, a sauce that deliciously projects local culinary tradition onto the blank, chewy palate of the snail meat. If you're using wild snails, it is important to correctly prepare the snails to be eaten—that is, to allow them the time necessary to purge all the contents of their insides to get rid of any off flavors (see Note). However, canned snails may be easier to find and are much easier to use. ✿

SERVES 4 TO 6

1 pound (450 g) snails, wild or canned and drained

2 tablespoons (30 mL) extra-virgin olive oil

1 onion, diced

1 sweet Italian green pepper, such as Cubanelle, diced

1 red pepper, diced

2 garlic cloves, minced

6 slices (100 g) Ibérico or Serrano ham, diced

1 small dried chile

3½ ounces (100 g) chorizo, sliced into thin coins

1 cup (240 mL) red wine

1½ cups (360 mL) tomato sauce (see page 192)

If working with wild snails, follow the directions for cleaning in the Note. If you're using canned or jarred snails, soak in clean water for 5 minutes and drain, discarding any broken or damaged shells. Set aside.

Heat the olive oil in a large pot over high heat. Add the onion, peppers, and garlic and sauté for about 10 minutes, lowering the heat to medium, until the onion is tender and transparent. Add the ham to the pan along with the chile.

Cook, stirring, until the ham begins to render, about 1 minute. Turn the heat up to high and add the chorizo. Cook, stirring, for 1 minute. Add the red wine and simmer the mixture, stirring occasionally, for about 2 minutes. Add the tomato sauce and ½ cup (120 mL) water, stir, and bring the mixture to a simmer. Add the snails to the sauce.

continued »

Lower the heat to a gentle simmer and cook for about 20 minutes. Serve warm.

Note If your snails are foraged: First allow them to rest for one week in a well-ventilated net. You can leave them with a bit of flour, and when their excrement is white, you can be assured the snails have expelled everything in their intestines. Clean the outside shell well and discard any snails that have not shown any activity. Then proceed with the standard cleaning method:

Add the snails to a pot filled with cold water. Allow them to rest overnight and let out slime. Change the water and place the pot over very low heat. When the snails come out of their shells, increase the heat a bit. Now turn the heat up to high and boil for a few minutes. Drain and repeat this process two more times until the water is totally clean. Proceed with the recipe.

EUSKAL PILOTA

JAI ALAI

Few Basque villages are without a *frontoia*. Nothing more than a two-sided wall, or in some cases a single wall, painted with a few lines or done up in green with the town's coat of arms, it nevertheless serves as the center of activity in the village. It is the nucleus of the village activity, a place where children gather and celebrations are held.

Its major purpose, however, is the game of *pilota*, or jai alai, as it is known in the United States. The national sport of the Basques, pilota (along with tennis) is a descendant of *jeu de paume* ("palm game"), which dates back to the twelfth century. The sport has adopted many evolutions throughout its lifetime; rubber balls were introduced in the nineteenth century, which meant faster and farther bounces. The advent of the *txistera*, a long, curved glove made of woven reed, made players more agile when handling the ball. These two evolutions changed the shape of the game; instead of facing each other, players faced the wall of a frontoia (outdoor court) or *trinketea* (indoor court) and hit the ball against it.

There is no one version of pilota—in fact, there are dozens of variations, counting regional twists. The easiest way to understand the variations is to look at the instrument used against the ball. *Esku pilota* is played using only the hands (*eskuak*), held cupped and rigid, to hit the ball against the wall. Then there are the games played with some sort of racquet, most commonly the *pala*, a flat, racquet-shaped wooden stick. A curious, not widely played version is *xare*, which uses a racquet strung with a loose net, a bit like the head of a lacrosse stick. And finally, there is the pilota played with the txistera, the famous throwing glove used in the *zesta-punta* version of the game, an impressive sight both on and off the court.

Gernikako Piperrak

GERNIKA PEPPERS

GERNIKA PEPPERS carry the name of the town made famous by Picasso's painting of its bombing during World War II. In reality, the peppers can come from anywhere in a 30-mile zone around the Cantabrian Sea. Brought to the region from the Americas at the end of the fifteenth century, they mellowed in the Cantabrian climate and now rarely pack a punch. Green and uniform in color, *Gernikako piperrak* are typically a bit larger than *pimientos de Padrón* and shishito peppers, ranging between 2 and 4 inches (5 to 10 cm) long.

Their arrival in late spring/early summer is heralded by ceramic serving plates stacked high on nearly every bar in the city, alongside plates of the more slender guindilla chiles (see page 175). The Gernikas are scooped up by the handful, dumped onto a plate, and sent back to the kitchen to be flash-fried in olive oil until blistered and tender, then drained and sprinkled with sea salt. The pleasure found in such sheer simplicity is a hallmark of Basque cuisine. ✣

SERVES 4 TO 6

½ pound (225 g) Gernika peppers
(about 24 peppers; see Note)

Olive oil, for frying

Flaky sea salt

Clean and dry the peppers well. If desired, prick each pepper with a fork or knife; this will prevent oil splatters.

In a large sauté pan, add enough olive oil to cover the bottom of the pan and heat to about 350°F (175°C). To test, add a single pepper to the oil: If it begins to sizzle immediately, the oil is ready. Add the peppers and cook without moving them for 1 minute, then flip them over one by one. Cook and turn as needed for 3 to 4 minutes more, or until the peppers are well blistered with a touch of gold color on some of them.

Remove with a slotted spoon and transfer to paper towels to drain. Transfer to a serving plate and sprinkle generously with the salt. Serve.

Note If you can't find Gernika peppers, Padrón or shishito peppers are fine substitutes.

Piquillo Piperrak

PIQUILLO PEPPERS

SILKY TEXTURED AND DEEPLY AROMATIC. Sweet and intensely red. Piquillo peppers have no equal. Known colloquially as Nafarroa's "red gold," they have been protected under a government designation since 1987, and for good reason. They're smaller than a bell pepper and more intensely flavorful. Harvested by hand in the early fall, they are roasted over an open flame, which lends them a smoky flavor; most are sold preserved in jars.

In pintxo bars, you can find piquillos stuffed with meat or fish (see page 27), but they are also served as a condiment for a main course, used in place of a sauce. The peppers are delicious straight out of a jar, but they are usually cooked gently in oil with garlic before serving, which takes them to another level.

This recipe replicates the best peppers served across Basque Country, those in the *erretegiak*, restaurants whose menus revolve around grilled foods. You cook them twice, first roasting and then confiting them, to approximate the incredible flavor of peppers left to languish in a corner of a grill, caramelizing at their ends, while a fat steak (see page 223) cooks over the flame. If you can't find raw piquillos, follow the instructions below for using preserved. ✤

SERVES 4

WITH FRESH PEPPERS

16 fresh piquillo peppers

¼ cup (60 mL) extra-virgin olive oil, plus more for drizzling

3 garlic cloves, sliced

Flaky sea salt

WITH PRESERVED PEPPERS

16 preserved piquillo peppers (1 jar, 390 g)

¾ cup (180 mL) extra-virgin olive oil, plus more for drizzling

3 garlic cloves, sliced

Flaky sea salt

If using fresh peppers: Preheat the broiler. Line a baking sheet with foil.

Toss the peppers with the olive oil and spread out on the baking sheet. Broil for about 5 minutes, turning halfway through.

Remove from the oven and close the foil over the peppers. Set aside to steam for about 10 minutes. Open the foil carefully, then peel the peppers, leaving the stem on. Arrange them on a platter.

Serve with a drizzle of olive oil and a sprinkle of flaky sea salt.

continued »

If using preserved peppers: Preheat the oven to 400°F (200°C). Line a baking sheet with foil.

In a large skillet, heat the olive oil and garlic over medium-high heat. When the garlic turns a light golden color, remove it with a slotted spoon and set aside.

Add the peppers to the pan and cook slowly for about 10 minutes. Reduce the heat so that the oil is just barely bubbling. Flip the peppers and cook for about 5 minutes more.

Carefully transfer the peppers to the prepared baking sheet. Bake for about 10 minutes, which will condense the flavor of the peppers and further caramelize them.

Gently transfer the peppers to a serving platter and scatter with the golden garlic.

To serve, drizzle the peppers with olive oil and sprinkle with flaky sea salt.

ERRIOXAKO ARDOA

RIOJA WINE

For a Basque in the provinces of Spain, there is only one red wine: Rioja. It's their default wine for drinking. And it's no wonder: La Rioja is one of the world's most celebrated wine regions. The Rioja DO (Denominación de Origin, or Designation of Origin) was created in Spain in 1925, although winemaking in the area dates back to Roman times. The region enjoys a superb microclimate, with a rainy winter that turns into a lovely spring and summer, with lots of sun and the occasional rainfall— basically the ideal climate for winemaking.

Rioja wine is classified into categories of varying cost and quality. In a local bar, you may often be asked to specify *del año* or *crianza*. That means choosing between a very young wine or a wine that has been aged for two years, one in a barrel of (typically) French or American oak. *Reserva*, a step above, is aged for three years, one of which must be in barrel. The final category, *gran reserva*, indicates that the wine has had at least five years of aging, two in barrel.

Reds, which make up about 85 percent of Rioja production, are full-bodied. They taste of tradition, fruity and perfectly balanced. Most Rioja is made from the tempranillo grape, with blends of garnacha, graciano, and mazuelo. The skins are pressed and removed, and the resulting liquid is passed to fermentation tanks, where it ferments for two to two and a half weeks before being passed to oak barrels. White Riojas, made with macabeo/viura grapes, also exist, and are quite underrated, with a hint of typical Rioja oak.

Wines from the Rioja Álavesa are fruity and a bit fresher, with a touch more acidity than their Spanish Rioja counterparts. Many prestigious wines come from this area, several—including Bodegas Bilbainas, Gómez Cruzado, La Rioja Alta S.A., López de Heredia, Muga, Roda, and CVNE—with more than one hundred years of history behind them.

Piperminak

PICKLED GUINDILLA PEPPERS

GUINDILLAS BEGIN TO APPEAR IN BASQUE MARKETS at the beginning of summer. These pickled guindilla peppers from Ibarra are technically chiles, *piperminak*, although they are most widely known as *Ibarrako piperrak*. They can be anywhere from 2 to 6 inches (5 to 15 cm) long when harvested, though the optimum size is around 4 inches (10 cm). In season, fresh guindillas are flash-fried and sprinkled with salt. However, they are easily preserved for use year-round, and are a vital addition to many traditional pintxos, such as the *gilda* (see page 23), and as an accompaniment to Tolosa beans (see page 176).

Fresh, the peppers are a bright, verdant green, with a smooth, tender skin, and their characteristics were tweaked to be grown at high altitudes and in heavy rain. The zone of production is less than one square mile, which is why most of these peppers don't make it out of Basque Country. Of course, the seeds can be planted and the peppers grown anywhere, but the climate of the zone produces sweeter and more delicate peppers than in other areas. Many pickled guindillas sold are grown outside of Basque Country, and they tend to be bigger, tougher, and spicier.

There is an old wives' tale that a few dried garbanzos in each jar will help keep the peppers bright green, but a more effective way to do so is to choose perfectly ripe peppers, discarding any that are past their prime, and cover them completely with liquid. ✿

MAKES 1 PINT (475 ML)

⅓ cup (80 mL) white wine vinegar, plus more if needed

⅓ cup (80 mL) filtered water, plus more if needed

¼ teaspoon kosher salt

¼ pound (115 g) fresh guindilla chiles

Put the vinegar, water, and salt in a 1-pint glass canning jar. Seal the lid and give it a few shakes to help dissolve and distribute the salt.

Wash the peppers well. Arrange them in the jar, one by one, with the stems upward. If the peppers are not covered completely by the liquid, add a bit more, using a 50:50 ratio of vinegar to water.

Refrigerate the peppers for at least 3 months before using. These are often served with stews, on pintxos, or as part of a salad.

Tolosako Babarrunak

TOLOSA BEANS

TOLOSA BEANS ARE A HARBINGER OF WINTER in the county of Goierri in Gipuzkoa. These small, purplish-black beans are from Tolosa, a village with posh aspirations, buried in the mountains. When the cold sets in, *kuadrillak* (groups of friends; see page 9) start to plan their *babarrunada*, a party featuring bean stew. The groups gather on a Saturday at the headquarters of their *txoko* (dining society) to prepare the Tolosa beans, eat them in a prolonged and late lunch, then drink digestifs until everyone is restless enough to head to a local bar. The beans are one of the rare examples in Basque cuisine of forgoing a first and second course for a single main dish.

The key to cooking such a simple dish lies in technique: Add the salt at the end, to help avoid the beans breaking. Never stir the beans; instead, shake the pot gently to keep them from sticking. With the addition of olive oil, the broth simmers into a lovely, rich liquid. Serve according to tradition, with what the Basques call the "sacraments": blood sausage (see page 203), pickled guindilla peppers (see page 175), and cabbage (see page 178). ✤

SERVES 6

1 pound (450 g) Tolosa beans

¼ cup (60 mL) extra-virgin olive oil

1 tablespoon kosher salt

Rinse the beans under cool water. Put them in a pot and add enough water to cover by 2 inches, about 2 quarts (1.9 L). Add the olive oil.

Bring the water just barely to a boil. Reduce the heat immediately to maintain a gentle simmer, shaking the pot gently every so often and skimming off any foam or scum that rises to the surface. The beans must always be covered in liquid, or they will break; add more water if necessary.

After about 2 hours, add the salt and shake. Simmer until the beans are totally tender and the cooking liquid is thick, 20 to 30 minutes more, adding water as needed to keep the beans covered.

Serve in shallow bowls, along with the accompaniments. You can serve the blood sausage, chiles, and cabbage family-style or individually with each bowl.

Aza

CABBAGE

CABBAGE IS AN OMNIPRESENT COLD-WEATHER VEGETABLE in the gardens of Basque country houses. It is rarely served outside of home kitchens, save in the case of its starring role as a complement to Tolosa beans (see page 176). This recipe is the traditional way of preparing cabbage to serve alongside, although it is quite delicious in its own right. The cabbage is blanched and then gussied up with a quick sauté in olive oil and garlic, a technique known as *refrito* in Spanish. If you want to add a touch of heat, a dried guindilla (or guajillo) chile, cut into rings, makes a nice addition to the refrito. ✣

SERVES 6

1 tablespoon plus 1 teaspoon kosher salt, plus more if needed

2 pounds cabbage (900 g), thinly sliced

3 tablespoons extra-virgin olive oil

4 garlic cloves, thinly sliced

Fill a large pot with water, add 1 tablespoon of the salt, and bring to a boil. Add the cabbage and boil, stirring occasionally to make sure all the cabbage is immersed, for 10 minutes. Drain in a colander. Run cold water over the cabbage or plunge into an ice bath to stop the cooking.

In a large skillet, heat the olive oil over medium-high heat. Add the garlic and cook until it begins to color. Add the cabbage and the remaining 1 teaspoon salt. Cook, stirring occasionally, for a few minutes, long enough to heat the cabbage through—some parts may even get a bit of color. Taste and adjust the seasoning.

Transfer to a serving plate and serve warm.

RURAL SPORTS

The most demanding rural tasks often grew into challenges between family members and neighbors, eventually escalating to *apustuak* (betting). This tradition, perhaps born out of boredom in the rural countryside, evolved into *herri kirolak*, a roster of competitions of brute strength unique to the Basque Country.

These sports are a strange and memorable sight. You might find yourself watching men climb onto a beech trunk, balancing as they swing their axes rhythmically until the trunk breaks in two. These *aizkolariak* (lumberjacks) participate in national championships, and there is even a league, the Urrezko Aizkora ("Golden Ax"). The *harrijasotzaileak* (stone lifters) are perhaps the most imposing. They lift giant rocks onto their shoulders, competing to see who can complete the most repetitions in a designated time. There are different categories, from "small" rocks (220 pounds)—with the record number of lifts being 1,000 in a 5-hour, 4-minute period—to larger ones, reaching up to 725 pounds. Naturally, for a farming society, there are also sports involving animals. The *probak* (tests) carry the name of the harnessed animal: *idi probak, zaldi probak* (ox and horse, respectively), to name a few. The animals are faced with the challenge of dragging an enormous stone a specified distance.

The list of herri kirolak is quite long, as there's a different sport for every household chore—milk churning, sack carrying, races, trials with agricultural tools, and on and on. Other herri kirolak are more familiar: *soka-tira*, tug of war; *sega* (literally "reaping"), where contestants use a scythe to cut grass at a rapid pace.

Nowadays, the rural sports are a staple at town fairs, a favorite spectator event. In Hegoalde (Southern Basque Country), however, it is still possible to witness a man-to-man challenge laid down in a country tavern. Bets are made, with neighbors throwing in a few coins each, and the games begin.

Piperrada

TOMATO-PEPPER STEW

ALONG WITH PARSLEY, peppers provide most of the color in Basque cuisine. *Piperrada*, a medley of stewed peppers and tomato, is served everywhere: piled atop salt cod, on a plate by itself, modernized on a pintxo with caramelized goat cheese, even alongside scrambled eggs. This dish has been so widely adopted on the French side of Basque Country that it is known worldwide by a Frenchified version of its Basque name, *piperade*.

The secret to a perfect piperrada is time. Allow the onions and peppers to caramelize and develop depth of flavor. You can add a pinch of dried Ezpeleta (Espelette) pepper (see page 219) for a hint of spice. You could also substitute duck fat for the olive oil for a more rustic and stronger-flavored option. ✤

SERVES 6

3 tomatoes (about 1 pound/450 g)

2 to 3 tablespoons extra-virgin olive oil

3 garlic cloves, thinly sliced

2 spring onions, julienned

Kosher salt

1 red bell pepper, julienned

2 sweet Italian green peppers, such as Cubanelle, thinly sliced

½ teaspoon Espelette pepper (optional)

Bring a pot of water to a boil.

Score the bottom of each tomato with an X and place them in the boiling water. Cook for 2 minutes, then drain and run under cold water. Peel the tomatoes (the skin should come off easily). Discard the skin and seeds, then finely dice the flesh. Set aside in a bowl.

In a large skillet, heat 2 tablespoons of the olive oil over medium-high heat. Add the garlic, and when it starts to "dance" and change color slightly, add the onions and a pinch of salt. Lower the heat to medium and cook, stirring, until the onions begin to caramelize, 15 to 20 minutes.

Add the red and green peppers, a pinch of salt, and if the mixture is looking dry, the remaining 1 tablespoon olive oil. Cook, stirring, until the vegetables are fully tender and the onions are caramelized, 15 to 20 minutes.

Add the diced tomatoes to the mixture, along with any juices that they have released. If using the Espelette pepper, add it now. Cook until the mixture has a homogeneous, stewlike texture, 20 to 25 minutes. Taste and adjust the seasoning.

Potxak Nafar Erara

NAVARRE-STYLE WHITE BEANS

IN THE MARKETS ACROSS BASQUE COUNTRY, nestled next to watercress and big, earthy mushrooms, are fresh beans, looking like dried white beans, except greenish, and plumper. They sit in unmarked plastic bags, topped with a tomato and a few small, green peppers and tied off for sale. These are *potxak*. The most celebrated are from Nafarroa, and they are often served as an accompaniment to game birds. During the prime of the season, late summer, the small town of Zangoza (Sangüesa) holds a special festival devoted to the bean, which includes an entire afternoon of village-wide bean shelling.

The term *potxa* can refer to any bean picked before it begins to dry, destined to be shelled and consumed immediately. However, in Basque Country, it almost unfailingly refers to a white haricot bean, similar to a navy bean. Picked at this age, the beans have a pale green tint, and don't need much cooking compared to their dry counterparts. When you make this recipe, keep an eye on the level of liquid—the beans should float in the lovely, slightly thick sauce. ✿

SERVES 4

1½ pounds (500 g) shelled fresh white beans

½ onion, cut into wedges

1 tomato, cut into 8 wedges

4 Gernika peppers (see Note)

2 garlic cloves, smashed

2 tablespoons olive oil

Kosher salt

Place all the ingredients except the salt in a pot and add cold water to cover by about 1 inch (2.5 cm). Bring just to a boil, then reduce the heat to maintain a constant, gentle simmer. Skim off any foam that rises to the top.

Simmer gently until the beans are tender and the sauce looks thickened and somewhat creamy, 20 to 40 minutes, depending on the freshness of the beans. Taste and season with salt and shake the pot to distribute. Simmer for 5 minutes more. Serve.

Note If you can't find Gernika peppers, Padrón or shishito peppers are fine substitutes.

Entsalada

SIMPLE BASQUE SALAD

IN KEEPING WITH THE PARED-DOWN NATURE of Basque cuisine, this green side salad is nothing more than loose-leaf green lettuce and thinly sliced spring onions brightened by apple cider vinegar and good-quality olive oil. It is on every table in Basque Country, and its versatility may just convince you to whip it up frequently, too. Serve it as an accompaniment to a grilled steak (see page 223), piquillo peppers (see page 170), and fried potatoes. ✺

SERVES 4

1 tablespoon extra-virgin olive oil

1 teaspoon apple cider vinegar

Kosher salt

1 head green-leaf lettuce

1 spring onion

Mix the olive oil and vinegar in a small bowl with a pinch of salt.

Tear the lettuce into bite-size pieces and put them in a bowl. Very thinly slice the spring onion using a knife or a mandoline. Add to the bowl.

When ready to serve, sprinkle the lettuce and onion lightly with salt. Add the vinaigrette and toss. Serve.

Onddoak Gorringoarekin

PORCINI MUSHROOMS WITH EGG YOLK

PORCINI MUSHROOMS ARE PRIZED across Basque Country and sell for high prices in the summer and fall. These mushrooms, large and cartoonishly perfect, have an excellent, forest-y flavor and meaty, luxurious flesh. *Onddo beltza* and *onddo zuri* (literally, "black mushroom" and "white mushroom") are served everywhere when in season, under the general umbrella name of *onddo*, or even the scientific moniker *boletus*.

Buy porcinis when in season at their cheapest and freeze them after cooking in single servings so you can enjoy them year-round. Here the porcinis are served simply with egg and sea salt. This dish is great at any time of day, but definitely try it for brunch with some crusty bread. ✥

SERVES 2

4 large porcini mushrooms (about 10 ounces/280 g)

1 large egg, at room temperature

2 tablespoons extra-virgin olive oil

Flaky sea salt

Preheat the broiler to high.

Tear the mushrooms into bite-size pieces, slice them, or cut them into cubes.

Separate the egg, putting the yolk in a small cup or ramekin and reserving the white for another use.

In a medium skillet, heat the olive oil over high heat. When it is very hot, add the mushrooms and sprinkle with a pinch of salt. Cook for about 1 minute before stirring, then stir and cook for about 2 minutes more, until the mushrooms are tender and wilted.

Transfer the mushrooms to a plate that can withstand high heat.

Make a well in the center of the mushrooms and gently slide the egg yolk on top, without breaking it. Place the serving plate under the broiler and broil to warm the yolk, about 1 minute.

Sprinkle salt on top of the yolk and serve immediately.

Patatak Errioxar Erara

RIOJAN POTATO-CHORIZO STEW

A PEASANT DISH, *patatak errioxar erara* (*patatas a la riojana* in Spanish) was created to fill the bellies of the very laborers responsible for the production of its components. It is not often found outside of the Rioja region, which is surprising, as it is both easy to make and composed of staple pantry ingredients: potatoes, onions, wine, and chorizo. Potatoes are the pride of the province of Araba, and one freshly dug from its soil is truly a revelation.

Just like any other vegetable, potatoes have a shelf life, so the fresher you can find, the better. However, this dish is a forgiving one; the fat from the chorizo, the starch from the potatoes, and the rich broth come together in a crowd-pleasing stew. ✿

SERVES 4 TO 6

5 tablespoons (75 mL) olive oil

1 small onion, chopped

2 garlic cloves, minced

10 small potatoes, preferably Monalisa, Kennebec, or Yukon Gold, peeled

1½ teaspoons kosher salt

1 link (8¾ ounces/250 g) Spanish chorizo (dulce or picante), sliced into thick coins

¼ teaspoon paprika

1 dried red guindilla chile (optional)

1 cup (240 mL) white wine

In a wide, shallow saucepan, heat 3 tablespoons of the olive oil over medium heat. Add the onion and garlic and cook, stirring, for 5 to 7 minutes, until soft.

Meanwhile, insert a knife about ½ inch (1.5 cm) into a potato and then rotate and lift the knife, breaking off an irregularly shaped piece. Rotate the potato and repeat; repeat with the remaining potatoes.

Add the potatoes to the pan and, if the pan looks dry, add the remaining 2 tablespoons olive oil. Season with the salt. Cook, stirring occasionally, for 10 minutes more. Add the chorizo, paprika, and chile (if using) and cook, stirring occasionally, for 2 to 3 minutes more. Raise the heat to medium-high and add the wine. Simmer until slightly reduced, about 3 minutes. Add water almost to cover and bring to a simmer, stirring occasionally to encourage the potatoes to break slightly. Cook until reduced to a thick sauce, about 15 minutes. Taste and adjust the seasoning, if necessary. Serve in shallow bowls with a glass of Rioja wine alongside.

Perretxiko Nahaskia

MUSHROOM EGGS

BASQUES ARE AVID FORAGERS, and the *perretxiko* (St. George's mushroom) is one of the first wild mushrooms to appear each year. (The term *perretxiko* is also used to refer to wild mushrooms in general.) The creamy-white mushroom has a smooth cap that can range from two to six inches in diameter. It has a perfect little stem and an earthy, faintly mildewy smell. The mushroom arrives in early spring—its name, in fact, derives from its appearance coinciding with St. George's Day, April 23—and is especially abundant in the province of Araba, where it is eaten during the festivities of the province's patron saint, San Prudentzio. In other areas, it goes by the names *ziza*, *xixa*, *seta de Orduña*, *zizazuri*, or *ziza/xixa de primavera*.

The combination of egg and mushroom is a classic one, and *nahaski*, a creamier, soupier scramble, is one of its most common riffs. At first glance, it should resemble very runny scrambled eggs. A slow, constant motion over low heat will help you achieve the perfect-size curd. Serve with a big chunk of bread to soak up every bit. You can make this recipe with any wild mushroom. ✤

SERVES 2 TO 4

3 tablespoons (45 mL) extra-virgin olive oil

⅓ pound (150 g) St. George's mushrooms or other wild mushrooms, torn or coarsely chopped

Kosher salt

8 large eggs

Cayenne pepper

1 teaspoon chopped fresh parsley

In a medium nonstick sauté pan, heat 2 tablespoons of the olive oil over high heat. Add the mushrooms. Season with a pinch of salt and cook, undisturbed, to sear the mushrooms. Stir and reduce the heat to medium. Cook, stirring, until the mushrooms are tender, about 5 minutes.

Beat the eggs in a large bowl and add the cooked mushrooms. Add a pinch of cayenne and a generous pinch of salt and beat once or twice to combine.

Wipe out the saucepan and set it back on the stovetop. Heat 1 tablespoon of the olive oil over medium heat. Pour in the egg mixture, reduce the heat to low, and shake the pan gently while stirring vigorously and continuously with a wooden spoon. Remove the pan from the heat almost immediately and stir until the pan cools a bit, then return it to the heat when the cooking slows. Repeat, removing the pan from the heat whenever the egg starts to scramble rapidly, until the egg is just barely set but still runny.

Sprinkle in the parsley and serve.

PERRETXIKO BILA

MUSHROOM FORAGING

Countryside foragers wake up early on weekends and set out on their mission, a wicker basket in hand. Thanks to the region's wet climate and large swaths of forest, the foraging culture of the Basques is the stuff of legend. Depending on the species of fungi, mushroom hunting is done in shady beech forests, tall pine groves, or clusters of oak trees, which populate the inland territory of Basque Country. The bounty foragers gather includes *perretxikoak* (St. George's mushrooms, or wild mushrooms in general; see page 190), *zizahoriak* (chanterelles), and *esnegorriak* (saffron milkcaps).

More serious mushroom hunters might duck into the woods in a random spot to throw off anyone following them before reorienting toward their true destination. Anyone with poor enough taste to inquire about the best place to forage will get a politely vague geographical reference and a tight smile. Mushrooms are more than just a food item; they are an activity, a topic of conversation, and a social gesture. Foraged mushrooms are shared when abundant and treasured when scarce. Mushrooms are a sign of the season, a most ephemeral gift from Mother Nature.

Tomate Frijitua

TOMATO SAUCE

EVERY BASQUE MOTHER has a tomato sauce recipe; it is a foundation of Basque and Spanish cooking. This smooth, reddish-orange sauce is not only a key element to many dishes, but also makes a quick, no-brainer meal when served with pasta or on top of tuna (see page 122). Basque tomato sauce is unique to the area—smoother than a marinara and fully vegetable based. Make extra, freeze it, and keep it on hand for last-minute meals. ✿

MAKES ABOUT 4 CUPS

¼ cup (60 mL) extra-virgin olive oil

1 onion, diced

2 garlic cloves, minced

1 sweet Italian green pepper, such as Cubanelle, diced

1 teaspoon kosher salt

2¼ pounds (1 kg) ripe tomatoes (about 5 large), chopped

In a large saucepan, heat the olive oil over medium heat. Add the onion, garlic, pepper, and ½ teaspoon of the salt to the pot. Cook, stirring occasionally, until the vegetables begin to color, about 15 minutes.

Add the tomatoes and the remaining ½ teaspoon salt to the pot. Cook, stirring occasionally to prevent sticking, for about 1 hour.

Puree the tomato mixture directly in the pot using an immersion blender, or let it cool slightly, then pass it through a food mill. Strain the resulting puree through a fine-mesh sieve, pressing to extract all possible liquid and discarding any solids, and return it to the pot.

Cook over medium heat for about 5 minutes, allowing the sauce to bubble and thicken slightly. Remove from the heat and let cool before using or storing. You can refrigerate it for 3 to 5 days, freeze it for up to 3 months, or go through a canning process for longer storage.

Xipister

HERB-PEPPER VINEGAR SAUCE

ON THE SPANISH SIDE OF BASQUE COUNTRY, the standard house vinaigrette is three parts olive oil to one part cider vinegar—a basic, simple dressing with no additions. *Xipister*, the standard vinaigrette in French Basque Country, is a far cry from such simplicity, an exuberant mix of herbs and staples like garlic, anchovies, and ground Espelette pepper (see page 219) resembling a Basque pantry dump. The French Basques keep a jar of xipister handy at all times for dressing salads, fish, and especially grilled foods.

With traditional vinaigrette ratios turned on their head, this sauce is an ideal accompaniment to fatty fish and meats. The sharp, tart vinegar and the bit of heat from the Espelette pepper cut through greasier fish or cuts of meat and meld with their juices. A jar of xipister will grow more flavorful with time, and will keep for up to 3 months when stored properly. ✿

MAKES 2 CUPS

1 small mild to medium-hot chile, fresh or dried	1½ cups (360 mL) apple cider vinegar or txakoli vinegar
1 bunch thyme	3 salt-cured anchovies
1 sprig rosemary	1 teaspoon Espelette pepper
1 sprig sage	1 bay leaf
½ cup (120 mL) extra-virgin olive oil	3 garlic cloves, unpeeled
	⅛ teaspoon kosher salt

Preheat the oven to 200°F.

Place the chile, thyme, rosemary, and sage on a baking sheet and heat in the oven for 5 to 10 minutes to bring out their flavors.

Meanwhile, in a medium saucepan, combine the olive oil, vinegar, anchovies, Espelette pepper, bay leaf, garlic, and salt. Heat over medium-low heat until warmed to just above room temperature.

Add the chile and herbs. Transfer the entire mixture to a storage bottle. Close and shake well. Set aside in a cool, dark place to infuse for 2 weeks.

Shake before using. The xipister will keep in a cool, dark place for up to 3 months.

Taloa

BASQUE CORN FLATBREAD

AFTER THE CONQUERING OF THE NEW WORLD, corn made its way to the fields of Basque Country, where it was ground into a new, cheaper flour. When wheat flour became too expensive, the *talo*, similar to a Mexican corn tortilla but made with untreated cornmeal, served as a substitute for bread across the countryside. It was also a common dinner or breakfast, soaked in milk and, with a bit of luck, honey or sugar.

In the late 1900s, better economic times set in and talo became something most often served at rural fairs and village celebrations. The women who make talo by the thousands at local fairs use wooden *palak* to pound out the talo in their laps before sliding them onto a mobile griddle, where they are flipped rapidly and served wrapped around a sausage like *txistorra* (see page 200) or modern additions like sheep's-milk cheese, bacon, or milk chocolate bars.

Much more important than the exact measurement of water is getting a feel for the dough, knowing when it is too dry or too wet and adjusting by sprinkling more corn flour or water into the mixture accordingly. Common knowledge says it takes thirteen attempts to get a talo to come out perfectly, so don't give up. The result should be very thin and pliable. ❧

MAKES 8

3 cups (300 g) corn flour (finely ground untreated corn— not cornmeal)

1 teaspoon kosher salt

Bring 1¼ cups (300 mL) water to a boil.

Mix the corn flour and salt in a large bowl. Add 1 cup of water to start. Begin to mix the dough with your hands or a wooden spoon, using a scooping-and-squeezing motion. Mix well, adding more water by the tablespoon if the dough appears dry or does not hold together. After a few minutes, the dough should become soft and velvety, not sticky; if it is sticky, add a bit more corn flour.

Pinch off enough dough to form a ball about 2 inches (5 cm) in diameter. Sprinkle your work surface with a bit of corn flour. Dust the dough with flour and pound it twice with your right hand. With your left hand cupped, turn it gently, forming it a bit along the side as you rotate it. Repeat the pat, pat, turn motion about five times, widening the talo each time. If you feel the talo begin to stick, sprinkle it with more flour and flip it over. Continue the pat, pat, turn motion for five more rounds, always avoiding sticking. When the talo is quite flat and about 7 inches (18 cm) in diameter, give it several quick pats to form the final shape and flatten out any uneven parts. It should be very thin. Repeat with the remaining dough, stacking the talo with sheets of wax paper in between.

Heat a dry pan or griddle over high heat. Add the talo one at a time and cook for 1 minute. Flip and cook for 1 minute or so on the second side; the talo should rise a bit.

Serve with your choice of filling.

SAINT THOMAS'S DAY

Santo Tomas Eguna, txorizoa eta ogia.
"Saint Thomas's Day, chorizo and bread."
—POPULAR BASQUE REFRAIN

On the morning of December 21, the streets of Bilbao and San Sebastián bustle with unusual activity: tents go up, makeshift griddles powered by butane burners are assembled, and temporary animal pens are hastily stuffed with hay. It is the Day of Saint Thomas, and the cities are about to erupt into a huge gathering of people, coming together in the street, donning their traditional garb, drinking cider, and eating sausage. This modern revelry has roots in one of the most important days of the year in Basque Country.

Santo Tomas Eguna has long marked the Basque calendar as a day when the countryside merged with the town. *Baserritarrak* (farmers and country folk) made their way into the city, carrying the yearly rent on their lands or homes to the wealthy landowners, payable either in coin or commodity, often wheat. They also brought a couple of handsome, fattened fowl as a gesture of goodwill. The country folk were not ones to squander a trip into town, however. They would bring along extra fruits and vegetables, as well as sausages and by-products of the recent slaughter, to sell to the city dwellers. This escalated into what is now a citywide country fair.

Farm animals from sheep to llamas are admired in their pens, but the star of the show is a gigantic sow, chosen as the finest and the fattest and consistently weighing in at over 700 pounds. The thin *txistorra* sausage (see page 200) has become emblematic of the day, and groups in traditional dress pound out corn *taloak* (see page 196) to wrap around them—an essential component of the festival, celebrated to this day.

Txistorra

BASQUE CHORIZO

A CADA CERDO LE LLEGA SU SAN MARTÍN—"Saint Martin's Day comes for every pig." When the chill of autumn begins to fall over Basque Country, the saying ceases to be a refrain about bad deeds being punished and regains its literal meaning. November 11, Saint Martin's Day, is the traditional beginning of the *txerri-hiltzea* season in Basque Country—when pigs are gathered for the slaughter before being separated into usable cuts and made into various sausages and hams.

To make *txistorra*, both lean and fatty scraps from the shoulder and other areas of the pig are ground and mixed with garlic, salt, and paprika to form thin reddish-brown sausages, which are then hung to lightly cure for anywhere from one day to ten days before being preserved—nowadays in refrigerators, and decades ago, packed in lard.

To make this sausage at home, a meat grinder and a sausage stuffer (or the equivalent attachments for a stand mixer) are the perfect tools. However, in a pinch you can get by with just a good food processor (see Note).

MAKES THREE 20-INCH (51 CM) SAUSAGES

2 pounds pork meat, a mix of 1 part lean and 2 parts fat, usually taken from the shoulder

2 tablespoons sweet paprika

1 tablespoon kosher salt

4 garlic cloves, finely minced

Natural sheep casings, 20/22 mm in diameter

Refrigerate the meat until very cold. Grind the meat into a bowl using the ¼-inch (6 mm) plate of a sausage grinder.

Add the paprika, salt, and garlic. Mix very well using your hands (or in the bowl of a stand mixer fitted with the paddle attachment) for up to 10 minutes, or until the mixture is homogeneous and the meat is threadlike in appearance. If desired, pull off a small portion of the mixture, cook it in a skillet, taste, and adjust the seasoning.

Rinse the casings with cold water. Slide the casing onto the sausage-stuffing mechanism, pushing it bit by bit until it is all on the nozzle.

Feed the meat mixture into the mouth of the stuffer. Add the meat gradually, a task that is easier with the help of a partner. Fill the casing with the meat. Tie off the casing with butcher's twine at one end, then tie it off at about 20 inches

continued »

(51 cm). Tie another knot right next to the last, and then another after 20 inches (51 cm) more. Repeat until all the sausage is tied off. With scissors, cut between the knots to separate the links. Loop each sausage into a circle and tie the twine at the ends together.

Prick the sausages in several places with a sharp knife or kitchen needle.

Hang the txistorra in a cool, dry place (50 to 55°F/10 to 12°C is ideal) to cure for at least 48 hours and up to 6 days. Refrigerate until ready to cook. It will keep for up to 10 days.

To cook, heat a dry skillet over high heat. Cut a txistorra into 3- to 4-inch (7.5 to 10 cm) pieces and fry, turning occasionally, until golden. Eat as is or serve sandwich-style on a crusty baguette. Pieces of txistorra on bread with a toothpick are perfect as part of a spread of pintxos.

Note If using a food processor to make the sausage, simply chop the meat into small cubes and chill, along with the food processor blade, for 30 minutes in the freezer. Process until the meat appears crumbly before proceeding with the recipe.

You can stuff the sausage without an attachment or stuffer by pressing in the meat with your fingers or by using a funnel.

Odolkia

BLOOD SAUSAGE

THE SMALL TOWN OF BEASAIN, deep in Gipuzkoa, is the *odolki* heartland. This sausage's texture is similar to that of superfine ground meat, mixed with caramelized vegetables (this is not the rice-studded blood sausage found elsewhere in Spain). The whole neighborhood would participate in its making (the Basque phenomenon of *auzolan*; see page 9), which happens in the fall. The reward? A string of sausages to take home.

It is also easy to make at home, though perhaps not for the faint of heart. Do not be put off by the ingredient list. Yes, this sausage is made with blood, but combined with the golden onions and fragrant spices, it has an amazing, rich flavor. You'll need to make friends with your butcher in advance, as he is the one who can get you pasteurized blood. Despite the rustic and almost graphic nature of this sausage, it is absolutely delicious. Serve it as an appetizer or as an accompaniment to bean dishes, like Tolosa beans (see page 176). ✿

MAKES 3 TO 5 SAUSAGES (ABOUT ¾ POUND EACH)

1¼ pounds (570 g) pork lard

8 onions, diced

1 leek, diced and rinsed well

2 tablespoons kosher salt

1 tablespoon ground cinnamon

2 teaspoons dried oregano

1 teaspoon cayenne pepper

½ teaspoon freshly ground star anise

7 tablespoons (100 mL) heavy cream (optional; see Note)

2¼ cups (540 mL) pasteurized pig's blood

Natural pig or cow casings, 34/36 mm in diameter

In a large saucepan, melt the lard over medium heat. Add the onions and leek and cook, stirring occasionally, until the vegetables have reduced and caramelized, about 40 minutes. Add the salt, cinnamon, oregano, cayenne, and star anise and cook, stirring until well mixed.

Remove from the heat and place in a large bowl. Add the cream (if using) and stir. Add the blood and stir well.

Rinse the casings with cold water. Slide the casing onto the sausage-stuffing mechanism, pushing it bit by bit until it is all on the nozzle.

Feed the mixture into the mouth of the stuffer. Add it gradually, a task that is easier with the help of a partner, filling the casing. Tie off the casing with butcher's twine at one end, then tie it off at about 15 inches (38 cm). Tie another

continued »

knot right next to the last, and then another after 15 inches (38 cm) more. Repeat until all the sausage is tied off. With scissors, cut between the knots to separate the links. Loop each sausage into a circle and tie the twine at the ends together.

Bring a pot of water just barely to a simmer. Add the sausages and simmer for 30 minutes. Transfer the sausages to a bowl of ice water to stop the cooking. Remove and hang in a cool, dry place for about 30 minutes.

Store the odolki in the refrigerator in an airtight container for up to 10 days.

To serve, rinse the odolki and place in a pot of cold water. Bring just to a simmer over medium-high heat. Reduce the heat to maintain a very gentle simmer and cook for at least 1 hour and up to 2 hours, until the casing is very tender and edible. Remove from the water and let rest for a couple of minutes before cutting open to eat.

Note Cream is not a traditional addition to odolki; milk was used as filler if blood was in short supply. However, the addition of heavy cream is a modern trick used by some butchers—although they might not admit it—to achieve a finer, creamier result.

Mondejua

LAMB TRIPE AND EGG SAUSAGE

THIS WHITE SAUSAGE, born out of a need to craft something edible from lamb leftovers, is a cousin of *odolki* (blood sausage; see page 203). A curious, likable mixture of tripe, leek, and eggs, *mondeju*'s texture is pleasingly reminiscent of scrambled eggs. Though its origins remain mysterious, geographically they are clear: the tiny county of Goierri in Gipuzkoa. The sausage was traditionally made in the fall, when the time for the slaughter of spring lambs neared. Historically, a black mondeju was made with sheep's blood, but refined modern tastes have left only the white mondeju standing.

To make this sausage at home, a meat grinder and a sausage stuffer (or the equivalent attachments for a stand mixer) are the perfect tools. If you do not have a meat grinder, you can chop the meat by hand. Pork casings are used for this sausage, as they are thinner than cow casings. The mondeju's pleasing firm texture makes it an ideal accompaniment for stews and beans, chopped and sprinkled on top to serve. You can also eat it as a main dish with cabbage (see page 178) alongside. ❖

MAKES TWO 15- TO 20-INCH (38 TO 51 CM) SAUSAGES

Natural pork casings, 34/36 mm in diameter

⅓ pound (150 g) lamb tripe, cleaned well

½ pound (225 g) lamb fat

1 leek, diced and rinsed well

1 tablespoon kosher salt

¼ teaspoon cayenne pepper

7 large eggs

Soak the pork casings in cool water to cover for 30 minutes to 1 hour.

Bring a pot of water to a boil. Add the tripe and boil for 1 hour. Drain and place in the refrigerator to cool.

In a medium pot, melt a handful of the lamb fat over medium-high heat. Add the leek, reduce the heat to medium-low, and cook slowly, stirring often, for about 15 minutes, or until the leek just barely colors. Add the remainder of the lamb fat and cook until melted, stirring.

Grind the cooled tripe into a bowl using the ¼-inch (6 mm) plate of a sausage grinder. Add to the pot with the leek-fat mixture and stir for about 2 minutes. The mixture will be quite liquid. Add the salt and cayenne and stir. Remove from the heat.

continued »

Rinse the pork casings with cool water. Cut them into manageable pieces, about 3 feet (1 m) long each. Slide the casing onto the sausage-stuffing mechanism, pushing it bit by bit until it is all on the nozzle. Tie off the end of the casing using butcher's twine, if necessary.

Beat the eggs together and add to the lamb-leek mixture. The texture will be similar to that of pancake batter.

Feed the meat into the mouth of the stuffer. Pass the meat through gradually, filling the casing with all the meat. Tie off the casing using butcher's twine at one end, and then tie again at about 15 inches (38 cm). Tie another knot right next to the last, and then another after 15 inches (38 cm). Repeat until all the sausage is tied off. With scissors, cut between the knots to separate the sausage into 15-inch (38 cm) links. Loop each sausage into a circle and tie together the pieces of twine at the ends.

Bring a pot of water to a gentle simmer. Add the sausages to the water and cook for 2 minutes, then prick with a sharp knife or a kitchen needle so the air can escape. Cook, moving the sausages occasionally to avoid sticking, for about 15 minutes. Hang the sausages in a dry, cool place until they are at room temperature, then store in an airtight container in the refrigerator for up to 6 days before using.

To finish cooking the mondeju, bring a pot of water just to a simmer and add the sausage. Cook for 20 minutes, then remove and let rest for a couple of minutes before serving.

ARTZAINAK
SHEPHERDS

While shepherds in other cultures are a forgotten relic, lost in the post–Industrial Revolution rush toward efficiency, they remain relevant and active in Basque Country. They have had an outsized impact on the language, diet, and landscape of a country that defines itself by language, diet, and landscape. The manicured aspect of the Basque Country's hills is the work of the sheep. Shepherds in Nafarroa still practice transhumance, leading the sheep through the desertlike terrain of Bardenas, singing "*Arriving to San Miguel, shepherds to the Bardena, to drink from the watering hole and sleep in the open air. Arriving to Santa Cruz, shepherds to the mountains, to drink water from founts and sleep in the cabin.*" Shepherds speak a highly local language that varies from pasture to pasture. They dress in blue pants made of rough linen, perhaps with a plaid shirt and a modern fleece vest, and the Basque beret, the *boina* or *txapela*, is practically obligatory, as is the shepherd's staff.

Some of the older traditions associated with shepherding have been lost. Cured sheep's meat was once a desired delicacy. Shearing was an important time in which the whole village participated and a fun, convivial atmosphere pervaded the town. However, it is a living and breathing profession and one that cannot afford to be stuck in the past. The formation of the European Union and Spain and France's integration in the 1980s meant problems for the shepherds, whose work was left on the fringes of legality under new EU laws. They formed societies and organized contests to celebrate the local Latxa breed, refusing to fade into unknown uniformity. They adopted technological advancements, but without sacrificing tradition. Shepherds now use SUVs and smartphones. In 1997, Gomiztegi shepherd school, a pioneer in the teaching of shepherding, opened in Arantzazu. Now the focus is on preserving native breeds, ethical treatment of animals, and responsible management of natural resources.

209
VEGETABLES
AND MEAT

Arkumea Txilindron Erara

LAMB IN CHILINDRÓN SAUCE

LAMB IS A POPULAR DISH in Basque Country in the springtime. *Chilindrón* sauce is purportedly named for a card game where players compete for a combination of three cards. This dish, by extension, is a combination of three favored ingredients: lamb, dried peppers, and potatoes. The inclusion of bay leaf signals that the dish hails from Nafarroa and La Rioja: In the provinces of Bizkaia and Gipuzkoa, bay was considered a sacred leaf and not typically used in cooking. ✤

SERVES 4

5 dried choricero peppers, or 2½ tablespoons choricero pepper puree

4 pounds (1.8 kg) suckling lamb, preferably the leg, lower ribs, and skirt steak, cut into 1½-inch (4 cm) pieces (ask your butcher to do this, or use a heavy cleaver)

Kosher salt and freshly ground black pepper

⅓ cup (40 g) all-purpose flour

¼ cup (60 mL) olive oil

2 garlic cloves, minced

2 large onions, diced

¼ cup (60 mL) white wine

¼ cup (60 mL) tomato sauce (see page 192)

2¾ cups (660 mL) chicken stock

1 bay leaf

4 potatoes, preferably Monalisa, Kennebec, or Yukon Gold

If you're using dried choricero peppers, heat 4 cups (1 L) water in a saucepan. Put the peppers in a bowl and pour enough hot water over the peppers to cover. Soak until they are soft, up to 1 hour, depending on the pepper. Drain and pat dry with a paper towel. Open each pepper with a knife, discarding the stems and seeds. Scrape the pulp from the skin of the peppers with the knife and discard the skin. Set the choricero pulp aside.

Season the pieces of lamb generously with salt and pepper. Put the flour in a bowl and dredge each piece of lamb in flour, shaking to remove any excess.

In a large pot, heat the olive oil over medium-high heat. Working in batches as necessary, add the lamb pieces, without crowding, and sear until golden brown on each side, about 2 minutes per side. Remove each piece as it browns and set aside on a large plate.

continued »

After you've browned the lamb, add the garlic to the pot. As it begins to "dance," add the onions. Reduce the heat to low and cover the pot. Cook the vegetables without browning, stirring often, for about 45 minutes. Return the lamb to the pot and raise the heat to high.

Add the wine and simmer for about 1 minute to cook off the alcohol. Add the tomato sauce and the choricero pulp (or puree, if using) and cook, stirring, until the mixture comes together, a minute or two. Add the stock and bay leaf and bring to a simmer. Cover and cook for about 25 minutes.

Peel the potatoes and cut them into large bite-size pieces by inserting a knife about ½ inch (1.5 cm) into a peeled potato and then rotating and lifting it, breaking off an irregularly shaped piece. Rotate the potato slightly and repeat; repeat with the remaining potatoes.

After the lamb mixture has cooked for 25 minutes, add the potatoes, cover, and cook for 20 to 25 minutes longer, until the potatoes are tender and fully cooked.

Taste, adjust the seasoning, and serve.

PILGRIMAGE

The mountains have always been the principal backdrop to pagan and religious rites in Basque Country. Pilgrimage walks are an important part of the festivals in many villages, carrying the goodwill and cheer of the party down winding paths and up to isolated peaks, finishing at a hermitage or other religious monument.

Hermitages are generally located on some sort of sacred site, be it an ancient pagan temple, the location of important remains, a fount of medicinal waters, or even where a malevolent spirit has been spotted. One such place is the hermitage of San Juan de Gaztelugatxe, constructed in the ninth century. It sits above the Bay of Biscay, 241 zigzaggy steps away from the outcropping of the mainland. In July, a pilgrimage from the nearby fishing village of Bermeo is celebrated, and inhabitants march their way to this famed hermitage, ring the bells (mystically supposed to cure any migraines in the public), and attend a mass before settling in for a snack.

Most *erromeriak* feature the promise to cure a certain illness. In the famed pilgrimage of San Prudentzio, the patron saint of Araba, tradition was to offer olive oil and balls of string in exchange for carving a bit of powder off one of the hermitage's rocks, said to cure psoriasis. Nowadays, as the religious beliefs of the modern Basque wane, the more secularly pleasant part of each erromeria remains: a walk in the fresh air, ending in a bit of eating and a bit of dancing. *Perretxikoak* (see page 190) and snails (see page 164) are the reward for those in San Prudentzio who make it to the Campas de Armentia, while *arkumea txilindron erara* (see page 211) or *potxak* (see page 183) with eels are part of the post-pilgrimage meal in the festivals in Nafarroa.

Txitxikis

PORK HASH WITH PAPRIKA

TXITXIKIS EVOLVED from the method of testing the seasoning of each batch of homemade chorizo. A bit of the marinated meat would be cooked to taste for salt and spice before being stuffed into casings. The dish's popularity grew such that now lean meat scraps are mixed with spices, left to marinate for up to a couple of days, and then quickly sautéed into hash.

Use the freshest ingredients possible. The word *txiki* in Euskara means "small," but you can experiment with the size and cut of the meat—txitxikis can range in size from a coarse grind to a larger dice. Add toasted bread and a fried egg to make an easy, complete meal. ❖

SERVES 4

1 pound (450 g) pork loin

6 tablespoons (90 mL) extra-virgin olive oil

1 tablespoon sweet paprika

1 tablespoon spicy paprika

1 teaspoon kosher salt

4 large eggs

Baguette slices, toasted

Very finely dice the pork loin and put it in a bowl. Add 2 tablespoons of the olive oil, the paprikas, and the salt and mix well. Store the mixture in the refrigerator overnight, covered in plastic wrap, or for up to 3 days, stirring every 12 hours.

When ready to eat, in a large sauté pan, heat 1 tablespoon of the olive oil over high heat. Add the marinated pork mixture to the pan and cook without stirring for about 90 seconds. Stir and cook until the meat is cooked through.

In a separate medium pan, heat the remaining 3 tablespoons olive oil over medium-high heat. Crack an egg and slip it into the oil, without breaking the yolk. Sprinkle with a bit of salt. Slip a spatula under the egg to make sure it is not sticking, then cook for about 1 minute. Repeat with the remaining eggs, one or two at a time.

Distribute the warm meat among four plates. Add an egg to the side on each plate. Serve each with a slice of toasted bread.

Txahal Masailak

BEEF CHEEKS

THIS RICH, TENDER MEAT is a new Basque favorite—despite its former life as an oft-discarded cut of beef. The slightly gelatinous nature of the cut makes it perfect for braising until super tender, similar to the short rib.

On weekends, *txahal masailak* are paraded out of the village butcher's shop in metal pots. They sit in a pool of thick, dark brown sauce, ready to heat and eat at gastronomic societies, the pot to be returned the following week. One of San Sebastián's most famous beef cheeks is from the pintxo bar Borda Berri, on the crowded Calle Fermín Calbetón. Bite-size pieces of beef are served over a potato puree laced with goat cheese and drizzled with tomato sauce and parsley oil. If you'd like to re-create their beloved pintxo, just trim the meat to pintxo size. However you serve it, this short rib–like dish will become a new favorite. ✿

SERVES 4

2 large beef cheeks
(about 1½ pounds/680 g)

Kosher salt and freshly ground
black pepper

3 tablespoons extra-virgin olive oil

1 onion, chopped

3 garlic cloves, smashed

2 carrots, coarsely chopped

2 leeks, coarsely chopped and
rinsed well

1 large tomato, coarsely chopped

1½ cups (360 mL) red wine

3 cups (720 mL) beef stock

1 tablespoon unsalted butter

Cut each cheek into three equal-size pieces. Season thoroughly with salt and black pepper.

In a Dutch oven, heat 1 tablespoon of the olive oil over high heat. When the oil is very hot, add the meat and sear without moving for about 2 minutes. Once browned on the first side, turn it over and reduce the heat to medium-high. Cook for about 2 minutes more, or until well seared on each side. Remove and set aside on a plate.

Add the remaining 2 tablespoons olive oil to the pot over high heat. Add the onion and garlic and cook, scraping up any browned bits from the bottom of the pan, for about 2 minutes. Add the carrots, leeks, and tomato, along with a pinch of salt. Cook over medium heat, stirring occasionally, for about 10 minutes.

Arrange the beef cheeks on top of the vegetables and raise the heat to medium-high. Add the wine and simmer for about 10 minutes to reduce. Add

continued »

the stock and bring back to a simmer. Cover and reduce the heat to low so the mixture is at a very gentle simmer. Cook for 2 hours, or until a knife inserted into each beef cheek comes out effortlessly.

Carefully remove the beef cheeks and set aside on a plate. Strain the mixture from the pot, discarding the vegetables. Return the strained liquid to medium-high heat and cook for about 10 minutes to reduce. Add the butter, stir, and cook for another minute. Return the beef cheeks to the pot with the reduced jus. If serving immediately, cook for about 10 minutes more, until the liquid is rich and glazed. If serving later, store the mixture in the refrigerator. When ready to serve, return to the heat and cook for about 10 minutes to reduce.

Serve the cheeks alone or on top of a bed of mashed potatoes.

ESPELETTE PEPPER

The two-story *baserriak*, squat and wide with their sloping roofs, could be anywhere in Basque Country, save for the dark red peppers that drape their sides. Hardly any of the facade is visible through the strings upon strings of red peppers. Long wooden poles hang at a slight curve, drooping a bit with the weight of hundreds of strings to which dozens of peppers are tied, every which way.

Welcome to Ezpeleta (Espelette, in French), and nine other villages around it, where the Espelette pepper (known as *Ezpeletako piperra* in Euskara and *piment d'Espelette* in French) is grown, sun-dried, ground, and oven toasted, to the tune of 200 tons per year. The fame that has been achieved by this single *Capsicum annum* has more than a little to do with the impressive sight of them hanging across villages. In October, during the pepper festival, the population of Ezpeleta swells from 2,000 to 20,000. Peppers and products made with the pepper are tasted, and, as only the French Basques know how, ancient traditions are approximated and made tourist-friendly in a showy display of capitalism-tinged patriotism.

Protected since the year 2000 by a French AOC (Appellation d'Origine Contrôlée, the French Designation of Origin), Espelette pepper is carefully regulated, produced without pesticides and under specific conditions. The ground pepper is low heat, smelling at first of smoke, hay, and fruit, with a sweet, slightly bitter flavor. The spice hits in the aftertaste, but never overpowers. Espelette pepper appears in descriptions of dishes on the menus of Paris's most exclusive restaurants, and it is a key ingredient in the famous Baiona (Bayonne) ham, rubbed over the exterior of the legs to preserve and cure the ham. In local cuisine, the pepper is often used in place of black pepper, in dishes from *axoa* (see page 220) to *piperrada* (see page 180).

Axoa

VEAL STEW WITH PEPPERS

VEAL STEW IS A COMMON DISH at festival lunches in the French Basque Country. A mix of chopped veal and smallish sweet peppers, it is often served alongside rice or potatoes, which can be cooked separately or, as in this recipe, in the pot as the stew finishes simmering. ✿

SERVES 4

¼ cup (60 mL) extra-virgin olive oil or duck fat

2 cups diced bell peppers

1 small onion, diced

Kosher salt

2 garlic cloves, minced

1 pound (450 g) veal, finely minced or ground

½ teaspoon Espelette pepper

⅓ cup (80 mL) white wine

1½ cups (360 mL) stock, preferably made from veal but beef, chicken, or trotter stock would do

2 small potatoes, peeled

In a large skillet, heat 2 tablespoons of the olive oil over medium-high heat. Add the bell peppers and onion, along with a pinch of salt, and reduce the heat to medium. Cover and cook, stirring occasionally, for 25 minutes. Reduce the heat to low, add the garlic, and cook, uncovered, for 15 minutes more, or until the vegetables are golden.

In a Dutch oven, heat the remaining 2 tablespoons olive oil over high heat. Add the veal, Espelette pepper, and another generous pinch of salt and cook without stirring for a few minutes to get the veal a nice golden brown. Reduce the heat to medium-high and cook, stirring, for 5 minutes, until cooked through. Add the wine and simmer for another minute.

Add the pepper-onion mixture to the veal and cook, stirring. Add the stock, which should be enough to cover. If it's not, add a bit more.

Cut the potatoes into large bite-size pieces by inserting a knife about ½ inch (1.5 cm) into a peeled potato and then rotating and lifting it, breaking off a piece. Rotate the potato slightly and repeat; repeat with the remaining potato.

Add the potatoes to the pot and bring to a simmer. Cover and cook, stirring occasionally, until the potatoes are tender, up to 30 minutes. Uncover and simmer for about 5 minutes more, if necessary, to thicken the mixture.

Txuleta

STEAK

THE *TXULETA*, OR BASQUE STEAK, is a celebrated item on the menu of every *erretegi* and *sagardotegi* in Basque Country. And all it requires is meat, salt, and fire—nothing more and nothing less. Starting at the butcher, make sure to get dry-aged beef, organic and grass-fed if possible. Calling ahead is essential to get a rib steak with the bone still in. The steak should be very thickly cut, from 2 to 3 inches. Bring your steak to a warm room temperature before cooking it; this relaxes the meat and yields better results. Do like the Basques and try it rare, deep brown on the outside and red on the inside. ✿

SERVES 2

1 (24- to 28-ounce/680 to 800 g) very thick bone-in rib steak

Flaky sea salt

Bring the meat to room temperature. This takes at least 3 to 5 hours.

Prepare a grill with high heat but no live flames. Do this an hour or two before use, so the (preferably hardwood) charcoal is smoldering and very hot. Push the charcoal to one side of the grill to create a warm and cool spot on the grill.

Place the steak on the grill grate. Cook the steak on one side for 5 to 7 minutes, without moving it, until a dark crust forms. Take care to avoid flare-ups caused by dripping fat. To make this even easier, you can try setting your grill on an incline, and the fat will drip away from the flame. When you are ready to flip the steak, salt it generously and turn it over. Cook for another 5 to 7 minutes, or until both sides are very well seared.

Remove to a cutting board. Cut the steak away from the rib bone, and then slice the separated meat into pieces about ½ inch (1¼ cm) thick. Use a metal spatula or the flat side of your knife to transfer the slices to a serving platter. Position the bone next to the slices, approximating its location before cutting. Sprinkle the steak generously with flaky sea salt. Serve.

NOTES: To cook steak inside, preheat the oven to 400°F (200°C). Sear the steak in a skillet over high heat, 1 to 2 minutes per side, before finishing it in the oven for about 10 minutes.

I salt the meat generously toward the end, but many cooks salt only minimally during cooking. Virtually everyone finishes the steak with large flakes of salt.

Cook times are approximations; it will all depend on the thickness of the steak. Give it a good sear and make sure to avoid overcooking the steak.

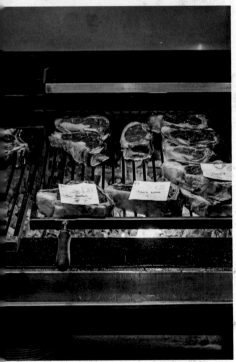

CIDER HOUSES

Txotx! With the shout of this one word, golden apple cider arcs through the air, spurting with the pressure of all 8,000 gallons in the *kupelak*, giant, 5-foot-diameter (1.5 m) wooden barrels, propped up on cement blocks. Those drinking have already formed a line along the barrels, and it moves jerkily as each hand holds out a thin, cylindrical glass to catch the cider. *Gutxi ta sarri*, as they say, get a little bit and serve yourself often, which keeps the cider from getting warm or oxygenated. When everyone has finished, the *sagardogile*, the proprietor serving the cider, returns the *txotx*, a thin wooden pin, to the small hole in the barrel.

Cidermaking was once common in all the provinces of the Basque Country, with written evidence of the practice dating back to the fourteenth century. But war and dictatorship in Spain from the 1930s to the 1970s were hard on the apple, and the custom fell off in Iparralde, Araba, and Nafarroa—even in Gipuzkoa—resulting in the abandoning of many orchards that have only recently begun to recuperate.

Ninety-five percent of Basque cider is produced in Gipuzkoa, in almost one hundred cider houses, and much of it specifically in the town of Astigarraga. *Sagardo* means literally "apple wine," and that is exactly what Basque cider is. Apples, selected for a desired balance between tart and sweet, are pressed in the *tolare* or *lagar*, and the juice is collected and fermented into cider.

Traditionally, new ciders are tasted in December, in a tasting ritual known as *probaketa*. Basque forefathers would ride over to the cider house, have an impromptu tasting with a snack of whatever was on hand, like salt-preserved sardines or hard-boiled eggs, to cleanse the palate between batches, and purchase their cider. While this was once reserved for acquaintances, who would then stock their farmhouse or restaurant with the cider if it was to their liking, in the middle of the twentieth century people began making a night out of it, bringing their own raw goods to slap on the grill. The cider house owners began to realize that attracting diners on weekends could be a real business, hence the modern cider house has become an all-you-can-drink prix fixe dining experience, albeit with roots in the ancient *probaketak*. Some are open even outside of season for curious tourists.

The food is fatty, rich, and simple. Often starting with an appetizer of chorizo cooked in cider (see page 39) or blood sausage (see page 203), the first real course is the salt cod omelet (see page 97). These dishes are brought out to long, wooden tables and served family-style alongside baskets of bread. Then there is salt cod topped with confit peppers and onions, which of course is punctuated by several trips to the barrels, where diners congregate to socialize and digest before the next course: *txuleta*, a giant, sizzling steak (see page 223) topped with coarse salt and served sliced and ready to devour. More trips to the barrels, and the meal is finished with boisterous talking and, typically, traditional singing over apple paste (see page 253), local sheep's-milk cheese, and walnuts cracked at the table.

ARABA

ARABA

SINCE THE BEGINNING OF TIME, ARABA (ÁLAVA IN SPANISH) HAS BEEN
the wheat belt of Basque Country, but its landscape was shaped permanently by
the importation of the potato from the Americas. Araba is a poorer province; its
agrarian landscape is speckled with haunting, dust-color villages whose churches
stand high above their two-story skylines.

Just like the other provinces of Basque
Country, Araba has a tradition of high-quality
ingredients. The region's earthy produce
may seem less glamorous than its coastal
neighbors' shiny, ephemeral fish, but the
products in Araba have staved off hunger in a
rustic, satisfying way for centuries. Chestnuts,
potatoes, beans, apples, birds, rabbits,
mushrooms, snails, crabs . . . this interior
province has nothing to envy the coast, apart
from its ability to market itself.

The potato, upon its arrival from the
Americas, was served mostly to animals.
However, the Real Sociedad Bascongada de
Amigos del País (Royal Basque Society of
Friends of the Country) brought it through
genetic selection for deliciousness and onto

the table in the early eighteenth century.
Potatoes were popularly called "steaks of the
garden," sold on the streets, roasted, and then
soon hit the sauté pan in the *tortilla* (see page
24). Until recent times, Araba dwellers would
likely eat a potato-leek soup for breakfast
instead of milk or porridge. And now this
humble, hunger-staving tuber has its own
quality label, the Eusko Label Kalitatea Patata
de Álava/Arabako Patata. There are a multitude
of varieties: Spunta, Red Pontiac, Jaerla, Fénix,
Maika, Nagore, and Baraka, with the Kennebec
and Monalisa varieties especially prized for
cooking.

Araba also contains a crown jewel of Basque
Country: La Rioja Alavesa. This zone of the Rioja
DO produces lovely reds that have a fruity,

fresh character thanks to its slightly cooler, wetter climate. Towns like Laguardia, Haro, and Elciego define themselves in splashes of *ardo beltza* (red wine), and are home to wine cellars more than one hundred years old as well as others designed by world-famous architects. Arabako Txakolina gets less attention, but is another fount of the Basque wine *txakoli*.

The largest city is Vitoria-Gasteiz, where the Basque government is headquartered, with 240,000 inhabitants. The next largest village is Laudio, with 19,000, but the majority of Araba is a quiet province with small towns and villages with populations fewer than 900 people. One curiosity is that the villagers have nicknames for which they are known across the province. Most of these have to do with food: *pantostaus* for those from Albéniz

and Urabain, because apparently they enjoy toast for breakfast; *sopicones* in Sendadiano, just because when they inaugurated the new church bells they had soup inside the bell tower; or *hueveros* for the villagers from Atiega, one of the towns that paid their tribute to the salt mines of Añana in eggs.

In Vitoria-Gasteiz, the patron saint San Prudentzio receives an especially Alavés homage. Thousands of locals make an *erromeri* (pilgrimage; see page 213) up to the sanctuary of Armentia, a couple of miles outside the town center. After a religious ceremony honoring the saint, they dig into scrambled eggs with *perretxikoak* (St. George's mushrooms; see page 190) and snails (see page 164). This day joins other curious religious celebrations across the region, like the burning of Judas in

Samaniego or the filtering of water through the gold-plated head of San Bittor Gauanako, from Elorriaga, which the faithful use to bless their home or sick loved ones throughout the year.

In the west part of Araba in Añana, there are thousand-year-old salt flats. Water from the River Muera is channeled through wooden terraces, where it is allowed to evaporate in special salt pans. The Salted Valley of Añana was nearly abandoned, with only one salt maker left in the year 2000. However, a resurgence in interest has helped with recovery, and now the product is a gourmet, local alternative to Maldon sea salt or French fleur de sel.

The other culinary legacies left by Araba continue along this line of fruits of the earth.

Babak "vitoriana" erara (see page 162), a simple stew of fava beans and ham, is a must on menus across the province. The entrenched link to the *txerriboda*, the pig slaughter, that Araba has, and its dependence on the resulting sausages, hams, and loins for food, has left a unique plate in the *txitxikis* (see page 214). *Patorrillos*, a beloved traditional offal dish in Nafarroa, are an absolute delicacy: lamb trotters wrapped in intestines, garnished with brains, livers, kidneys, and everything else that nobody wanted. And, in reality, there are many more dishes—*bolo, litiruelas, croquetas de patatas, oblada, arrope*—awaiting a culinary awakening to bring them back to relevance and smooth their rough rustic edges.

GAZTA IZOZKIA
Cheese Ice Cream | 235

INTXAUR SALTSA
Walnut Cream | 237

ETXEKO BISKOTXA
Gâteau Basque | 238

MAMIA
Basque Sheep's
Curd | 243

SAGAR ERREAK
Roasted Apples | 245

ARRAUTZA ESNEA
Pudding | 263

ARROZ ESNEA
Rice Pudding | 264

ESNE TORRADA
Fried Milk | 266

OGI TORRADA
Caramelized
Custard Bread | 269

GURIN OPILA
Brioche Buns with
Buttercream | 271

GOZOAK

SWEETS

PANTXINETA
Almond-Cream
Tart | 246

TXANTXIGORRI OPILA
Chicharrón Sweet
Bread | 249

SAGAR DULTZEA
Apple Paste | 253

ARROZ PASTELA
Bilbao Custard
"Rice" Tarts | 255

GAZTA TARTA
La Viña Cheesecake | 258

ERROSKILAK
Anise-Scented
Fritters | 261

BIZKOTXOA
Yogurt Cake | 274

SAGAR TARTA
Apple Tart | 276

GOXUA
Basque Trifle | 279

KREMAZ BETETAKO
HODITXOAK
Basque Cannoli | 282

TEILAK
Almond Cookies | 287

SAN BLAS OPILA
Anise Sugar
Cookies | 288

GABONETAKO KONPOTA
Christmas
Compote | 293

THE BASQUES HAVE NEVER BEEN PARTIAL TO the sugary dessert traditions of France or the honey-soaked customs of the Arabs. Perhaps due to geographical, cultural, and linguistic isolation, or to the tendency to survive off fruits from local farms, the native dessert tradition was long rustic and undeveloped. There are few desserts that can claim the deepest of roots in Basque Country. And those that do stick out, for their simplicity and their unique names: *intxaur saltsa*, a pudding of stewed walnuts; *mamia*, curdled sheep's milk or junket; or *opil*, a category of sweet breads and cakes that takes on exactly as many variations as there are villages. With the influx of French baking influence and techniques, the Basques began to acquire an affinity for puff pastry, breeding a new tradition of Basque tarts and replacing old standbys like roasted chestnuts and *morokil*, corn flour dissolved in water and mixed with milk and sugar.

There is a dichotomy in Basque cooking of "kitchen desserts" and "bakery desserts." Stirred by worn or wrinkled hands, with time and patience as major ingredients, kitchen desserts are humble and comforting. In contrast, bakery desserts prize quickness and precision, and rely on the science of baking, which is not usually a home cook's strong suit. Until the beginning of the 1900s, ovens capable of controlling temperature precisely enough to produce delicate cakes were the sole property of bakeries. In the home, you would find desserts cooked on the stovetop, such as the classic puddings *arrautza esnea* (literally "egg milk") and *arroz esnea* (rice pudding). Abundant frying fats, from lard to olive oil, mean that fried desserts like *esne torrada* (fried milk) and *erroskilak* (fritters) are also popular at-home desserts.

"Bakery" desserts are a bastardization of French techniques and simple maneuvers with puff pastry, all redolent of cinnamon, lemon, and perhaps a bit of anise or clove. The result is a collection of sweets that all seem reminiscent of one another. This does not impede the Basques from showing immense pride in their pastry tradition, claiming existence of famous pastries from nearly every village: *guardia civiles* cakes from Areatza; *ignacios*, almond-egg tarts from Azpeitia; *mantecadas* cookies from Orduña; *piperopil*, *arrigoxo*, *artopil* . . . the list is endless, but they are more often than not riffs on the same ingredients. They also help to form the Basque dessert identity, rich in aromatics, flavored milks and custards, cinnamon and citrus. Anise gets a starring role as well, sprinkled into various doughs and icings. Almonds and almond meal sit right next to wheat flour on every baking shelf.

In Basque Country, desserts are often the only item purchased premade for a dinner, everyday or celebratory. They are conduits for social customs rather than items offered with the beaming homemade pride common in other cultures: *opilak*, party breads and cakes requisite for gifting; *espetxekoak*, filled bonbons invented in Vitoria-Gasteiz during the Civil War as a way to deliver liquor to prisoners; and the almond puff-pastry tart *pantxineta*, required dining for feast days but almost never made at home.

The most famous Basque dessert is most definitely the *gâteau Basque* (French for Basque cake), known and made the world over, albeit often incorrectly. I've included an authentically delicious recipe for this lovely tart, so familiar to the French Basques it is known as the "house cake" (*etxeko biskotxa*). The Basques also proffer some of the most famous chocolate in Europe, the chocolate from Baiona. However, ask almost any local, and they are sure to tell you they prefer a good cheese, *sagar dultzea* (apple paste), and some fresh walnuts to a rich cake any day.

Gazta Izozkia

CHEESE ICE CREAM

ALL OF THE BASQUE CAPITALS celebrate the festival of Aste Nagusia ("Big Week"), for no good reason aside from summer. It sits smack-dab in the middle of August, the hottest month of the year, its main activities being fireworks, street theater, concerts, and . . . ice cream. In San Sebastián, the order goes like this: dinner, fireworks show, and ice cream cone while strolling the main promenade; repeat for seven days in a row.

For a dairy-loving culture on the coast, ice cream wasn't a hard sell with the advent of freezers. The Basques have a notable preference for milky flavors in their ice cream: yogurt ice cream, mamia ice cream, yogurt ice cream with berries, cheesecake ice cream and, simply, cheese ice cream. This ice cream includes the local cheese, Idiazabal. You can use the plain, cured Idiazabal or the orange, smoked Idiazabal—whichever you can find. You'll need an ice cream maker for this recipe, but it is so worth the machinery and the wait. Served next to the *ogi torrada* (custard bread; see page 269); it makes a not-too-sweet counterpoint. And it is an absolute revelation. ❧

SERVES 4

3 cups (720 mL) whole milk

1 cup (3½ ounces/100 g) grated Idiazabal or other hard sheep's-milk cheese

12 ounces (340 g) cream cheese

2½ ounces (71 g) glucose syrup or corn syrup

½ teaspoon kosher salt

In a medium saucepan, combine the milk and Idiazabal cheese and heat over medium-high heat until just steaming. Remove from the heat and set aside to cool for at least 20 minutes.

Blend the mixture thoroughly in a blender or directly in the pot using an immersion blender. Pass the mixture through a fine-mesh sieve into a bowl; discard the solids.

Add the cream cheese, glucose, and salt to the infused milk and blend in a blender or with the immersion blender until homogeneous.

Freeze the mixture in an ice cream maker according to the manufacturer's instructions. Serve with your favorite sauce or topping.

Intxaur Saltsa

WALNUT CREAM

INTXAUR IS "WALNUT" IN EUSKARA, and this walnut cream is one of the most ancient desserts in the Basque repertoire. Walnuts, crushed in a mortar or pulverized with a rolling pin or wine bottle, were sprinkled into a pot of steaming milk, hanging over an open fire. They were left to stew down into a creamy mush, perhaps with a bit of egg or bread crumbs thrown in to thicken the mixture. The result was a delicious, creamy pudding.

Intxaur saltsa has only recently begun to reappear on restaurant menus, in a self-consciously retro nod with patriotic undertones. It is a dish made with ingredients available around the *baserri*, walnuts from the ground and milk from the cows, so it's rustic and without pretensions. This version is straightforward yet can be quite elegant, a surprising dessert that is simple and healthy. Walnuts from Basque Country are a revelation—plump, with a flavor that makes them seem more fruit than nut—so toasting them would be overkill. However, if top-quality, fresh walnuts aren't available where you are, you can toast the walnuts before grinding them to bring out their flavor. The size of the pieces is a matter of personal taste, but a mixture of powdery and crumblike bits is best. ✺

SERVES 4

4 cups (960 mL) whole milk

1 cinnamon stick

2 cups (250 g) top-quality shelled walnuts, plus more for garnish (see headnote)

¾ cup (150 g) sugar

Place the milk and the cinnamon stick in a saucepan. Heat over high heat until the milk is steaming. Just before it starts to simmer, remove from the heat and set aside to infuse for at least 10 minutes.

Meanwhile, chop or crush the walnuts very finely by putting them in a clean kitchen towel and rolling them repeatedly with a rolling pin or by pulsing them in a food processor, but be careful not to overprocess. There should be a mixture of powdery and small, crumblike pieces. The powdery pieces will thicken the mixture; the crumblike pieces will give it a pleasant texture.

Add the sugar and walnuts to the milk. Return the pot to high heat and bring the mixture to a very gentle simmer. Lower the temperature to medium and cook, maintaining a gentle simmer and stirring often, until the pudding has a creamy texture, about 30 minutes. Let cool to room temperature, or chill and eat cold.

Garnish with extra nuts, if desired.

Etxeko Biskotxa

GÂTEAU BASQUE

IT IS ONLY FITTING that one of Basque Country's most famous baked goods hails from Iparralde, French Basque Country. Iparralde is infamous among the Basques for allowing its culture to be influenced greatly by the French. While this has been detrimental in certain aspects, it has been a boon to the otherwise simple Basque baking tradition. The gâteau Basque, while exquisite and impressive as a finished product, is also simple: The golden crust of the cake is an enriched pâte sablée with both all-purpose flour and almond meal. Inside, it hides a filling of either pastry cream, as in this recipe, or a layer of cherry preserves (see Variations). Nowadays, there are chocolate versions, too.

The *etxeko biskotxa* ("house cake"), as it is called in Basque, has its origins in the Sunday breads that were made in the *baserriak* during the seventeenth century. Marianne Hirigoyen, a baker from Cambo-les-Bains, France, is credited by some for creating the modern rendition in the mid-1800s. She passed the recipe on to her daughters, and the cake originally called "the cake from Cambo" became known as "Basque cake." In a clever bit of Iparralde marketing, it has its own festival in Cambo-les-Bains and a dedicated museum in nearby Sare. ✺

SERVES 8

FOR THE DOUGH

1 cup (200 g) sugar

¾ cup plus 2 tablespoons (200 g) unsalted butter

1 large egg

2 egg yolks

2½ cups (310 g) all-purpose flour

1¼ cups (125 g) almond meal

1 teaspoon baking powder

½ teaspoon kosher salt

Grated zest of 1 lemon

FOR THE PASTRY CREAM

1 cup (240 mL) whole milk

1 cup (240 mL) heavy cream

½ vanilla bean

½ cup plus 2 tablespoons (125 g) sugar

¼ teaspoon kosher salt

4 egg yolks

⅓ cup plus 1 tablespoon (50 g) cornstarch

3 tablespoons dark rum

Unsalted butter, for the pan

All-purpose flour, for dusting

1 egg, for egg wash

Confectioner's sugar, for sprinkling (optional)

Make the dough: In the bowl of a stand mixer fitted with the paddle attachment, beat the sugar and butter until smooth. Add the egg and the yolks and mix until combined. Add the flour, almond meal, baking powder, salt, and lemon zest and mix until combined.

Turn the dough out onto your work surface and divide it into two pieces, one slightly bigger than the other. Form each piece into a ball and wrap them in plastic wrap. Refrigerate for at least 2 hours or, for best results, up to overnight.

Make the pastry cream: In a saucepan, heat the milk and the cream over high heat. Using the point of a knife, halve the vanilla bean lengthwise and scrape the seeds into the milk mixture. Add the bean pod and bring the mixture just to a simmer.

Meanwhile, in a bowl, whisk the sugar, salt, and the egg yolks vigorously, until they begin to lighten in color and are thick and creamy. Whisk in the cornstarch.

Remove the vanilla bean from the milk mixture and remove the pan from the heat. While whisking continuously, carefully pour about half the milk mixture into the egg mixture and whisk to combine (this tempers the eggs so they won't curdle). Add the egg mixture to the saucepan with the remaining milk mixture. Return to medium heat and cook, stirring vigorously with a whisk to avoid lumps, until the cream begins to thicken. Continue stirring for about 1 minute. Remove from the heat and stir in the rum.

Pour the pastry cream into a bowl and press plastic wrap directly against the surface to prevent a skin from forming. Refrigerate the pastry cream until completely cool.

Preheat the oven to 350°F (175°C). Butter a 9-inch (23 cm) round tart or cake pan, dust it with flour, and tap out the excess.

On a generously floured surface, roll out the larger ball of chilled dough until it is about 2 inches (5 cm) wider than the pan, to form the sides of the tart. Carefully center the dough in the bottom of the prepared pan, pressing with your fingers to fit it snugly along the bottom and sides. Trim any overhanging dough flush with the top of the pan.

Whisk the cooled pastry cream to loosen it. Spread the cream evenly over the dough in the cake pan.

Roll out the second piece of dough until it is just large enough to cover the pastry cream. Place it carefully on top—it may help to fold it in half, center the fold on the pastry cream, and then unfold it carefully. Smooth any bumps on the top by patting lightly. Using the underside of a spoon, seal the top layer of dough

continued »

to the bottom layer, applying pressure down and then up against the sides of the pan, scraping away the excess dough. Continue around the entire tart.

Using a fork, lightly score the tart in a crosshatch pattern; do not tear the dough. Beat the egg in a small bowl. Brush the top with the egg wash and sprinkle with a bit of sugar.

Bake for about 50 minutes, until golden brown. Let cool on a wire rack before serving. To serve, slice into individual pieces and, if desired, dust with confectioner's sugar. The cake is best eaten the day of or a day after making it. Store in an airtight container.

Variations

To make the gâteau Basque with cherry jam, just add 1 cup (325 g) to the first layer of dough instead of the pastry cream.

You could also make this in individual mini tart pans. Line the pans with dough, fill with pastry cream, and top with a second layer of dough as for the full-size cake. Cut the baking time down to 30 to 40 minutes.

Mamia

BASQUE SHEEP'S CURD

THE BASQUE DESSERT PAR EXCELLENCE is a lesson in simplicity itself. *Mamia*, also known as *gaztanbera*, *gatztu*, *putxa*, *kaillatu*, and *gatzatun*, is nothing more than sheep's milk, heated and curdled with a bit of rennet. It is often served with honey and walnuts—ingredients found in the hills of Basque Country. Traditionally it was made in a *kaiku*, the ancient receptacle used to collect milk. A rock, called the *esne harria* ("milk stone"), was left on an open fire to heat, then dropped into the milk-filled kaiku with a bit of chopped and smashed sheep's stomach. The rock warmed the mixture, leaving it with the distinct burnt taste characteristic of mamia. Mamia is an acquired taste, but it's a beautiful example of a local dessert, one that dates back thousands of years. ✿

SERVES 6 TO 8

4 cups (960 mL) raw sheep's milk (see Notes)

Kosher salt

¼ teaspoon rennet (see Notes)

Walnuts, freshly shelled, for serving

Honey or sugar, for serving

In a medium saucepan, heat the sheep's milk and a pinch of salt over high heat, just until it comes to a boil. Remove from the heat and let it sit until it cools to about 130°F (50°C).

Meanwhile, add 3 drops of the rennet to each serving bowl. When the milk has cooled to temperature, divide it among the prepared serving bowls and let sit, totally undisturbed, for 10 minutes.

Eat immediately or cover and chill until ready to serve. The ideal temperature for serving is a cool room temperature, around 60°F (15°C), so if you do refrigerate the dessert, remove it from the refrigerator about 1 hour before serving.

Serve with walnuts and honey to drizzle on top. Leave the honey on the table, as it is customary to drizzle it on layer by layer as you eat the dessert.

Notes Check the Internet to see if raw sheep's milk can be sold where you live. You can substitute other milks for the sheep's milk, but you'll have to experiment with the levels of fat and milk solids, or the mamia may not set correctly.

Rennet is an enzyme used in cheesemaking and is readily available online (see Resources, page 317). When using animal rennet, bring the milk up only as far as body temperature, 98°F (37°C).

Sagar Erreak

ROASTED APPLES

APPLE TREES HAVE GROWN IN BASQUE COUNTRY for thousands of years; in the Middle Ages, travel descriptions say that one could go from Baiona to Bilbao on the boughs of apple trees. The *sagar-lurra* ("apple earth"), equivalent to 5.58 meters—the space between apple trees—was an oft-used measurement. Destroying five or more fruit-bearing apple trees meant the death penalty in those days. It makes sense, then, that apples hold a prominent spot at the dessert table.

Today, there are dozens of apple varieties grown throughout Basque Country, bearing evocative names like Mendiola, Urbete, Aretxabaleta, Larrabetzu, Gezamina, Mokoa, Txalaka, and Pelestrina. The sweetheart is the Errezil, a local variety of the Reinette (*reineta de Regil*) apple. Tart, golden, and with a slightly smashed appearance, this apple lasts months and months in storage. Apples in the Russet family are the closest substitute, but you can also use Golden Delicious.

Make this healthy dessert during the peak of apple season, when it will be at its most flavorful. ✿

SERVES 4

4 apples, preferably Reinette, Russet, or Golden Delicious

6 tablespoons (75 g) granulated or brown sugar

2 teaspoons ground cinnamon

4 teaspoons (20 mL) anisette liqueur

½ tablespoon unsalted butter, cut into 4 pieces

Preheat the oven to 375°F (180°C).

To prepare the apples, cut out the core from the top in an upside-down cone-shaped piece. Do not cut a hole all the way to the bottom; only cut through three-quarters of the apple. Discard the cone-shaped piece. With a sharp knife, make a thin incision in the skin around the diameter of the apple, halfway between the base and the equator of the apple. This prevents the apple from bursting and helps it to keep its shape.

Arrange the apples upright in a small square baking dish. Distribute the sugar evenly among the apples. Depending on the size of the apple and the size of the hole, you may need a bit more or a bit less sugar. Sprinkle the cinnamon on the top, dividing it evenly among the apples. Pour 1 teaspoon of the anisette into each apple and top with a piece of butter.

Bake until golden, tender, and bubbling, about 25 minutes. Let cool and serve.

Pantxineta

ALMOND-CREAM TART

IN SAN SEBASTIÁN, there are protocols to meals at the dining societies (see page 91), despite their relaxed appearance. And on certain days of the year, like the evening before San Sebastián Day, the sweet protocol calls for one dessert only: the *pantxineta*. This simple tart, made from pastry cream sandwiched between two layers of puff pastry and sprinkled with almonds, was born in the early 1900s during the Belle Epoque, when French royalty and French culinary influence flooded the beaches and promenades of the city.

Casa Otaegui, a bakery founded in 1886 and still open today, employed some of the French cooks brought in with the Belle Epoque wave, creating an incubator for a deeply French pastry tradition. These bakers, working with the little raw materials they could find in times of war-induced scarcity, put together the simple, key elements in this circular, two-layer tart. The owner's wife, Emilia Malcorra, improperly (or cleverly, according to one's point of view) used a Basqueified bastardization of *frangipane* (almond cream) to baptize the tart, and the pantxineta was born.

This recipe comes as close to the original as possible, down to its humble, off-white pastry cream. If you prefer a rich, yellow, eggy pastry cream, you can substitute the recipe on page 279. Eat the tart slightly warm—either before it has the chance to cool completely or for leftovers, reheated in the oven to a pleasant lukewarm temperature. ❖

SERVES 8

2 cups (480 mL) whole milk

1 cinnamon stick

1 strip of lemon zest, peeled with a vegetable peeler

½ cup (100 g) sugar

2 large eggs

2 tablespoons cornstarch

2 tablespoons all-purpose flour

2 sheets (about 500 g) high-quality store-bought frozen puff pastry, defrosted

1 egg yolk

1 tablespoon heavy cream

¾ cup (75 g) chopped blanched almonds

In a medium saucepan, combine the milk, cinnamon stick, and lemon zest. Bring just to a simmer over high heat and remove the mixture from the heat. Set aside to infuse for about 10 minutes.

continued »

In a medium bowl, whisk the sugar and eggs well. Whisk in the cornstarch and the flour.

Remove the cinnamon stick and lemon zest from the milk. While whisking continuously, carefully pour about half the milk into the egg mixture and whisk to combine (this tempers the egg so it won't curdle). Return the egg mixture to the saucepan with the remaining milk. Return the pan to medium heat and cook, stirring vigorously with a whisk to avoid lumps, until the cream begins to thicken, about 5 minutes. Remove from the heat.

Pour the pastry cream into a bowl and let cool to room temperature. Press a piece of plastic wrap onto the surface of the cream to prevent a skin from forming. (The pastry cream can be made ahead of time and then refrigerated until ready to use. Bring to room temperature before using.)

Preheat the oven to 400°F (200°C).

Roll out half the puff pastry, or, if using store-bought puff pastry, open up one sheet. Cut a circle with a 9-inch (23 cm) diameter (it helps to use the bottom of a 9-inch/23 cm springform pan as a guide).

In a small bowl, whisk the egg yolk with the heavy cream. Using a pastry or kitchen brush, paint the borders of the pastry circle with the egg-cream mixture. Spread the pastry cream evenly over the pastry, keeping within the painted borders.

Roll out the second half of the puff pastry, or, if using store-bought puff pastry, open up the second sheet. Cut a circle with a 10-inch (25 cm) diameter. Place it carefully over the smaller circle and the pastry cream. Press around the border with your fingertips to seal the edges.

Paint the entire top of the tart with the egg-cream mixture. Cover generously with the chopped almonds. Bake for 25 to 30 minutes, until the outer edges are nicely browned.

Serve warm.

Txantxigorri Opila

CHICHARRÓN SWEET BREAD

THIS SWEET BREAD FROM NAFARROA takes its name from its distinguishing ingredient, the *chicharrón*, or pork rind. A hyperlocal delicacy that is most famous in the town of Olite, *txantxigorri* was traditionally made between the Day of Saint Martin and the Day of Saint Anthony, which is pig slaughter season. When the pork fat was rendered, the clean, pure-white fat was reserved for storage and cooking. Neighbors would bring the mix of gristle and fat left behind to the local bakers, such as the Vidaurre family, to put it to good use. This part-fatty, part-solid mixture would be incorporated into a breadlike dough, with a generous cinnamon sprinkling.

The result is something that can win over both savory and sweet lovers. The Vidaurre's *torta de txantxigorri* became famous when travelers began to take it to the *opila* blessing in Pamplona during San Blas (see page 288). Their version also features unleavened "host" bread as a base, which made it more portable. Here the tortas can be rolled out and cut into individual servings, or they can be rolled out and baked in a sheet, a more rustic form of serving that would be lovely for an outdoor fall gathering. ✿

SERVES 4 TO 6

½ cup (120 mL) warm water (body temperature is fine, but no hotter than 150°F/65°C)

1 envelope (7 g) active dry yeast

2 cups (250 g) all-purpose flour, plus more for kneading

½ teaspoon salt

5 tablespoons (75 g) lard, at room temperature, plus more for greasing the bowl

1 cup (65 g) chicharróns, or pork rinds

⅓ cup plus 2 tablespoons (100 g) sugar

1½ teaspoons cinnamon

In a large bowl, mix the warm water and yeast. Sift in the flour and salt. Stir until the ingredients are well combined and form a ball of dough. Turn the dough out onto a floured work surface and knead for about 10 minutes, or until the dough is elastic and smooth. Sprinkle with more flour if necessary to keep the dough from sticking.

continued »

Grease a clean bowl with a bit of lard. Add the dough and cover with a damp tea towel. Let it rise until it more or less doubles in size, about 1 hour, depending on the room's temperature.

Grind the chicharróns in a food processor to a fine texture. Some small bits are fine—they will give the torta a more interesting texture. Set aside.

Turn the dough out onto a floured work surface and punch it down. Add the lard, the ⅓ cup (75 g) sugar, and the cinnamon to the risen dough and fold and knead it for a few minutes, until the lard is fully incorporated and the sugar no longer feels grainy against your hands. Sprinkle the ground chicharróns over and fold and knead again, until the bits are distributed evenly throughout the dough. Roll the dough into a ball shape and place back in the oiled bowl. Let it rest for about 10 minutes.

Preheat the oven to 450°F (225°C). Line a baking sheet with a nonstick silicone mat or a lard-greased piece of parchment paper.

Turn the dough out onto the prepared baking sheet. With your palm and fingers, pat it out to an 8 by 10-inch (20 by 25 cm) rectangle, no more than ½ inch (1.5 cm) thick.

Sprinkle with the remaining 2 tablespoons sugar. Lower the oven temperature to 400°F (200°C) and bake for about 15 minutes, or until fragrant and beginning to turn golden. Remove from the oven and cool on a wire rack. Serve slightly warm or at room temperature.

Sagar Dultzea

APPLE PASTE

THE BASQUE HOLY TRINITY OF AFTER-DINNER EATING is a rich, tart, solid paste made with stewed apples and sugar, sliceable and photogenic, accompanied by cheese and walnuts. Many Basques make their own *sagar dultzea* (also known as *sagar-gozokia*), the Basque answer to Spanish *membrillo*, quince paste.

This is a staple dessert in the cider houses, but on your table it will make a lovely addition to any cheese board. Make sure to include some Idiazabal cheese on the board, as it is apple paste's ideal pairing. The apple paste is also delicious sliced and served pintxo-style on pieces of bread with a bit of cheese and walnuts.

If you're working with shelled walnuts that aren't the best quality, toast them to help coax out their flavor. The paste lasts for months in the refrigerator and indefinitely in the freezer, so make a big batch and enjoy it with abandon. ✤

SERVES 6

1½ pounds (680 g) apples (about 4), preferably Reinette, Russet, or Golden Delicious

Juice of ½ lemon

2½ cups (500 g) sugar

Idiazabal cheese, for serving

Whole walnuts, for serving

Cut the apples into medium-size chunks, discarding the cores. Place in a pot with the lemon juice and ⅓ cup (80 mL) water. Bring to a simmer over medium-high heat and cook until the apples are soft, 30 to 40 minutes. Let cool slightly.

Transfer the mixture to a blender and puree. The mixture should be dense with a bit of texture. Return the puree to the pot and add the sugar. Cook over low heat, stirring continuously, until the puree thickens to a jamlike consistency and comes away from the bottom of the pan when stirred, about 20 minutes.

Line an 8½ by 4½-inch (22 by 12 cm) silicone mold or baking pan with a piece of plastic wrap (this makes it easy to remove the paste once it's chilled). Choose a mold that will hold the paste to a depth of 2 to 3 inches (5 to 7.5 cm).

Pour the apple paste into the prepared mold and let cool, either at room temperature or in the refrigerator. The paste will firm up as it cools.

Remove from the mold and plastic wrap, and serve with cheese and walnuts.

Notes To adjust the recipe to a specific number of apples, just keep in mind that the sugar should weigh 75 to 80 percent as much as the apples.

The color of the final paste can be darkened by lightly caramelizing the sugar before adding it to the apples.

Arroz Pastela

BILBAO CUSTARD "RICE" TARTS

THE JOKES ABOUT *BILBOTARRAK*, residents of Bilbao, are endless, but they nearly always insinuate that the city's residents think the world revolves around them. Deep down, it comes from a sense of pride and belonging to a city that, until recently, didn't have much superficial charm and was lovable only to those born within its borders. This patriotism allows Bilbao's residents to claim that the *arroz pastela* ("rice cake") is an invention of the city's bakers; however, it closely resembles the famous *pastéis de nata* from Portugal, or even the Southern chess pie.

A simple, cinnamon- and citrus-infused custard mixture poured into miniature puff pastry bases doesn't look like much going into the oven. During baking, the custard puffs up like a muffin, but do not fear: Upon cooling, the tarts settle right down and turn out perfectly. The result is a gradual transition from a crunchy pastry to an almost cheesy, flan-type custard with a slightly browned skin on top.

There is no rice anywhere to be found in this tart. Some theorize that the recipe was brought from the Philippines, where the flour used was rice flour instead of wheat. However, midcentury recipe books seem to suggest otherwise, featuring arroz pastela recipes made with a rice pudding filling (see page 264). This recipe can also be made in a larger format, using a springform pan, with or without the puff pastry. Eat these the same day they are made; the puff pastry tends to get soggy after sitting under the custard overnight. ✿

MAKES 9 INDIVIDUAL TARTS

5 tablespoons (70 g) unsalted butter, melted, plus unsalted butter for greasing

⅔ cup (85 g) all-purpose flour, plus more for dusting

1⅓ cups (320 mL) whole milk

1 cinnamon stick

Zest of 1½ lemons, peeled with a vegetable peeler

1 sheet (about 8½ ounces/245 g) puff pastry, homemade or store-bought (if store-bought, thaw before using)

2 large eggs

½ cup (100 g) sugar

Preheat the oven to 440°F (225°C). Position an oven rack in the top third of the oven. Grease nine wells of a muffin tin or nine individual small molds with butter and then sprinkle evenly with flour. Tap out any excess.

continued »

In a medium saucepan, combine the milk, cinnamon stick, and lemon zest. Bring just to a simmer over high heat and remove the mixture from the heat. Set aside to infuse for about 10 minutes.

Roll out the puff pastry, or, if using store-bought puff pastry, open up one sheet. Cut out 9 circles about 4 inches (10 cm) in diameter—the dough circle should be large enough to come to the top of each well of the muffin tin or individual mold when pressed in. Press the dough circles lightly into the prepared tin or molds, smoothing out the sides. Place the tin or molds in the freezer while you proceed with the recipe.

In a large bowl, whisk the eggs and sugar by hand. Pour in the melted butter, which should be only slightly warm. Whisk again. Sift the flour into the mixture and stir to combine.

Remove the cinnamon stick and lemon zest from the infused milk and while whisking continuously, gradually add the milk to the egg mixture. When all is well combined, remove the muffin tin or molds from the freezer and fill each of the shells to the very top, without overflowing.

Bake for about 25 minutes, until the custard is set and the tops are browned. Check after 15 minutes; if the tops are not browning, move the rack closer to the heating element.

Allow the tarts to cool. These are best the day they are made.

CHEESE

Before there was Idiazabal, Roncal, or even Ossau-Iraty, there was *etxeko gazta*, house cheese. After baby lambs were weaned, their mothers' milk would fulfill a new destiny. The milk was collected and mixed, raw, with natural rennet from the stomachs of the lambs. The rennet would typically be hung in little sacks from the porch of the farmhouse, drying in the cool air. When needed, the cheese maker would pull one down, clean the rennet, and mix it into a paste to add to the milk. After a short while, about an hour, the cheese maker would mix the milk, "cutting" the curds to separate them from the whey. The curds were gathered, drained, and placed in a *zumitza* mold to be pressed. After the pressing, the rounds were immersed in a brine (*gatzuna*), then drained and placed on shelves to dry. For two weeks, they were turned daily. And that was how cheese was made for approximately the last thousand years in Basque Country.

With the onslaught of modern legalities, the creation of AOCs and DOs has meant putting a name to this cheese, and pinpointing its distinguishing qualities. Three different cheeses surfaced:

OSSAU-IRATY

Supposedly the first cheeses ever made in France, Ossau and Iraty cheeses are made with the milk from local Manech sheep. These cheeses have a nutty aftertaste and are generally somewhat softer than Idiazabal and Roncal.

IDIAZABAL

The cheese is made from the raw milk of only two breeds of sheep: Latxa and Karranza. It can be aged anywhere from 2 to 10 months, and it often appears in a smoked format that is a vestige from the days when the cheese was aged near the family hearth, which lightly smoked the rind.

RONCAL

This cheese is made from Latxa and Rasa sheep's milk, which can be legally gathered from anywhere in Nafarroa. However, the cheese must be made in one of the seven towns in the Roncal Valley to bear the name Roncal.

Gazta Tarta

LA VIÑA CHEESECAKE

THE WALLS AT LA VIÑA, a bar at the end of San Sebastián's Calle 31 de Agosto, are lined with stack upon stack of cheesecakes, still in their springform pans. They come down gradually as the day goes on: a steady stream of the most famous cheesecake in all of Europe. Cheesecake is an ancient baked good, and this Basque adaptation conquers the hearts and stomachs of foreigners from everywhere, even visiting Manhattanites schooled in the art of cheesecake eating.

Somewhere between a New York cheesecake and a flan, La Viña cheesecake sets the gold standard in Basque Country. Part of this dessert's joy is its abundance. Tall, creamy, and downright sinful, the combination of five simple ingredients is ethereal. This cake needs no crust—the parts of the cake in contact with the pan brown faster, forming a natural crust that transitions gradually into the creamiest of cheese custards. Serve with a glass of sherry. ✿

SERVES 12

1¾ cups (350 g) sugar

2¼ pounds (1 kg) cream cheese, at room temperature

¼ teaspoon kosher salt

5 large eggs

2 cups (480 mL) heavy cream

¼ cup (30 g) all-purpose flour

Preheat the oven to 400°F (200°C). Grease a 10-inch (25 cm) springform pan and line it with parchment paper, leaving 2 to 3 inches (5 to 7.5 cm) overhanging the top of the pan. (You can cut a circle to fit the base and then cut a band of paper to fit neatly around the sides, but the more rustic and simple method is to press an entire sheet into the pan, pleating the paper where it begins to crease.)

In a large bowl using a handheld mixer or in the bowl of a stand mixer fitted with the paddle attachment, cream the sugar and cream cheese until smooth. (This can be done by hand as well—beat with a wooden spoon for about 5 minutes.) Add the salt and mix. Incorporate the eggs one by one and stir until fully incorporated. Whisk in the cream. With a sifter, add the flour to the mixture and fold it in gently.

Pour the batter into the prepared pan and bake for 50 minutes, or until browned and almost burned-looking on top. This can really vary oven to oven, so it helps to have your eye on the cheesecake from 50 minutes forward. The center will still be quite jiggly, but the cake is ready. Remove from the oven and cool.

Before serving, remove the outer part of the springform and gently tug away the parchment paper. Serve at room temperature.

Erroskilak

ANISE-SCENTED FRITTERS

IT MAY SEEM STRANGE how a single sweet can suggest both the warmth of a flame on an open hearth and the cold mist hanging over a town surrounded by mountains. The scent of *erroskilak* does just that. A dough laced with *anisado*, an anise liqueur, cooks to a golden brown and releases the sweet scent of fried dough with a hint of anise. The *erroskila's* big moment is at the country fair, where it's sold in bags or freshly fried, tossed into a pile of white sugar and served warm.

Form the fritters by rolling the dough between your hands or on the counter like a snake and folding it around back onto itself. You could also make a knot where the dough meets. Mass-produced or bakery-made fritters are more doughnutlike in appearance, but homemade erroskilak have a charm of their own, with their uneven ends and imperfect circular shape. ✿

MAKES 20 TO 30

2 large eggs

½ cup (100 g) sugar, plus more for dusting

½ cup (120 mL) anisette liqueur

⅔ cup (160 mL) sunflower or olive oil

3½ cups (440 g) all-purpose flour, plus more for dusting

4 teaspoons baking powder

Pinch of kosher salt

Olive, sunflower, or vegetable oil, for frying

In a large bowl, whisk together the eggs, sugar, anisette, and oil.

In a separate large bowl, mix together the flour, baking powder, and salt.

Mix the dry ingredients into the wet ingredients in two additions, mixing well after the first before adding the second. Stir just until all the flour is combined.

Dust a clean work surface with flour and dump the dough out onto the surface. Knead it, giving it a few turns and adding a bit more flour if necessary to make the dough easy to work. Once it has fully come together, form into a ball and let rest for about 10 minutes.

Meanwhile, pour oil into a heavy-bottomed pot to the depth of about 1½ inches. Heat the oil over high heat to between 350 and 400°F (175 and 200°C).

To shape the erroskilak, pinch off a walnut-size piece of dough. Roll it out into a rope about 4 inches (10 cm) long and then bring the edges together and press to seal, forming a circle. Working in batches to avoid crowding the pan, carefully

continued »

place the circles of dough in the hot oil and fry for about 2 minutes, or until golden, turning once so they cook evenly.

Remove the erroskilak with a slotted spoon as they finish cooking and drain on paper towels. Pour some sugar on a plate or shallow bowl and toss each piece in the sugar to coat.

Serve. Store any leftovers in an airtight container at room temperature for up to a few weeks. Not that they would ever make it past a few days . . . or a few hours.

Note The size of the erroskilak is up to you. These are on the small side. However, you can make them larger—say, the size of a doughnut—if you'd like.

Arrautza Esnea

PUDDING

IN BASQUE, *arrautza esnea* translates literally to "egg milk," a rustic way to refer to an elegantly thickened crème anglaise perfumed with vanilla, citrus, and cinnamon.

When heated slowly and constantly, the egg in the pudding cooks, thickening the sauce evenly until it has a spoonable texture. This is an easy dessert, but you need to pay close attention because it will separate if it goes over 180°F (82°C).

Serve with a plain cookie on top, sprinkled with a dash of cinnamon. ✤

SERVES 4

2 cups (480 mL) whole milk

Zest of 1 lemon, peeled with a vegetable peeler

½ cinnamon stick

½ vanilla bean

½ cup (100 g) sugar

5 egg yolks

Ground cinnamon, for dusting

4 María cookies or digestive biscuits, for serving

In a medium saucepan, combine the milk, lemon zest, and cinnamon stick. With the tip of a knife, halve the vanilla bean lengthwise and scrape the seeds into the milk. Add the pod and bring just to a simmer over high heat, then remove the mixture from the heat. Set aside to infuse for about 15 minutes.

In a medium bowl, whisk the sugar and the egg yolks vigorously, until they begin to lighten in color and are thick and creamy.

Remove the cinnamon stick and lemon zest from the milk. While whisking continuously, carefully pour about half the milk into the egg mixture and whisk to combine. Return the egg mixture to the saucepan with the remaining milk. Return to medium heat and cook, stirring continuously with a silicone spatula, for about 15 minutes. Do not allow the mixture to boil, and keep the temperature below 180°F (82°C) or the eggs will curdle and separate. You can use a candy thermometer to watch the temperature, especially on your first couple of times making this. Do not heat faster or attempt to shortcut; if you notice that the mixture begins to separate, remove it quickly from the heat and whisk vigorously; if this doesn't reincorporate the mixture, you'll have to discard it and start again.

When the mixture reaches a creamy, thick consistency, divide it among four serving bowls. Sprinkle with cinnamon and set one cookie in the center of each bowl. Refrigerate until chilled and serve when desired.

Arroz Esnea

RICE PUDDING

RICE PUDDING remains one of the most deeply entrenched desserts in all of Spain, especially in the north, where cows are more abundant. Rice is cooked in milk, with aromatics and sugar, until it begins to let out its starches. The milk reduces, the rice absorbs the milk, and the mixture becomes uniformly thick.

This rice pudding is flavored with cinnamon and citrus. Rice pudding can be made with any type of rice, although long-grain tends to disintegrate by the end of the cooking time. It's an easy, economical dessert that is simple, stunning, and refreshing when served chilled. ✣

SERVES 6

½ cup (100 g) short-grain rice, preferably bomba or another rounded variety (see headnote)

4 cups (960 mL) milk, plus more if needed

1 cup (240 mL) heavy cream (see Notes)

2 cinnamon sticks

Zest of 1 lemon, peeled in strips with a vegetable peeler

½ cup (100 g) sugar

Ground cinnamon

Fresh mint leaves, for garnish (optional)

Rinse the rice in a fine-mesh sieve. Transfer to a large bowl, add enough water to cover, and soak for about 10 minutes. (See Notes.) Drain.

In a large pot, combine the milk, cream, rice, cinnamon sticks, and a few strips of lemon zest. Bring to a simmer over medium-high heat. Reduce the heat to low and cook, stirring every 5 minutes or so to avoid sticking, until the rice is nearly tender. Add the sugar and cook, stirring continuously, until the mixture is very creamy. This can take anywhere from 20 minutes (after which the rice will be tender) to 40 minutes (for a better, creamier result). If at any point before reaching a very tender stage the rice looks dry, add a bit more milk.

Remove the cinnamon sticks and lemon zest and let the pudding cool a bit. Distribute among six individual bowls. Rice pudding can be eaten warm, at room temperature, or chilled until cold. When ready to serve, sprinkle with cinnamon.

Notes Soaking the rice for 10 minutes or so before cooking allows some of the starch to be released, resulting in a less dense rice pudding. It's optional.

The heavy cream is included to achieve an ultra-creamy result, but also to simulate the thick, farm-fresh milk originally used in the making of arroz esnea.

Esne Torrada

FRIED MILK

ESNE TORRADA translates literally to "fried milk," a whimsical concept that belies a seriously seductive dessert. It could be thought of as a sweet croquette, with a thick, velvety pastry cream taking the place of béchamel, lightly coated in flour and flash-fried until golden and crispy.

Found in pastry shops and restaurants around Basque Country, fried milk is, at its heart, a homey dessert. Its origin is unknown, as old as home cooking. It gets claimed by several regions of Spain, but each region adds a personal twist. In Basque Country, rather than being coated with bread crumbs, the pastry cream gets the traditional batter: flour, then egg, and on to the hot oil.

This is an ideal dessert to prepare in advance. You don't have to fry the pieces immediately after preparing, and you don't have to eat them immediately after frying, either—esne torrada is nearly always fried and eaten at room temperature later that day. The texture changes: Out of the oil, it is almost crunchy and extra creamy; after a few hours, the outside softens and the inside becomes a more solid mass of pudding. ✿

MAKES 6

3 cups (720 mL) whole milk	4 egg yolks
1 cinnamon stick	¼ cup (30 g) all-purpose flour, plus more for dredging
2 strips of orange zest, peeled with a vegetable peeler	
2 strips of lemon zest, peeled with a vegetable peeler	⅔ cup (130 g) sugar, plus more for sprinkling
1 vanilla bean	¼ cup (28 g) cornstarch
	1 large egg
Sunflower or vegetable oil, for greasing and frying	Ground cinnamon, for sprinkling

In a medium saucepan, combine the milk, cinnamon stick, 1 strip of orange zest, and 1 strip of lemon zest. Using the tip of a knife, halve the vanilla bean lengthwise and scrape the seeds into the pan. Add the pod and bring just to a boil over medium-high heat. Remove from the heat and set aside to infuse for at least 15 minutes. Strain the milk and set aside.

Grease an 8-inch (20 cm) square glass or metal baking pan with a bit of oil.

In a large bowl, whisk together the egg yolks, flour, sugar, and cornstarch until mixed well. Little by little, whisk the milk mixture into the egg yolk mixture. Once all the milk is incorporated, return the mixture to the pot and heat over medium-high heat for 5 minutes, keeping it just below a boil and stirring continuously with a spatula to prevent sticking or burning.

Pour the mixture into the prepared baking pan. Cover with plastic wrap, pressing it directly against the surface to prevent a skin from forming. Let cool completely, then refrigerate for at least 2 hours and preferably overnight.

Remove the firmed-up pastry cream from the refrigerator and cut it into squares or rectangles. (Some prefer triangles; choose whatever you like best.)

In a heavy-bottomed skillet, heat about 1 inch (2.5 cm) of oil with the remaining strips of orange and lemon zest over medium heat until it reaches about 350°F (180°C). To test the oil, throw in a bit of flour; when it sizzles on contact, the oil is ready. When the oil is hot, remove the zest.

Pour some flour over a plate. In a shallow bowl, beat the egg until it loosens up. Pass the pastry cream shapes through the flour, turning to coat each side. Shake and brush off any excess flour. Dip the pastry cream in the egg, letting any excess drip off.

Working in batches as necessary to avoid crowding the pan, place the coated pastry cream shapes in the hot oil and fry for about 2 minutes, until the first side begins to turn a golden brown. Flip and fry on the other side for another minute or two. Remove and drain on paper towels. Repeat with the remaining pieces of pastry cream.

Serve immediately or at room temperature, sprinkled with cinnamon and sugar.

Note If desired, the squares of pastry cream can be frozen. Just pass through the flour first, and freeze on a baking sheet. When ready to use, allow to defrost halfway and, when still quite cold, pass through the flour and egg and proceed with the recipe.

Ogi Torrada

CARAMELIZED CUSTARD BREAD

HOMEMADE BREAD was a necessity for many centuries in the isolated *baserriak* of Basque Country. It was made from millet, and later, after the discovery of America, from corn—the two products share the same name in Euskara, *arto*. A riff on *pain perdu* was an excellent way to use bread that was too stale for the dinner table.

In other parts of Spain, the bread might be soaked in wine, but in Basque Country, the *ogi torrada* is most often made with rich, buttery brioche, soaked in a bath of flavor-infused full-fat dairy.

This recipe is a modern version, using an eggless batter and a big, blocky cut on the bread for a nicer presentation. The bread pieces are cooked in a hot pan, seared on all four sides, and sometimes finished with another layer of sugar caramelized with a kitchen torch (see Notes). The result is a crispy exterior that hides a creamy, warm, French toast–like texture. ❧

SERVES 4 TO 6

1 cup (240 mL) heavy cream

1 cup (240 mL) whole milk

½ cup plus 6 tablespoons (175 g) sugar

1 cinnamon stick

½ loaf brioche or white bread (around 7 ounces/200 g), a few days old

6 tablespoons (85 g) unsalted butter

In a medium saucepan, combine the cream, milk, ½ cup (100 g) of the sugar, and the cinnamon stick and heat over medium-high heat, stirring to dissolve the sugar, until steaming. Remove from the heat. Let cool to room temperature. Strain the milk mixture, discarding the solids.

Cut the bread into rectangular bars, about 2 inches (5 cm) high and 2 inches (5 cm) wide. The length may be determined by the loaf, though each bar should be about 4 inches (10 cm) long. Place the bread pieces on a rimmed baking sheet. Pour the milk mixture over evenly and let soak for about 10 minutes.

In a large sauté pan, melt 2 tablespoons of the butter and 2 tablespoons of the sugar over medium-high heat. While that mixture is melting, remove 2 pieces of bread from the milk mixture. Set on a paper towel to drain any excess liquid. Once the butter and sugar have fully melted, add the 2 pieces of bread to

continued »

the pan. Cook for 1 minute before flipping 90 degrees. Cook for another minute on that side, then flip 90 degrees again. The sugar and butter should be beginning to caramelize. Flip again and, after another minute, flip to the last side and cook for about 30 seconds. Finally, swirl the pan around to distribute the caramelized sugar-butter mixture and flip the bread pieces once more, with the most presentable side down. Cook for 1 minute. Very gently remove the bread with a spatula and set on a serving plate, with the most presentable side up. Repeat with the remaining bread in batches of two, using 2 tablespoons of the remaining butter and 2 tablespoons of the remaining sugar for each batch.

Serve warm.

Notes To finish with a kitchen torch: Melt only the butter in the pan, no sugar. Cook the bread slices as directed, then remove from the pan, sprinkle the sides of the bread with sugar, and run the flame of a kitchen torch back and forth over it until the sugar melts and then caramelizes, like a crème brûlée. The caramelized sugar cools into a crunchy coating.

To finish with the broiler: Preheat the broiler. After heating the pieces of bread in the pan with the butter and sugar, sprinkle the tops with extra sugar and place them under the hot broiler, as close to the heat as possible. Allow the sugar to melt and caramelize (keep your eyes on it, as it will only take about a minute under the hot broiler) and then remove.

Gurin Opila

BRIOCHE BUNS WITH BUTTERCREAM

GURIN OPILA, a filled brioche bun that everyone loves, is the darling of Bilbao. At first glance, it appears to be a simple brioche bun with a streak of sugar across the top. Gurin opila is more than just a brioche, however. After baking, the buns are split with a serrated knife and spread with a creamy filling, which varies both in the amount added (anywhere from a thin spread to a full half inch) and in how it's made. At its most basic, the filling is butter whipped until aerated with a thickened sugar syrup. More common is a filling like this one, which includes egg yolks, in the style of French buttercream. It is a satisfying breakfast or afternoon snack, and the recipe is quite foolproof. ✤

MAKES 12

FOR THE BUNS

¾ cup (180 mL) milk, lukewarm

0.6 ounce (17 g) fresh baker's yeast or 1¾ teaspoons (5 g) active dry yeast

4 large eggs

½ cup (100 g) sugar, plus more for dusting

½ teaspoon kosher salt

4½ cups (560 g) all-purpose flour

½ cup (113 g) unsalted butter, at room temperature

Sunflower or other neutral oil, for greasing

2 tablespoons milk or heavy cream

FOR THE BUTTERCREAM

1 cup (200 g) sugar

2 egg yolks

1 cup (225 g) unsalted butter, at room temperature

Make the buns: Line two baking sheets with parchment paper or silicone baking mats.

In a large bowl, combine the warm milk and the yeast. Whisk to dissolve. Allow it to sit for a few minutes to be sure the yeast is going to activate. Once it begins to foam, whisk in 3 eggs, the sugar, and the salt until combined.

With a handheld mixer or wooden spoon, incorporate the flour in two additions, stirring well after each. The dough will become hard to stir. Continue stirring or beating on low speed for a few minutes more.

Add the butter in tablespoon-sized pieces, mixing to incorporate after each addition.

continued »

If you're using a mixer, beat the dough for 10 to 15 minutes more, or until smooth, shiny, and stretchy—you should be able to pick it up in one piece.

If you're mixing the dough by hand, after the last bit of butter has been added and incorporated, dump the dough out on a clean work surface coated with a bit of oil. (It also helps to rub a bit on your hands to work easily with the dough.) Knead the dough until it becomes smooth and elastic, scraping up any pieces that stick to the surface with a spatula or bench scraper and reincorporating them. Knead for about 10 minutes, or until the dough is smooth and shiny.

Transfer the dough to an oiled bowl and let it double in volume, 1 to 2 hours.

Break off pieces of dough weighing between 2½ and 3 ounces (70 to 85 g), a bit smaller than a baseball. Form each piece into a ball by placing the dough on your work surface, between your cupped hands, and rotating the ball in a circle, applying light pressure and guiding the dough into a smooth round shape. Repeat with the remaining dough.

Take each ball of dough and roll it lightly back and forth to form an elongated shape about 4 inches (10 cm) long. Place on the prepared baking sheets. Cover with a kitchen towel or plastic wrap and set aside until doubled in size, 30 minutes to 2 hours, depending on the temperature of the room.

Preheat the oven to 400°F (200°C).

Separate the remaining egg, discarding the white or reserving it for another use. Mix the yolk and the milk or cream in a small bowl, beating well. With a kitchen or pastry brush, paint the tops and sides of each bun with the mixture. Generously sprinkle a line of sugar down the middle of the bun.

Bake until light golden, 10 to 15 minutes. Let cool.

Meanwhile, make the buttercream: In a small pan, heat the sugar and ½ cup (120 mL) water to a boil and cook until it thickens and reaches about 230°F (110°C). The syrup will be thick and almost to soft-ball stage; if you take a bit between your thumb and second finger, the syrup will begin to leave a thread when you separate your fingers but will quickly break. Let cool to lukewarm.

In a medium bowl using a handheld mixer or a whisk, beat the egg yolks well. While mixing, add the mostly cooled syrup in a thin stream and beat for about 1 minute. Let cool completely.

In the bowl of a stand mixer fitted with the paddle attachment, beat the butter until it lightens in color. When the egg-syrup mixture has completely cooled, with the mixer running, add it to the butter in a steady stream. Beat well until smooth.

To assemble, split the cooled buns along the equator with a serrated knife. Open and spread with the buttercream, using at least a generous, heaping tablespoon per bun. Place the tops back on each bun and serve.

Bizkotxoa

YOGURT CAKE

BIZKOTXO IS A SIMPLE CAKE, moist from the inclusion of olive oil and tenderized with yogurt, yet its charm lies in its preparation—the first ingredient into the bowl is the yogurt, and then the yogurt container is used to measure out the remaining ingredients, from the sugar to the flour.

It is not the most attention-getting cake, but it tastes distinctly Basque. One bite is enough to take most Basques back to the breakfast table, set with Cola Cao hot chocolate, or a *merienda* (midafternoon snack) at the corner café, with a steaming *kafe* (coffee). In a rural setting, the cake is often made with heavy, unpasteurized cream in place of the yogurt and/or the olive oil. This cake has most definitely evolved according to tastes over the years, and the current version is lightly sweet and easy to love. It's quite moist, so if necessary you can bake it one day and eat it the next. ✤

SERVES 6 TO 8

½ cup (120 mL) extra-virgin olive oil, plus more for greasing

½ cup (120 g) plain yogurt

4 large eggs

1 cup (200 g) sugar

1¼ cups (155 g) all-purpose flour

1 tablespoon baking powder

½ teaspoon kosher salt

Preheat the oven to 350°F (180°C). Grease an 8½ by 4½-inch (22 by 12 cm) glass loaf pan with a bit of olive oil.

In a large bowl, combine the yogurt, eggs, and sugar. Beat well until the mixture is combined. While whisking continuously, stream in the olive oil and whisk until the mixture is homogeneous.

In a separate medium bowl, sift together the flour, baking powder, and salt.

Fold the dry ingredients into the wet ingredients, stirring just to blend. Pour the batter into the prepared loaf pan. Bake until the cake is golden brown and a toothpick inserted into the center comes out clean, about 35 minutes. Let cool before removing from the pan.

Note This recipe, measured in 120 g yogurt containers, is 1 container of yogurt, 2 of sugar, 3 of flour, and 1 of olive oil.

Sagar Tarta

APPLE TART

A STANDARD IN THE BASQUE REPERTOIRE, the apple tart is one of the handful of pastries guaranteed to be found in any bakery, from Bizkaia to Iparralde. It is a riff on those three favorite dessert components: puff pastry, pastry cream, and apples. While some bakers put an apple compote or even *frangipane* under the layers of sliced apples, most rely on pastry cream as the cement between the apple and the pastry.

This dessert is versatile—simple enough for a weeknight treat but pretty enough to serve on holidays. The shape can change according to the occasion: Large and round, to be sliced and shared. Rectangular, cut into a few segments to serve. Individual circles, with apple spiraling to the center. Here the puff pastry is divided into three rectangles, which makes apple placement, and sharing at a crowded table, easier. ✺

SERVES 12

FOR THE PASTRY CREAM

1 cup (240 mL) whole milk

Zest of ½ lemon, peeled with a vegetable peeler

½ cinnamon stick

¼ cup (50 g) sugar

2 egg yolks

1 tablespoon cornstarch

½ tablespoon unsalted butter

FOR THE TART

1 sheet (about 8½ ounces/245 g) puff pastry, homemade or store-bought (thawed if store-bought)

2 apples, preferably Reinette, Russet, or Golden Delicious

1 egg yolk

1 tablespoon milk or heavy cream

2 tablespoons unsalted butter, cut into tiny pieces

2 tablespoons sugar

2 tablespoons apricot jam

Make the pastry cream: In a medium saucepan, combine the milk, lemon zest, and cinnamon stick. Bring just to a simmer over high heat and remove the mixture from the heat. Set aside to infuse for about 10 minutes.

In a medium bowl, whisk the sugar and the egg yolks vigorously, until they begin to lighten in color and are thick and creamy. Whisk in the cornstarch.

Remove the cinnamon stick and lemon zest from the milk. While whisking continuously, carefully pour about half the milk into the egg mixture and whisk to combine (this tempers the eggs to prevent them from curdling). Return the egg mixture to the saucepan with the remaining milk. Return to medium heat and cook, stirring vigorously with a whisk to avoid lumps, until the cream begins to thicken, about 5 minutes. Remove from the heat and whisk in the butter until melted and incorporated.

Pour the pastry cream into a bowl and let cool to room temperature. Press a piece of plastic wrap onto the surface of the cream to prevent a skin from forming. (The pastry cream can be made ahead of time and then refrigerated until ready to use. Bring to room temperature before using.)

Make the tart: Preheat the oven to 400°F (200°C).

Roll out the puff pastry, or, if using store-bought puff pastry, open up one sheet. Cut it into three rectangles, about 12 by 5 inches (30 by 13 cm) each. Arrange on a baking sheet. The tarts won't spread much, so they can be placed fairly close together.

Peel and core the apples. Using a mandoline or a sharp knife, slice the apples into ⅛-inch-thick (3 mm) slices.

Spread a layer of pastry cream over each puff pastry rectangle, leaving the border uncovered. Place the apple slices in a row down the middle, overlapping each piece by about half, to cover the whole surface of the pastry cream.

In a small bowl, beat the egg yolk with the milk. Using a small pastry or kitchen brush, paint the border of the tart, covering it completely. Dot the apples with the butter and sprinkle each tart with sugar over its entire surface.

Bake for 35 minutes, or until golden brown.

Meanwhile, in a microwave-safe bowl, combine the apricot jam and 2 teaspoons water and microwave for 15 to 30 seconds, or until liquid. Stir, picking out any fruit lumps.

Brush the apricot glaze over the cooled tarts. Serve.

Goxua

BASQUE TRIFLE

COMBINING TWO POPULAR DESSERTS INTO ONE and soaking them with alcohol could only turn out one way—delicious. *Goxua*, whose two literal meanings are "sweet" and "delicious," is akin to tiramisu. A soft, génoise-style sponge cake is soaked in rum and layered with whipped cream and pastry cream, and the whole thing is topped with a touch of crunchy caramel.

An argument over the invention of this layered dessert has yet to be settled. The debate is between several bakers in the Vitoria region, and dates as far back as the 1920s. It's traditionally served in a tiny earthenware casserole dish. You can take a page from the modern versions of the dessert and layer it in a glass dish or with plastic cake collars so the layers can be appreciated. ✥

MAKES 6

FOR THE PASTRY CREAM

2 cups (480 mL) whole milk

Zest of ½ lemon, peeled with a vegetable peeler

½ cinnamon stick

4 egg yolks

½ cup (100 g) granulated sugar

2 tablespoons cornstarch

1 tablespoon unsalted butter

FOR THE CAKE

Unsalted butter, for greasing

4 large eggs, separated

1½ cups plus 2 tablespoons (325 g) granulated sugar

1 cup (125 g) all-purpose flour

1 tablespoon whole milk (optional)

2 tablespoons rum or brandy

1⅔ cups (400 mL) heavy cream

½ cup (60 g) confectioners' sugar

Make the pastry cream: In a medium saucepan, combine the milk, lemon zest, and cinnamon stick. Bring just to a simmer over high heat and remove the mixture from the heat. Set aside to infuse for about 10 minutes.

In a bowl, whisk the egg yolks and granulated sugar vigorously, until they begin to lighten in color and are thick and creamy. Whisk in the cornstarch.

Remove the cinnamon stick and lemon zest from the milk. While whisking, carefully pour about half the milk into the egg mixture and whisk to combine. Return the egg mixture to the saucepan with the remaining milk. Return to medium heat and cook, stirring vigorously with a whisk to avoid lumps, until the

continued »

cream begins to thicken, about 5 minutes. Remove from the heat and whisk in the butter until melted and combined.

Pour the pastry cream into a bowl and let cool to room temperature. Press a piece of plastic wrap onto the surface of the cream to prevent a skin from forming. (The pastry cream can be made ahead of time and then refrigerated until ready to use. Bring to room temperature before using.)

Make the cake: Preheat the oven to 400°F (200°C). Grease a 10 by 15-inch (25 by 38 cm) rimmed baking sheet with butter and sprinkle with flour to coat.

In a large bowl using a whisk or a handheld mixer, beat the egg whites until they hold stiff peaks.

In a separate large bowl, whisk together the egg yolks and ½ cup plus 2 tablespoons (125 g) of the granulated sugar. Sift in the flour and stir to combine. If the flour is difficult to incorporate, it may be the egg yolks were a bit on the small side. In that case, add the milk and continue incorporating.

Gently fold the egg whites into the mixture until just combined.

Pour the batter into the prepared baking sheet, smoothing the top. Tap it once on the counter to remove any air bubbles. Bake for 8 minutes, or until a toothpick inserted into the center comes out clean. Let cool before using.

In a medium saucepan, combine ½ cup (120 mL) water, ½ cup (100 g) of the granulated sugar, and the rum and bring to a simmer over high heat. Cook until thickened, about 5 minutes. Remove from the heat and let the syrup cool slightly.

Cut circles out of the cooled cake that correspond with the size of your serving vessels. With a pastry or kitchen brush, paint each circle of cake with the spiked syrup. Allow to soak in the cake for a few minutes, then paint the cake again.

In the bowl of a stand mixer (preferably chilled in the freezer beforehand) fitted with the whisk attachment, combine the cream and confectioners' sugar. Beat until the cream holds stiff peaks. (Alternatively, whip the cream in a large bowl with a whisk or handheld mixer.)

Divide the whipped cream among six parfait glasses, to create a nice base. Place the soaked cake on top of the whipped cream. If desired, paint the cake once more with the spiked syrup. Divide the pastry cream among the parfait glasses. Sprinkle the remaining ½ cup (100 g) granulated sugar evenly over the top of each. Hold the flame of a kitchen torch just above the sugar and move it in circles until the sugar melts and then caramelizes into a thin layer. Serve immediately.

Note If you don't have a kitchen torch, you can use the broiler to caramelize the sugar. Use oven-safe bowls or ramekins; set the broiler to high and watch carefully so as not to burn the sugar.

FESTIVALS

A charming reflection of the fame and pride of each village, Basque *jaiak*, town festivals, remain an entrenched tradition and one that surely makes Basque Country a unique corner of the world.

In fall, festivals are predominantly related to themes of the farmhouse: the harvest and the slaughtering of animals, especially the pig. Winter brings festivals related to carnival, *inauteriak*, and certain towns are especially known for their form of celebration: Tolosa, Zuberoa, Zubieta, and Lantz, for example, attract townspeople from the entire province. The past is threaded through with the maintenance of traditions, like the presence of Zaldiko, a half-man, half-horse creature, or Momotxorro, a particularly menacing half bull, half man.

The jaiak of the summer, however, is the stuff of myth. From San Fermín, Pamplona's world-famous running of the bulls, to the Big Week (Aste Nagusia) in every capital, millions of people gather in main squares for fireworks, concerts, sports, cooking competitions, and more. It is most definitely not limited to the populous big cities, however. Every single village celebrates its patron saint, animating a long weekend in summer with the addition of a good dose of small-town charm. Those in attendance know each other, smiling and waving in the streets during the daytime festivities and drinking from the vendors in the *txosnak*, improvised taverns set up during festivals. They rotate among the village's bars, practicing the art of *guapasa*, or staying up all night partying.

Some villages have distinctive fingerprints on their jaiak. Zumaia, for example, has a town festival that smells of the dried octopus waving in the wind. Lekeitio's Antzar Eguna features a sort of tug-of-war in the port with a one-on-one between a goose, a man, and gravity. All are united with a unique festive spirit.

Kremaz Betetako Hoditxoak

BASQUE CANNOLI

THE INSTANTANEOUS REACTIONS when dough hits hot oil are multiple: Liquid evaporates, air bubbles are created, and sugars and proteins are coaxed to golden brown. Cooks in Basque Country have perfected this fried dessert without delving into the science. The simple dough is enriched with olive oil (or lard), shaped into a cone or tube, fried around a mold, and then filled with pastry cream. As with its Italian cousin, the cannoli, the *kremaz betetako hoditxoa* (literally "cream-filled tube") was introduced by the Arabs and then adapted to local tastes. In a very popular variation, it can also be made with puff pastry, in which case it earns the suffix "from Bilbao."

You will need 10 to 12 conical metal pastry molds to form the cannoli shells. Making cannoli is an easy task if you employ some helpers. Get friends or family in the kitchen to help you make the *hoditxoak*, assembly-line-style. ✣

MAKES 10 TO 12

FOR THE PASTRY CREAM

2 cups (480 mL) whole milk

Zest of ½ lemon, peeled with a vegetable peeler

½ cinnamon stick

½ cup (100 g) sugar

4 egg yolks

2 tablespoons (30 g) cornstarch

1 tablespoon unsalted butter

FOR THE CANNOLI

½ cup plus 2 tablespoons (150 mL) whole milk

¼ cup (60 mL) olive oil

1 teaspoon fresh lemon juice

2 cups plus 3 tablespoons (295 g) all-purpose flour, plus more for dusting

Kosher salt

Sunflower or vegetable oil, for frying

Sugar, for garnish

Make the pastry cream: In a medium saucepan, combine the milk, lemon zest, and cinnamon stick. Bring just to a simmer over high heat and remove the mixture from the heat. Set aside to infuse for about 10 minutes.

In a bowl, whisk the sugar and egg yolks vigorously, until they begin to lighten in color and are thick and creamy. Whisk in the cornstarch.

Remove the cinnamon stick and lemon zest from the milk. While whisking continuously, carefully pour about half the milk into the egg mixture and whisk to combine (this tempers the eggs so they don't curdle). Return the egg mixture to the saucepan with the remaining milk. Return to medium heat and

continued »

cook, stirring vigorously with a whisk to avoid lumps, until the cream begins to thicken, about 5 minutes. Remove from the heat and whisk in the butter until melted and combined.

Pour the pastry cream into a bowl and let cool slightly. Transfer to a pastry bag and set aside. This can be made ahead and refrigerated until ready for use.

Make the cannoli: In a medium bowl, combine the milk, olive oil, and lemon juice. Whisk to combine well. Sift the flour into the wet ingredients. Add a generous pinch of salt and mix until the flour is completely incorporated. Turn the mixture out onto a clean, lightly floured countertop and knead by hand until the dough is smooth and pliable.

Roll the dough into a ball and wrap it in plastic wrap. Let rest in the refrigerator for at least 30 minutes.

With a flour-dusted rolling pin, roll out the chilled dough until very thin, ⅛ to ¼ inch (3 to 6 mm). With a sharp knife, cut the dough into strips about 1 by 6 inches (2.5 by 15 cm). Wrap these strips around the metal molds, overlapping the strips slightly as you wind them up the molds.

In a heavy-bottomed pot, heat oil a few inches deep over medium-high heat to 320 to 350°F (160 to 180°C). Working in batches to avoid crowding the pot, add the dough-wrapped cones to the hot oil and fry until the pastry is deep golden, about 2 minutes. Remove from the oil with a slotted spoon and drain on paper towels. Repeat with the remaining dough. Let cool, then remove the cannoli shells from the molds.

When ready to serve, position the pastry bag in the opening of a completely cooled shell and squeeze, filling the shell with pastry cream. Roll in or sprinkle with sugar. Repeat with the remaining shells and serve.

BASQUE DANCE

Dantza pervades the air of any celebration in Basque country. Voltaire once even referred to the Basques as the people who skip around the foothills of the Pyrenees. To the tune of the *xirula* or the *txistu*, Basque flutes, dancers perform the oldest of dances: dances for men (*mutil dantzak*), dances for both sexes, dances with swords (*ezpata dantzak*), and dances that are actually games, like the *alki dantza*, which in some versions becomes a type of musical chairs. *Jauziak* (jumps) mark many of the dances, done elegantly with a lighter-than-air lift by men in traditional dress and *espartinak* or *abarketak*, Basque espadrilles.

The procession of *ttunttun-xirula*, a drum-flute combo, is a tradition dating back five hundred years in Zuberoa. The Zuberoako Maskarada, a set of theatrical performances during Carnaval, features one of the most famous feats in Basque dance culture: a breathtaking moment in the *godalet dantza* ("glass dance") in which one of the dancers hops onto a small cider glass without breaking it. The pastoral includes song and parades, battles enacted with music. Basque dances of Iparralde were even incorporated into classic ballet, in the step *pas de basque*, proof of their widespread fame.

The *aurresku* is the dance of honor, present at political acts, weddings, and other public events. Dancers hold hands or handkerchiefs (a holdover from more conservative days), and perform the *soka dantza* (rope dance) in a line. *Aurresku* means "first hand," and it was the name given to the dancer first in line. Nowadays, the aurresku has been singled out of the soka dantza to stand alone in a ceremonial version, *ohorezko aurresku*, a dance of high kicks and jumps, performed to honor someone on a special occasion.

Teilak

ALMOND COOKIES

LEGEND HAS IT THAT THE *TEILA*, a tile-shaped almond cookie, was created by
Luís María Eceiza. Hailing from a family of bakers who founded the eponymous
Eceiza bakery in 1924, Luís created the teila when his friend Julian asked for a
simple dessert to serve in his steakhouse. While the teila is reminiscent of the
French tuile, like all things Basque, it tends toward the rustic. Traditional recipes
forgo luxuries like melted butter and pastry flour, and use the entire egg instead
of just the white.

 When making these cookies at home, a rolling pin serves nicely to form
the cookie's curved shape; a wine bottle can work in a pinch. Working quickly
is important, because once cooled, the *teilak* won't bend into shape. You can
substitute chopped almonds for the almond meal and part of the flour for a more
country-style cookie. ❀

MAKES 2 TO 3 DOZEN

Unsalted butter, for greasing
(optional)

¾ cup plus 2 tablespoons (175 g) sugar

1½ cups (165 g) almond meal

½ cup (60 g) all-purpose flour

¼ teaspoon kosher salt

3 large eggs

Grated zest of 1 lemon

½ cup (60 g) slivered almonds

Preheat the oven to 350°F (180°C). Line two baking sheets with parchment paper
or silicone baking mats, or grease very well with butter.

 In a large bowl, mix the sugar, almond meal, flour, and salt. Add the eggs and,
with a wooden spatula, mix well until completely combined. Add the lemon zest
and mix well.

 Make small mounds of batter, about a heaping teaspoon, on the prepared
baking sheets, spacing them 2 to 3 inches apart. With the back of a spoon, smooth
the batter into thin circles, wetting the spoon with water after every other mound.
Sprinkle with the slivered almonds.

 Bake, turning halfway through, until the golden color at the edges gets dark
and begins to creep toward the center, 11 to 13 minutes. Remove the pan from the
oven, and, working quickly with a metal spatula, press each cookie gently against
a round mold or rolling pin to achieve the roof tile shape.

 Once the cookies harden completely (less than a minute), you can remove them
from the mold/pin and transfer to a sealable plastic bag or airtight container.

San Blas Opila

ANISE SUGAR COOKIES

BAKERIES ARE FRAGRANT WITH ANISE around the day of San Blas. The patron saint of the sore throat is celebrated around Basque Country on February 3, and this customary sweet is said to protect those who enjoy it from throat-related illness. The San Blas cookie is a flat, plain cookie, often shaped with undulating cutters, topped with a plain, white icing—all of it scented with anise. *Torta de San Blas* is an example of the *opil*, a sweet that has evolved from the breads used as offerings in ancient pagan rites. They vary across the region, with shapes and flavors molded to each area and each celebration. With the passage of time, the cakes and cookies have adapted themselves not only to modern Christianity but also to modern baking.

These cookies are typical of Eibar and Elgoibar, two neighboring villages on the border of Bizkaia and Gipuzkoa. Although they are often made with butter, they are better and more tender when made with the traditional lard. Both the dough and the icing have anisette liqueur added. It can be an acquired taste, but it's one the Basque have definitely acquired. "*San Blas*" is often written across the top in chocolate. Historically, the cookies were carried to churches and hermitages to be blessed, along with the house's salt supply and a cord, which was tied around the throat for eight days in a row after the blessing, then thrown into the fire.

These cookies keep well. Double the recipe to be sure you have enough on hand, especially during cold and flu season when Blas's blessing might come in handy. ✤

MAKES EIGHT 3-INCH (7.5 CM) COOKIES

¼ cup (50 g) lard, at room temperature, plus more for greasing

7 tablespoons (88 g) granulated sugar

1 large egg

1 tablespoon plus ½ teaspoon anisette liqueur

1⅔ cups (208 g) all-purpose flour, plus more for dusting

¼ teaspoon table salt

¼ teaspoon baking powder

1 egg white

1 cup plus 3 tablespoons (150 g) confectioners' sugar

Preheat the oven to 350°F (180°C). Grease a baking sheet lightly with lard or line it with a silicone baking mat.

continued »

In a large bowl using a wooden spoon or handheld mixer, cream the lard with the sugar. Add the egg and 1 tablespoon of the anisette, mixing well until incorporated. Sift the flour, salt, and baking powder into the bowl and mix until just combined.

Gather the dough into a ball and wrap in plastic wrap. Stick the dough in the refrigerator or freezer for about 10 minutes to firm up.

Flour a clean work surface and roll the dough out until it is between ½ and 1 inch (1.5 to 2 cm) thick. Using a cookie cutter or a knife, cut into the desired shape. Place on the prepared baking sheet and bake until the sides are just beginning to color, about 15 minutes, turning halfway through.

Meanwhile, in a small bowl, beat the egg white until it holds stiff peaks. Sift the confectioners' sugar over the egg white and fold gently until fully incorporated. Gently fold in the remaining ½ teaspoon anisette.

As soon as you remove the cookies from the oven, ladle the icing over them with a spoon, spreading so that it falls off the borders and covers the cookies entirely. The icing will dry in a shiny, thin layer as long as it is applied to warm cookies. If desired, decorate with optional chocolate writing (see Notes) and serve.

Notes The shape of the San Blas cookie varies: It can be square, circular, or rectangular, often with a wavy or pinched border.

The cookies are often decorated with the words *San Blas* in chocolate. To do so, heat 1 cup (175 g) chopped chocolate with 2 teaspoons oil in the microwave until just melted, stirring halfway, about 2 minutes. Immediately spoon the chocolate into a pastry bag and write the desired message on the cooled cookies.

The anisette liqueur can be replaced with anise extract; use just a few drops of extract.

BASQUE SANTA CLAUS

A roughshod, scruffy man, he is dressed in a sheepskin vest and black shirt with woolen socks pulled over his coarse pants. His *txapela* (beret) is cocked over his eyes, which seem to sparkle above his rosy red cheeks, so-hued thanks to a weakness for red wine. This is Olentzero, a figure who evolved from a terrifying mountain man devoted to making charcoal and scaring children into the Basque Santa Claus.

Although he seems to have been around forever, Olentzero's link with Christmas is actually fairly recent, with written record dating back only to the 1920s. Many children of the time remember threats of Olentzero cutting their throats with his sickle should they break the pre-Christmas fast, not clean the hearth, or stay up too late on Christmas Eve. But in the 1960s, the figure of Olentzero began to change, with figurines and images of his smiling face donning cards of the season. And in the 1980s, it began to circulate that it was actually Olentzero doing the gift giving, leaving presents and a bit of coal in children's shoes. It was also around this time that Olentzero got a girlfriend, Mari Domingi, who nowadays appears by his side in official acts and depictions.

The etymology of his name is associated with "the good season," or the winter solstice. Some versions of his origin have him as the only pagan figure who can see the advent of *Kixmi*, or Jesus Christ. The *jentilak*, pagan giants, went into hiding in the Sierra de Aralar, but Olentzero proclaimed the news from village to village.

Gabonetako Konpota

CHRISTMAS COMPOTE

THE BASQUE ANSWER TO CRANBERRY SAUCE, *konpota* (compote) is synonymous with the holiday season and is an absolute mandatory addition to any Christmas table. A medley of fruits sits abundant in an engraved crystal bowl, ready to be heaped onto dessert plates and drizzled with its thick, ruby red syrup.

As for what makes these fruits (dried figs, peaches, plums, and grapes) so Christmasy, the answer likely goes to times when winter meant nothing fresh but the apples and the winter pear in this fruit stew. On Christmas Eve, when a bounty is called for, stored summer fruits would be resuscitated in a syrup boiled down from red wine, water, and sugar. The hint of cinnamon and star anise are vital to the compote, but some people add citrus peel or juniper berries, too.

The only trick to konpota is timing the reduction of the liquids to a thick syrup with the perfect tender texture of both the dried and fresh fruit, which is done by staggering the incorporation of each fruit. This is a highly flexible dish and tastes quite delicious with whichever dried fruits you can get your hands on. ✿

SERVES 8

3 cups (720 mL) red wine, preferably Rioja

1 cup (200 g) sugar

1 cinnamon stick

1 star anise

¾ cup (about 4½ ounces/125 g) dried peaches (no sugar added)

1 cup (about 6 ounces/170 g) prunes, pitted

¾ cup (about 4½ ounces/125 g) dried figs

1 cup (about 4½ ounces/125 g) raisins

2 apples, preferably Reinette, Russet, or Golden Delicious

1 winter pear, such as Comice

In a pot, heat 3½ (840 mL) cups water, the wine, sugar, cinnamon, and star anise over high heat. Bring to a simmer and cook for 2 to 3 minutes to cook out the alcohol and allow the liquid to begin reducing.

Add the dried peaches and simmer for 10 minutes. Add the prunes, figs, and raisins and simmer for about 25 minutes, or until almost but not quite tender.

Meanwhile, peel the apples and the pear, core them, and chop into 1-inch (2.5 cm) pieces. Add them to the pot. Simmer for about 15 minutes, or until the fresh fruit is tender. If the liquid is reducing too quickly, cover the pan. Or, if the mixture looks quite dry, add a bit more water, keeping in mind that the end product should be fruit bathed in a syrupy, deep red liquid.

Serve at room temperature or chilled.

IPARRALDE

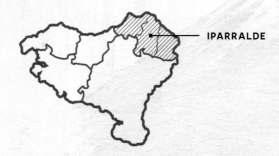

IPARRALDE

THE THREE PROVINCES ON THE FRENCH SIDE OF BASQUE COUNTRY—
Nafarroa Beherea, Lapurdi, and Zuberoa—comprise Iparralde. They often get
lumped together, in part due to their much smaller population, in part because the
maintenance of the cultural traditions in Iparralde has taken a different path than
the southern provinces of Basque Country. The cuisines of the three provinces bear
much more similarity to one another than to the southern provinces, and they
have striking differences from the Spanish Basque Country.

The indelible mark that French techniques
and cuisine have left on Iparralde's Basque
cuisine is delicious, if a bit less historically
authentic than in the other provinces. To the
horror of their neighbors in Hegoalde, those
in Iparralde are known to dress their fish
with sauces, even mixing in (gasp!) butter,
herbs other than parsley, and citrus. At French
Basque farms, geese are taken out to pasture
with the sheep, and duck is ever present.
Seared and roasted duck is frequently found on
menus and in homes, and foie is revered.

Traditional dishes are few, and prepared
mostly for festival lunches or in homes,

behind closed doors. If you spot one on a
restaurant menu, you're most likely in a tourist
trap. Some of the traditional dishes are even
willfully forgotten, as is the case with *arto sopa*,
a milky soup in which cornbread was soaked
before eating. This disconnect with tradition
is a reflection of the geopolitical situation of
the province. Located in the South of France,
the tradition has always been agricultural,
with little industry, meaning poverty and
dependence on the state. The moneymaker in
Iparralde is tourism, which experienced such a
boom in the twentieth century that the Basque
traditions and roots have evolved to be for

show, marketed to a point that authenticity is only a memory.

The most famous eating from Iparralde comes in the form of products, not plates. The ham from Baiona (Bayonne) is celebrated worldwide, along with its chocolate. Jews, expelled from Spain and Portugal, propagated the chocolate-making tradition, one of France's first, and by the late 1600s the chocolate makers in Baiona were already banding together to form boards and associations. From the dried red chile from Ezpeleta (see page 219), known worldwide, to the cherries from Itxassou, experiencing their renaissance, the products of Iparralde are celebrated. A resurgence of farming among young people is also under way, helping to bring heritage seeds, like the famous red corn, back to the table.

The heavenly hills of Nafarroa Beherea, or Lower Navarre, are softly rolling and so close together it is easy to get lost in their valleys. It is home to the Irouléguy AOC, a wine region that produces enthralling, earthy reds, whites, and rosés from mostly Tannat grapes (locally called Bordelesa Beltza) grown on its reddish terrain. It is said that the wine-making tradition dates back to the Middle Ages, initiated by the monks in Saint-Jean-Pied-de-Port and Roncesvalles, perhaps to supply the pilgrims on the Camino de Santiago with wine.

Lapurdi is the glamorous Basque coast that includes the sparkling Biarritz, the hippie-surfer vibe of Guéthary and Bidart, and the small-town charm of Saint-Jean-de-Luz. Fish soup (see page 72) takes on a different form here, in *ttoro*, a brothy melange of local fishes that often features mollusks and Espelette pepper. *Garbure*, a famous stew of duck or ham, cabbage, and other vegetables, is enjoyed throughout Iparralde, but originated here. It is served as two dishes—first the broth and then the pieces of meat, often alongside toasted bread with butter and cheese. The *gâteau Basque* (see page 238) also grew famous in the area around Sare and Cambo-les-Bains.

Zuberoa is home to Ossau-Iraty cheese, which is actually two cheeses, purportedly among the first to ever be made in France. A variation of the Iparralde dish *piperrada* (see page 180) exists in this region, a poor man's adaptation that makes the best use of extra bits of bread. This *piperrada zuria*, or white piperrade, was soaked pieces of bread fried in pig fat with peppers and garlic. To finish, a bit of tomato or tomato sauce was added along with a beaten egg. *Tripot*, a variation of *odolki* (blood sausage; see page 203) with a meatier stuffing, is also made and served with apples fried in animal fat, *xagarrada* in local dialect.

The Basques in Iparralde still live from agricultural endeavors, and with the help of the French state, many are returning to their roots. Idoki, an association formed in 1992, is devoted to supporting the producers of and promoting seventeen local products, which is a bit of hope for this heavily touristed, sparsely populated Basque region.

EDARIAK

DRINKS

THERE IS NOTHING MORE NATURAL TO A BASQUE than to say *"Goazen zeozer hartzera."* Literally "Let's go and take something," this is a proposition made to friends, family, and colleagues to simply get together and chat, but always over a drink. The natural tendency to socialize outside of the home in Basque Country (rather than inviting people over) lends itself to chance encounters and ... more drinks. However, what seems natural and organic is actually a very codified, deeply rooted social infrastructure with its own (delicious) rules and norms.

Each of the Basque capitals lays claim to the most bars per inhabitant or square mile in the world. While no one has firm proof of this, a stroll through the cities' streets proves its plausibility, and it definitely makes for a lively drinking culture. The drinks you'll find in this chapter are made for celebrations and socializing with friends.

The drinking ritual reaches maximum expression when Basques go out to eat. Mealtime is often preceded by an alcoholic drink to "open" the appetite, often a beer or a *marianito*, a small, cold red vermouth. Wine, cider, and *txakoli* (see page 139) are the most prevalent drinks during a meal. An espresso shot served alone (*hutsa*) or with a bit of milk (*ebakia*) comes after dessert, and is often followed by a digestif. The digestif can be broken into two stages as well: a small shot of an herbal liqueur, usually with anise tendencies (such as *patxaran*), and then a liquor–soft drink mix, such as a gin and tonic.

During *jaiak*, the celebrations of various patron saints and traditions that happen throughout the year in every town in Basque Country, the drinking routine shifts to accommodate the party. It's not at all unusual for townspeople and visitors to spend the entire day in the street, socializing, dancing, singing, and drinking. Naturally, the beverages of choice tend to be a bit less alcoholic and a lot easier to drink, like *kalimotxo* (red wine and cola) across Basque Country and *zurrakapote* (sangria) in the Rioja Álavesa.

Marianitoa

VERMOUTH

SWEET RED VERMOUTH has a 150-year history in Spain, and a much longer
one beyond the country's borders. One of the hotbeds of artisan vermouth
production has always been the Cataluña region of Spain, but in the last few years
the drink has seen a major resurgence in popularity across the peninsula. *Fer el
vermut*, "have a vermouth" in the Catalán language, is so common a phrase that it
has evolved to mean having *any* drink before a meal, whether beer, vermouth, or
a glass of wine. But it is on Sundays when you see young and old alike with this
reddish-brown drink in hand, floated with an olive and an orange slice.

At its most basic, vermouth is simply poured over ice with an olive plopped
in. This version is one seen in many bars in Basque Country, where two clear
glass bottles with spouts often sit on the bar, one filled with a bright red liquid
and the other with a transparent one. Bartenders liberally splash in these secret
ingredients, which are actually Campari and gin, to doctor up their house
vermouth. It is the perfect aperitif, traditionally accompanied by olives, potato
chips, and simple pintxos like *entsaladilla errusiarra* (see page 35). For a modern
presentation, shake the ingredients instead of stirring, and pour into cocktail
glasses. ✿

SERVES 4

½ orange

4 Manzanilla olives, pitted

2 cups (16 ounces/480 mL) sweet
red vermouth

4 teaspoons (⅔ ounce/20 mL)
Campari

4 teaspoons (⅔ ounce/20 mL) gin

Angostura or orange bitters

Seltzer (optional)

Prepare the garnish by cutting the orange in ½-inch (1.5 cm) slices, and then
cutting the round slices into half-moons. Skewer one olive on each of four
toothpicks and then slide on the orange slices.

Fill four short tumbler glasses with ice. Divide the vermouth evenly among
the glasses. Add 1 teaspoon of Campari and gin to each, and give them a stir.
Shake a dash of bitters into each glass.

If using the seltzer water, which is traditionally used to lighten up the drink,
add a splash. Place the olive-orange skewer into each glass, swirling slightly for
one last stir. Serve.

Patxarana

BASQUE SLOE LIQUOR

EVERY CULTURE HAS ITS HOMEMADE LIQUOR, and the Basques are no different. From the wooden shelves of country home sheds to the wine cellar of Arzak, the three-Michelin-star restaurant in San Sebastián, you'll find glass bottles filled with a ruby red liquid, sometimes with small, half-inch orbs rolling around in the bottom. This is *patxaran*, a sweet, anise-scented digestif.

The fruit of the blackthorn plant (*Prunus spinosa*) is called a sloe. Sloes look like berries, but are actually stone fruits, sharing more in common with a plum than a blueberry. (In fact, in Euskara, *aran* means "plum" and *pattar* means "liquor.")

The first written mention of patxaran was made in 1441 by a group of nuns in Segovia who noticed that the queen of Nafarroa took a spoonful of a red liquid to help with stomach pains. This suggests that making patxaran, which was always done at home and for family use, dates even further back than this mention.

Patxaran is nothing more than aniseed, liquor, and macerated sloe berries. Some people add coffee beans or cinnamon sticks to their patxaran during maceration, though this is considered anathema by patxaran purists and the body that governs its production. In and around Nafarroa, a special anise liquor base is sold for patxaran. It has a higher grade of alcohol and a softer hint of anise. This recipe uses a mixture of alcohols to water down the strength of available anise liquors and achieve the same result. ✿

MAKES 32 OUNCES (1 LITER)

1 to 1½ cups (150 to 225 g) sloe fruits (see Resources, page 317)

⅓ cup (80 mL) sweet anise (with about 35% alcohol)

3½ cups (840 mL) vodka

¾ cup plus 1 tablespoon (165 g) sugar

Place the sloe fruit in a colander. Dip the colander in a bowl of water and shake to rinse, removing any stems or fruits that float to the surface. Set aside to dry.

In a bowl, combine the sweet anise, vodka, and sugar and blend with an immersion blender until the sugar has totally dissolved.

Place the sloe fruits in a 32-ounce (1 L) glass jar or jug. Pour the alcohol mixture into the bottle, over the fruit. Seal the jar and set aside in a cool, dark place for 3 months. Once a day, turn the bottle upside down to encourage even infusion with the sloe berries.

After 3 months, strain the liquid through a fine-mesh sieve. Discard the fruits. Pour into a clean glass vessel and seal. Store in a cool place for up to 1 year.

Karajilloa

SPIKED COFFEE

THE *KARAJILLO* is far from a Basque invention—this alcoholic coffee has roots in the Spanish conquisition of Cuba. However, it has an important place at any weekend meal at a Basque restaurant or *txoko* (dining society; see page 91). On days when a more leisurely pace is the rule, the coffee between dessert and the digestif is often spiked with alcohol. Although the karajillo is sometimes reduced to coffee with a shot of alcohol, this recipe gives it more attention, flambéing the alcohol and adding a cold, velvety layer of cream on top. ✿

SERVES 4

6 ounces (175 mL) heavy cream

4 strips of lemon zest, peeled with a vegetable peeler

4 ounces (120 mL) rum, whiskey, or brandy

8 teaspoons (30 g) sugar

6 coffee beans

12 ounces (350 mL) brewed espresso or strong hot coffee

Ground cinnamon (optional)

In a bowl or a jar, use a whisk to gently beat the cream for 1 to 2 minutes, until the cream begins to thicken. Do not whip the cream; it should remain pourable.

In a small saucepan, combine the lemon zest, rum, sugar, and coffee beans. Heat over high heat until warm. Carefully remove from the heat and, with a long match or a lighter held near the liquid, set the mixture on fire. Allow it to burn until it goes out, or for no more than 10 seconds.

Strain the mixture through a fine-mesh sieve and divide it evenly among four short tumblers or glass mugs. Add 3 ounces of coffee to each glass. Divide the cream among the glasses, without stirring. Garnish each with a dash of cinnamon, if desired.

Kalimotxoa

RED WINE-COLA COCKTAIL

ON SUMMER SATURDAYS or the festival days of winter, drinking all afternoon and night is a favorite Basque pastime. Young people walk through the streets or perch on walls and park benches with giant one-liter bottles of Coca-Cola tucked under their arms. The nondescript contents look like cola, but in reality, the bottle is filled with *kalimotxo*, a mixture of equal parts red wine and cola that is a festival favorite in Basque Country.

The mix of Coca-Cola and red wine predates the term *kalimotxo*, a name whose use began in the 1970s and is popularly attributed to a group of friends from Getxo, a port village outside of Bilbao. Apart from a plastic soft drink bottle, it is often served from a *katxi*, an oversized plastic cup.

Such a simple, widely embraced drink has, naturally, several variations. The Coca-Cola can be replaced by orange soda; that drink is called a *pitilingorri* or *caliguay*. The use of lemon soda is also widespread, and is referred to as *kasimotxo*, literally "almost (kali)motxo."

Serve kalimotxo in tall glasses. Mix it over ice, directly in the glass. The red wine doesn't have to be anything special—this is a drink with its roots in economy. However, it is worth seeking out Coca-Cola made with cane sugar, not corn syrup, such as imported Mexican Coke. It should, however, be Coca-Cola not Pepsi, which experts say is too aggressively carbonated for this drink. Large ice cubes, which melt more slowly, are the final ingredient. ✿

SERVES 4

Large ice cubes

16 ounces (475 mL) red wine

16 ounces (475 mL) Coca-Cola, preferably made with cane sugar instead of corn syrup

4 lemon wedges

Place a handful of ice in each of four tall glasses.

Pour 4 ounces of wine into each glass. Slowly pour 4 ounces of cola into each glass. Gently give a half stir with a spoon, then add a lemon wedge to each glass, squeezing the lemon slightly before dropping it in.

THE STAND-UP POET

Neurriz eta errimaz
kantatzea hitza
horra hor zer kirol mota
den bertsolaritza.

Meter and rhyme
the singing word
behold *bertsolaritza*
as a form of sport.

—XABIER AMURIZA, THE FIRST BERTSOLARI
TO IMPROVISE IN EUSKARA BATUA

Euskara, the Basque language, lived most of its lengthy life on the margin of print, passing instead from mouth to mouth and generation to generation. Much of its life has been channeled into song, and one of the by-products is the *bertsolariak*, singers of discourse in rhyming Euskara.

A *bertso* is spontaneous, meaning it can erupt at the end of a long meal, around a table scattered with napkins, ashtrays, and empty glasses. In true Basque style, challenges between two improvisers often cropped up in social settings, bars, and cider houses. By the 1800s, *bertsolaritza* had evolved into a musical sport, with its own champions, competitions, and set of rules to play by. A mixture between stand-up comedy, a poetry slam, and a concert, participants must "answer" a rhyme presented by their colleague, selecting words to fill the lines (*koplak*). Crowds in the thousands gather to watch the competitions, and champions enjoy fame throughout the provinces.

The pose of the bertsolari is solitary and striking; he (or she—female bertsolariak are now commonplace) steps up to a microphone, solitary and humble, gaze fixed somewhere far off but not distant, shifting back and forth as lines of text fly through his mind. The bertsolari's mouth opens and the verse flows forth, in monochromatic tone that takes slow, deliberate steps up and down the musical scale to a haunting, vintage quality. Euskara is alive, being shifted and manipulated to create double meaning and form witty retorts, which the audience often sees coming and erupts into applause before the line is finished.

Gin-Tonic-a

GIN AND TONIC

MAKING A PROPER GIN-TONIC is an art form in Basque Country, with entire bars devoted to the drink. Their shelves sit heavy with the 240 gins available in Spain, the world's third-biggest market for the liquor.

But there are some differences in the Basque version in the proportions, the ingredients, and the method. The ratio of gin to tonic lowers drastically from 1:1 to 1:4. Logically, then, tonic takes on a protagonist role in the cocktail, which has prompted widespread use of premium tonics, made with sugar and real quinine.

A Basque gin-tonic is served in a special glass, which has the same form as a burgundy wineglass. Alternatively, it is often seen in a *vaso de sidra*, a cider glass, similar to a tumbler but usually wider and of a medium height. The most important thing is that the glass be large enough to comfortably fit the ingredients with plenty of ice, a key component. If at all possible, splurge on large, industrially frozen ice, which melts slowly and won't taste like a freezer. It's these little details that make this drink so special. ✤

SERVES 1

1¾ ounces gin

1 (6¾-ounce) bottle premium tonic water, chilled

1 green lemon or lime (see Note)

Juniper berries (optional)

Add large pieces of ice to a glass until it's about two-thirds full. With a long-handled spoon, move the ice in circles, vigorously, for about 10 seconds to cool down the glass. Using a cocktail strainer, drain any water that has melted and top off the glass with more ice.

Pour the gin over the ice to chill before adding the tonic. Pour the tonic over the ice *very* slowly. Insert a long-handled spoon to the bottom of the glass and gently give a half stir.

Hold the green lemon over the glass, and with the large hole of a citrus zester, remove one strip of peel and allow it to fall into the glass. Repeat twice more to allow the citrus's essential oils to mist the drink—whether the last two peels fall in the drink is up to you. Add a few juniper berries, if desired, and serve.

Note Green lemon is preferred for its unique and highly aromatic oils. It is simply lemon that has been picked before fully ripening.

Zurrakapotea

BASQUE SANGRIA

ZURRAKAPOTE is at its heart a festive, social drink. It marks the Semana Santa festivals of the Rioja Álavesa, and is poured in quantities that call to mind Jesus changing water into wine. The few written recipes that exist for this drink call for very generous quantities of wine, often cited in antiquated measurements, such as the *cántara*, whose equivalent is cited to be eight clay pitchers, a dozen bottles, or something completely different, depending on whom you ask.

Kuadrillak (groups of friends; see page 9) gather in their *locales* (spaces in public buildings), *bajeras* (cellars), and *chabisques* (huts)—the places where they meet to talk, eat, drink, and hang out. They make the zurrakapote (or *zurracapote* in its Spanish form) in a giant container about a week before the festival, with lower-quality wine, to hand out to guests who stop by during the festivities.

Zurrakapote should be made with red wine from the Basque area of La Rioja, the Rioja Álavesa, but in the lower area of La Rioja you can often find it made with *clarete*, a dark pink wine that has a longer maceration than rosé. And while other wine-based drinks of the Iberian peninsula rely on the addition of sodas and liquor, zurrakapote is about sweetening the base with a simple syrup; in this way, it adheres much closer to its wine-country roots. ✤

MAKES 1 LITER

½ cup (100 g) sugar

1 cinnamon stick

1 (750-mL) bottle red wine, preferably from the Rioja Álavesa

1 lemon

1 peach, fresh or canned

In a medium saucepan, combine ⅓ cup (80 mL) water, the sugar, and the cinnamon and heat over high heat, stirring, until the sugar has dissolved. Set the simple syrup aside.

Empty the wine into a container with at least a 1-liter capacity. Add the simple syrup (including the cinnamon stick) to the wine. With a vegetable peeler, peel the zest of the lemon, avoiding the white pith, and add the zest to the wine mixture.

Cut the lemon in half and juice one half. Stir the lemon juice into the wine mixture. Cut the peach in half and add to the wine mixture. Close the bottle and set aside in a cool place for at least 3 days before serving. Stir or shake, then refrigerate and serve cold.

ACKNOWLEDGMENTS

In reality, this book began to take shape almost ten years ago, and every person whom I have met along the way has contributed to furthering my understanding of the Basque people and, by extension, their tables.

A special thank-you to the A-team: to Simon Bajada for the amazing photographs and endless font of great attitude; to Susana Suarez for the prop sourcing and styling (and friendship, which goes for Gorka, Sasha, and Ane, too); and to Sonia Tapia for the food styling, beautiful smile, and hours in the kitchen. And, of course, to Artisan for believing in this project, and to especially my editor, Judy Pray, for her patience and encouragement in my first time through this process. This book is thanks to *you*.

Thanks to the Mimo family, especially Jon, Nicole, and Charles, for the understanding and support in what was the most difficult season. Thanks to my former bosses and mentors—Frank and Pardis Stitt, John Rolen, and Tasia Malakasis—for their help every step of the way. Thanks to Katharine Cobb and Kim Sunée for advice in the beginning stages. Thanks to Guille Viglione and Ana Alcover for their help in getting this project off the ground, as well as their unparalleled hospitality.

A big thank-you to Juan Manuel Garmendia and the Cofradía Vasca de Gastronomia for their knowledge, kindness, and physical space. Another special one to Mikel Erquiaga for the highly enjoyable trips through the French Basque Country. And to Paddy Woodworth for checking my facts and inspiring me from the beginning.

Thank you to all of those who helped with my research, opening doors, setting tables, and answering messages at all hours (in no particular order): Ander González of Astelena, Edorta Lamo, Pablo Loureiro, Nicolas from Tubal, Pilar and Juan Mari Idoate, Roberto Ruíz, Alberto Luque, Javier de la Maza, Javier Barrolo, Maypi Gomez, everyone at Ganbara (José Ignacio, Amaia, Amaiur, and of course Itxaso), the team behind Elkano (Aitor Arregui, Pablo Vicari, Asier, and Faustino to name a few), Aitor Zugasti, gastronomic consultant, for his culinary expertise, Felix (Susana's brother-in-law), Javi (Susana's brother), Txema Huici from Gros's best bar, Margari and the talo team from Ataun, Harrobialde Finca, Urtzi, Imanol and Felipe Ugarte, Luis Irizar and Ramon Roteta, Kentuene Jatetxea, Saltoki, Keramik, Hönnun, the Loaf Bakeries (for the beautiful bread pictured in this book and the year I spent at its ovens), Maisor, Reyno Gourmet and Itziar Inza Elía, Leslie and Manuel Recio, Jorge Deheza, Josema Azpeitia, Iñigo Galatas,

Álvaro Mina, Adrián of Zoco *patxaran*, the town of Zamudio, its mayor, Igotz Lopez, and Igor Llodio, Mireya, Ander and Miren at Rezabal, Kevin (and the Bens), Inés Susaeta, Jaime Burgaña at Aroa, Sylvain at Zaporejai, Telmo and the Orio rowing team, Jose Mari and the team at Vidaurre, Pedro and Tere from Martín Txiki, the Muñagorri family and their butcher shop, Hugh McCorcoran, Arturo and everyone from Maitenia, Aitor from Patxikuenea, Pampi and Leire Iturralde from Astoklok, Aran Goyoaga, Juan Mari and Elena Arzak, José Andrés, Xabier and Enrike Juanena from Venta Halty, Pierre and Catherine Oteiza (and their pigs and devoted work), Bixente and Frédérique of the Gâteau Basque Museum, Aitor Alonso of El Correo Araba, Andoni de Irala, Marina Amantegui and the neighbors born in the *casero* of Etxebarri, and to its current owner, Bittor, who has fed me for the last eight years and took valuable time to write me a prologue.

And, finally, to my dear friends and family who stood by me and kept me hanging on through all of this. Mom, Dad, Katharine, Bryan . . . I know you have my back always and for anything. You too, Danny and Grandma. To Xabier de la Maza, whom I was lucky enough to meet my first year in San Sebastián and who connected me with everyone and answered every Basque language doubt at every hour. To Maite Roso, who was my devoted friend and Basque language policewoman and partner in all kinds of cocktail crimes, as well as the International Society for the Preservation and Enjoyment of Vermut. To Majo, for her expertise and help. To Stefani, Bekah, Louise, Emily, Jen, Katie—my emergency line to sanity and friends for life. Katerina, Naike, Leire, Iñigo, Ane, Eider, Sofia, Mikel Lasa, Michael Broadbent, Hannah, my consistent Cait, I love y'all so much. Clyde and Rosa, where would I be without your help this year? There are so many more of you . . . thanks for supporting me through the good and bad. And last but not least, mi rey Chesko—te quiero, gracias por tu apoyo y amor.

Finally, the biggest of thanks to my daughter for understanding at just nine years old how important this project was, and for (almost) never complaining about bacalao dinners or weekends spent around the house. Buckley, you are truly the most amazing Basque of them all.

RESOURCES

Basque cooking is all about the ingredients. When possible, invest time and funds into sourcing the absolute best you can. Here is a list of some great places to shop and some of my favorite artisans, and tips for buying from both. Not surprisingly, quite a few of these ingredients are also for sale on Amazon.com.

ONLINE SHOPS

Delicias de España
tiendadelicias.com
This Spanish food retailer has been in business for more than twenty years.

Despaña
shop.despanabrandfoods.com
Despaña is a Spanish storefront with a wide selection of goods.

La Tienda
tienda.com
La Tienda has had the market on Spanish goods cornered since before the internet era, and apart from Spanish produce, it has a modest yet well-curated selection of Basque goods.

Mimo
shop.mimofood.com
This San Sebastián–based company is small, but their selection of products and wine is fabulous and comes with stellar customer service.

Spanish Table
spanishtable.com
This handy shop sells everything from paella burners to pintxo sticks.

NOTES ON INGREDIENTS

Anchovies
There are several quality anchovy suppliers. Always make sure the anchovies are from the Cantabrian Sea (it should say on the label). My favorites are from Maisor (maisor.com), which also ships internationally.

Choricero Peppers
Dried choricero peppers and the *pulpa de choricero* are relatively easy to find. The household brand in Basque Country is Zubia.

Chorizo
Be sure to use Spanish-style chorizo, not Mexican. The difference is important—the Spanish stuff is cured, unlike fresh, crumbly Mexican chorizo. It's ready to slice and eat.

Cider

Basque cider is becoming more available worldwide every year, both from retailers and at restaurants. Any cider house exporting will have a decent standard of quality. Family-run Zapiain (zapiain.eus/en) has a well-developed export business and produces a dependable, quality cider from right in the middle of Astigarraga.

Guindilla Peppers

These slender green peppers, a few inches long, are actually produced and pickled all over the peninsula. However, the most exquisite are those from Ibarra, so check product labels carefully.

Idiazabal

Got to love those government regulatory bodies . . . any Idiazabal granted the classification won't steer you too wrong. Smoked Idiazabal (with an orangey rind) is the most common in the United States, but in Basque Country the unsmoked variety is virtually the only kind served.

Olive Oil

Much of the olive oil used in Basque Country is, by default, made from Arbequina olives. The virgin and extra-virgin designations affect the flavor of a finished dish, sometimes more than others. The single biggest factor is to use a fresh bottle, not one that's been whiling away on a sunny shelf.

Piment d'Espelette

This rich, spicy red pepper is widely distributed. Just make sure to buy one printed with AOC—this means it is true Espelette pepper, certified by the French government. Maison Arosteguy (arosteguy.com) is a classic producer of the stuff, based in Biarritz, and they ship internationally.

Rennet

Thanks to a burgeoning DIY cheese culture, liquid rennet (natural or chemical/vegan) is widely available online and at natural foods stores.

Salt

Many Basques use Maldon as their flaky sea salt; however, there is a local salt from Araba that is quite popular as well: Sal de Añana. It's difficult to find stateside, but Mimo (opposite page) can ship several of its products to you internationally.

Sloe Fruits

Most sloes for sale are from vendors in the United Kingdom. You can find dried sloes on both Amazon and eBay, as well as from U.K. vendors that are willing to ship abroad for an extra fee. Try Just Ingredients (justingredients.co.uk).

Tolosa Beans

These hyperlocal beans are quite difficult to find. Your best bet is La Tienda (opposite page), which sells the Tolosa bean, although it has been grown in another province.

Tuna

The most important thing to look for when buying Spanish or Basque canned tuna is the phrase "bonito del norte." This ensures that you are getting the correct species, which is an important start. The "ventresca," as the belly is usually referred to on labels, is the most exquisite cut. There are several quality purveyors from the area that sell internationally. Ortiz is widely available and of satisfactory quality. If you want to go all out, you can order from a smaller artisan, like Olasagasti (conservasolasagasti.com).

TRANSLATION GUIDE

ENGLISH	BASQUE	SPANISH	FRENCH
PINTXOS			
Anchovy, Pepper, and Olive Skewer	gilda	gilda	gilda
Spanish Omelet	patata tortilla	tortilla de patata	omelette aux pommes de terre
Stuffed Peppers	piper beteak	pimientos rellenos	poivrons farcis
Croquettes	kroketak	croquetas	croquettes
Potato Salad	entsaladilla errusiarra	ensaladilla rusa	salade de pommes de terre
Cider-Braised Chorizo	txorizoa sagardotan	chorizo a la sidra	chorizo au cidre
Anchovies in Vinegar	antxoak ozpinetan	boquerón	anchois marinés au vinaigre
Garlic Potatoes	patatak baratxuriarekin	patatas al ajillo	pommes de terre à l'ail
Shrimp Kebab with Pepper Vinaigrette	ganba brotxeta	brocheta de gamba	brochette de crevette
Spanish Ham, Goat Cheese, and Sun-Dried Tomato Pintxo	urdaiazpiko, ahuntz gazta eta tomate lehor pintxoa	pintxo de jamón, queso de cabra, y tomate deshidratado	pintxo au jambon, fromage de chèvre, et tomates séchées
Foie Gras Terrine	foie micuit-a	foie micuit	foie gras mi-cuit
SOUP			
Beef and Chicken Broth	salda	caldo	bouillon de volaille
Fish Broth	arrai salda	caldo de pescado / fumet	fumet de poissons
Leek and Potato Soup	porrusalda	porrusalda	soupe paysanne aux poireaux
Garlic Soup	baratxurI zopa	sopa de ajo	soupe au pain et à l'ail
Fish Soup	arrai zopa	sopa de pescado	soupe de poissons
Salt Cod and Bread Soup	zurrukutuna	sopa de ajo con bacalao	soupe au pain, à l'ail et à la morue
Tuna and Potato Stew	marmitakoa	marmitakoa	marmite de thon
FISH & SHELLFISH			
Elvers (Young Eel)	angulak	angulas	civelles
Salt Cod Croquettes	bakailao kroketak	croquetas de bacalao	croquettes de morue
Scorpion Fish Pâté	krabarroka pastela	pastel de cabracho	flan de rascasse
Salt Cod Omelet	bakailao tortilla	tortilla de bacalao	omelette à la morue
Salt Cod Stew	ajoarriero bakailaoa	bacalao ajoarriero	morue à l'ajoarriero
Salt Cod in Biscayne Sauce	bakailaoa bizkaiko erara	bacalao a la vizcaína	morue à la biscayenne
San Sebastían–Style Spider Crab	txangurroa donostiar erara	txangurro a la donostiarra	araignée de mer farcie à la donostiarra
Fried Anchovies	antxoa Frijituak	anchoas fritas	anchois frits
Kokotxas in Pil-Pil Sauce	kokotxak pil-pil eran	kokotxas al pil pil	joues de poisson pil-pil
Grilled Sardines	sardinak parrilan	sardinas a la parilla	sardines grillées
Oil-Cured Tuna	hegaluze ontziratua	bonito en conserva	thon en conserve
Tuna and Tomato Salad	hegaluze eta tomate entsalada	ensalada de bonito y tomate	salade de tomates au thon
Tuna with Tomato Sauce	hegaluzea tomatearekin	bonito con tomate	thon à la sauce tomate

ENGLISH	BASQUE	SPANISH	FRENCH
FISH & SHELLFISH			
Grilled Tuna Belly	hegaluze mendrezka	ventresca de bonito	ventrèche de thon
Grilled Turbot	erreboiloa parrilan	rodaballo a la parrilla	turbot grillé
Squid with Caramelized Onions	txipiroiak pelaio erara	chipirones pelayo	chipirons aux oignons
Squid in Ink Sauce	txipiroiak bere tintan	chipirones en su tinta	chipirons à l'encre
Hake with Clams in Salsa Verde	legatza txirlekin saltsa berdean	merluza en salsa verde con almejas	merlu sauce verte aux palourdes
Rice with Clams	arroza txirlekin	arroz con almejas	riz aux palourdes
Fried Monkfish	zapo frijitua	rape frito	lotte frite
Navarre-Style Trout	amuarraina nafar erara	trucha a la navarra	truite à la navarraise
VEGETABLES & MEAT			
Spring Vegetable Stew	barazki menestra	menestra de verdura	jardinière de légumes
White Asparagus with Mayonnaise	zainzuriak maionesarekin	espárragos con mahonesa	asperges blanches et mayonnais
Vitoria-Style Fava Beans	babak "vitoriana" erara	habas a la vitoriana	fèves à la vitoriana
Snails	barraskiloak	caracoles	escargots
Gernika Peppers	gernikako piperrak	pimientos de Gernika	poivrons verts de Gernika
Piquillo Peppers	piquillo piperrak	pimientos del piquillo	poivrons piquillos
Pickled Guindilla Peppers	piperminak	guindillas	piments au vinaigre
Tolosa Beans	tolosako babarrunak	alubias de Tolosa	haricots rouges de Tolosa
Cabbage	aza	berza	chou
Tomato-Pepper Stew	piperrada	piperrada	piperade
Navarre-Style White Beans	potxak nafar erara	pochas a la Navarra	haricots blancs frais à la navarraise
Simple Basque Salad	entsalada	ensalada	salade
Porcini Mushrooms with Egg Yolk	onddoak gorringoarekin	hongos a la plancha con yema	cèpes sautés à la plancha et jaune d'oeuf
Riojan Potato-Chorizo Stew	patatak errioxar erara	patatas a la riojana	pommes de terre à la riojana
Mushroom Eggs	perretxiko nahaskia	revuelto de perretxikos	oeufs brouillés aux cèpes de Saint-Georges
Tomato Sauce	tomate frijitua	tomate frito	sauce tomate
Herb-Pepper Vinegar Sauce	xipister	chipister	sauce Xipister
Basque Corn Flatbread	taloa	talo	crêpe à la farine de maïs
Basque Chorizo	txistorra	chistorra	chorizo basque
Blood Sausage	odolkia	morcilla	boudin noir
Lamb Tripe and Egg Sausage	mondejua	mondeju	boudin blanc aux tripes d'agneau
Lamb in Chilindrón Sauce	arkumea txilindron erara	cordero al chilindrón	agneau en sauce chilindrón
Pork Hash with Paprika	txitxikis	chichiquis	porc au piment mariné
Beef Cheeks	txahal masailak	carrilleras	joues de boeuf
Veal Stew with Peppers	axoa	axoa	Axoa de veau
Steak	txuleta	chuleta	côte de bœuf
SWEETS			
Cheese Ice Cream	gazta izozkia	helado de queso	glace au fromage
Walnut Cream	intxaur saltsa	sopa dulce de nueces	soupe sucrée aux noix
Gâteau Basque	etxeko biskotxa	pastel vasco	gâteau basque
Basque Sheep's Curd	mamia	cuajada	caillé de brebis
Roasted Apples	sagar erreak	manzanas asadas	pommes rôties
Almond-Cream Tart	pantxineta	panchineta	tarte aux amandes
Chicharrón Sweet Bread	txantxigorri opila	torta de chanchigorri	tourte sucrée de chanchigorri

ENGLISH	BASQUE	SPANISH	FRENCH
Apple Paste	sagar dultzea	dulce de manzana	confit de pommes
Bilbao Custard "Rice" Tarts	arroz pastela	pastel de arroz	gâteau de riz
La Viña Cheesecake	gazta tarta	tarta de queso	gâteau au fromage blanc
Anise-Scented Fritters	erroskilak	rosquillas	beignets
Fried Milk	esne torrada	leche frita	lait frit
Pudding	arrautza esnea	natillas	crème anglaise
Rice Pudding	arroz esnea	arroz con leche	riz au lait
Caramelized Custard Bread	ogi torrada	torrija	pain perdu
Brioche Buns with Buttercream	gurin opila	bollos de mantequilla	petits pains au beurre
Yogurt Cake	bizkotxoa	bizcocho	gâteau au yaourt
Apple Tart	sagar tarta	tarta de manzana	tarte aux pommes
Basque Trifle	goxua	goxua	dessert à la crème recette basque
Basque Cannoli	kremaz betetako hoditxoak	canutillos	biscuits cigarettes
Almond Cookies	teilak	tejas	biscuits aux amandes
Anise Sugar Cookies	san blas opila	torta de San Blas	tourte de La Sainte-Blaise
Christmas Compote	gabonetako konpota	compota	compote de Noël
DRINKS			
Vermouth	marianitoa	marianito	vermouth
Basque Sloe Liquor	patxarana	pacharán	liqueur de prunelle de Navarre
Spiked Coffee	karajilloa	carajillo	café alcoolisé
Red Wine–Cola Cocktail	kalimotxoa	kalimotxo	cocktail vin rouge Coca Calimocho
Gin and Tonic	gin-tonic-a	gin-tonic	gin tonic
Basque Sangria	zurrakapotea	zurracapote	sangria basque Zurracapote

FURTHER READING

25 Años de la Nueva Cocina Vasca.
  Mikel Corcuera (2002).
Amar a Euskalerria Conociendola.
  Juan Jose Lapitz (1978).
Artzaintza.
  Gema Arrugaeta (2016).
Arzak Secrets.
  Juan Mari Arzak (2015).
Bacalao.
  Andoni Luis Aduriz (2003).
The Basque Country.
  Paddy Woodworth (2007).
The Basque History of the World.
  Mark Kurlansky (1999).
Calendario de Nuestra Cocina Traditional.
  Martín Berasategui (2001).
Cocina Riojana.
  Eduard Gomez Gonzalez (1995).
Cocina Vasca: Las Recetas de Toda la Vida.
  Karlos Arguiñano (2009).

Curiosidades de la Cocina Alavesa.
  Fernando Gonzalez de Heredia (1995).
El arte de la parrilla.
  Jose G Salizar (1995).
Euskal Sukaldaritzaz.
  Hasier Etxebarria (2012).
Fiestas de Invierno.
  Juan Garmendia Larrañaga (1993).
Gran Cocina de Navarra.
  Pedro Ma Diaz de Rada Turumbay et al. (1992).
Guía de La Gastronomía Popular.
  Enrique Ayerbe Echebarria (2000).
La Cocina de Bizkaia: Placer y Salud.
  Jesús Llena Larrauri (2005).
La Cocina de Nicolasa.
  Nicolasa Pradera (1933).
La Cocina Vasca.
  Ana Maria Calera (1971).

La Cocina Vasca De Los Pescados y Mariscos.
  José María Busca Isusi (1981).
La Joven Cocina Vasca.
  Martín Berasategui (1996).
Life and Food in the Basque Country.
  Maria Sevilla (1989).
Manual de Cocina Económica Vasca.
  Jose Castillo (1968).
Mugaritz.
  Andoni Luis Aduriz (2012).
Orhipean: The Country of the Basque.
  Xamar (2006).
Recetas de cocina de abuelas vascas.
  Jose Castillo (1983).
Treiñeru Estropadak.
  Agustín Zubikarai (1987).

INDEX

Note: Page numbers in *italic* refer to photographs.